The Epistle of Paul the Apostle to the ROMANS

The Epistle of Paul the Apostle to the Romans

by

Oliver B. Greene

THE GOSPEL HOUR, INC.
Oliver B. Greene, Founder
Box 2024, Greenville, S. C. 29602

Foreword

For some time I have felt led of the Lord to reprint and enlarge our Commentary on *The Epistle of Paul the Apostle to the Romans.* The original volume was done when we had very limited printing equipment and the finished product left much to be desired.

Finally, under the leadership of the Holy Spirit, this Commentary has been made more comprehensive and covers some points more extensively. This is by no means to be interpreted as a "revision" because nothing has been *revised* in the interpretation of the Scriptures. The truth contained in this edition is simply more detailed than in the first publication, and the new type style is much easier to read.

I trust, as this new volume goes out, that it will prove a blessing to Christians and a message of salvation to the lost.

To God be the glory!

Oliver B. Greene

Contents

Contents

Introduction

There is no doubt that Paul is the writer of the Epistle to the Romans (chapter 1, verse 1). The date of writing—the sixth in chronological order of Paul's writings—was about A.D. 60. He wrote the Epistle while in Corinth, during his third visit to that city (II Cor. 13:1). In the Epistle, Paul makes known his intention and his burning desire to soon visit Rome, and announces before his coming the distinctive truths which God had revealed to him, and which God would make known to the Romans through him—and not only to the Romans, but to all believers down through the Dispensation of Grace, the Church Age. He desired the Christians in Rome to have his own statement on the doctrine of God's grace, a doctrine so bitterly attacked in that day by the legalistic teachers. Paul was a "pure grace" preacher. On many occasions he declared that his message, as having to do with redemption, was a singular message: *The cross*—and certainly the cross and grace are inseparable.

1

Verse 1 in Romans clearly sets forth the theme of the Epistle: *the Gospel of God.* The Gospel of God is the very widest possible designation of the whole body of redeeming truth. The God whom Paul magnifies in this Epistle is no respecter of persons (Rom. 2:11). He is not the God of the Jews only, but He is the God of the Gentiles also (Rom. 3:29). And because He is the God of all, Paul clearly sets forth that all the world is found guilty before God (Rom. 3:19), and therefore a redemption as great as the great need must be provided and revealed. This redemption must be provided for all, on a basis that all can meet; namely, simple, childlike faith.

Not only does the Epistle to the Romans set forth in the fullest way the doctrine of the marvelous grace of God in relation to our redemption from sin and in relation to our salvation, but three outstanding chapters (chapters 9, 10, and 11) give the great promises God made to Israel—promises concerning the Gentiles and the fulfillment of God's promise to Abraham to the fullest extent; and the Epistle to the Romans clearly shows us that the completion of God's promises to Abraham can never be a reality until the completion of the Church is a reality and the Church (the bride of Christ) is caught up to meet Jesus, the Bridegroom, in the air. Then, and only then, can the Deliverer out of Zion appear (Rom. 11:25-27).

As we study the Book of Romans, you will notice

2

the key phrase in the Epistle is "the righteousness of God" (Rom. 1:17; 3:21, 22). There is no true righteousness apart from the righteousness of God in Christ Jesus. It matters not how good, how upright, nor how honest we may be, our righteousnesses are "as filthy rags" (Isa. 64:6). Paul sets forth this tremendous truth in Romans.

Almost all outstanding Bible scholars and commentators of the past divide the Book of Romans into *seven parts,* or divisions, as follows:

1. We learn that the whole world is guilty before God, and there is not one person or nation that is less guilty than all others (1:18 through 3:20).
2. In the second division, we clearly see that justification is through the righteousness of God by faith. We clearly see that God's righteousness as set forth in the Gospel, is the only remedy for sin and man's guilt toward God (3:21 through 5:11).
3. In the third place, we will learn as we study this Epistle, that we are crucified with Christ when we truly believe on Him and accept His righteousness on the terms of the Gospel. We are crucified with Christ, we are resurrected to new life in Christ, and we walk as the Spirit of God leads day by day because the Spirit leads every son of God. If any have not the Spirit, they do not belong to God (5:12 through 8:13).
4. As we study chapter 8, verses 14-39, we will see the full result in the blessing of the Gospel,

made possible through the sacrificial death, burial, and resurrection of Christ; that He died for us, and God commended His love toward us only because of God's grace.

5. The fifth division of Romans is very, very important. Paul clearly teaches that the Church is not a continuation of Israel. The Church did not inherit the promises God made to Abraham and Israel, and the Gospel does not do away with the covenant promises that God gave to Israel (9:1 through 11:36).

6. In the sixth division of the book, we are clearly taught Christian life as it should be lived daily, and Christian service as it should be practiced from a heart filled with gratitude and love for God's marvelous grace in Christ Jesus (12:1 through 15:33).

7. In the seventh division, there are 27 verses— chapter 16:1-27. These verses teach that love automatically flows from a Christian heart. After all, the very essence of Christianity is love.

Personally, I believe the Holy Spirit led the men who arranged the books of the New Testament, in placing Romans at the very beginning of the Epistles. There were five other Epistles written before Romans, but I believe this Epistle holds its rightful place in the arrangement of the books of the New Testament.

The body of truth revealed to Paul and penned down in these sixteen chapters had been "kept secret since the world (ages) began, but now is made manifest" (Rom. 16:25, 26; Eph. 3:5-7). Paul, under inspiration, begins to reveal this age-old mystery to the believers at Rome. Paul tells us that all Scripture is given by inspiration of God, and all Scripture is profitable to us (II Tim. 3:16). These great truths were first revealed to the Roman believers, but they are yours and mine as we study this gold mine of the Epistles.

As we study Romans, my heart's desire and prayer to God is that the Holy Spirit will use these studies to give to those who read these lines a clear understanding of the wonderful truths set forth in Romans, and I trust these truths will be accepted and will cause many to be established in the faith once for all delivered to the saints. Paul, in Romans, speaks of "Him that is of power to *stablish* you according to my Gospel, and the preaching of Jesus Christ, according to the revelation of the mystery, which was kept secret since the world began" (Rom. 16:25).

Many believers consider Romans a book hard to understand; but it is not difficult to understand if we will "let God be true, but every man a liar" (Rom. 3:4), and if we will read what Romans says and *believe* it instead of refusing to believe what we read. Many believers must confess that their besetting sin, as having to do with Bible study, is the sin of unbelief. They read a clear statement in God's Holy Word and then they stop, raise their eyebrows, scratch their forehead, and say, "I wonder what that means." Just let God be true and every man a liar! The Word of God says what it means, and means what it says.

There are parables in the Word of God, and there are symbols in the Word of God; but the Holy Spirit always makes it clear when parables are employed to illustrate a tremendous spiritual truth. So when you read a clear statement such as "For sin shall not have dominion over you . . ." (Rom. 6:14), do not ask, "What does that mean?" It is clear: When one receives Jesus as Saviour, Jesus is our victory over sin; and if He who is in us is defeated by him who is on the outside of us, then the latter is greater than the former. You will understand if you will read I John 4:4: "Ye are of God, little children, and have overcome them: *because greater is He that is in you, than he that is in the world.*" John is telling us that Jesus Christ is greater and more powerful than the devil. Every believer has within him Jesus in the Person of the Holy Spirit; and Jesus within is greater than the devil without. Therefore "we are more than conquerors through Him that loved us" (Rom. 8:37).

The Book of Romans speaks with authority. The words in Romans were penned down by the accredited representative of the risen Christ, one who was called and ordained of God to bear this message—not only to the Romans, but to all the

Gentiles. The words we read in Romans are God-breathed (II Tim. 3:16). So as we read and study these sacred lines, verse by verse, chapter by chapter, should we not feel as Moses felt when God said that he should remove his sandals from his feet because he was standing on holy ground? (See Exodus 3:1-5.)

Perhaps someone is asking here, "Just what do we mean when we refer to the Scriptures as being verbally inspired?" We know that not one word of the New Testament had been written when Jesus Christ ascended back to heaven, but we have in God's Word plain truths that declare His Word to be God-breathed, or verbally inspired.

In the first place, Jesus plainly said before He went away that He would leave the revelation of truth unfinished (John 16:12), but He promised that the revelation of truth would be completed after He ascended back to the Father, where He was before He came to earth in a body (John 16:13). Also, He chose certain men to receive additional revelation from time to time, and to be His witnesses, His preachers and teachers, after He ascended back to the Father. (Read John 16:13; 15:27; Matthew 28:19, 20; Acts 1:8 and 9:15-17.) These words, penned down by holy men called and ordained by God, are precisely the same in authority and power as the words spoken by the very lips of Jesus Himself. (Read Matthew 10:14, 15; Luke 10:16; John 13:20 and 17:20.)

I do not believe the Bible CONTAINS the Word of God; *I believe the Bible IS the Word of God!* I believe every word in the Bible is inspired of God and penned down by holy men called and ordained of God, and they wrote as God's Holy Ghost dictated to them the words they were to pen down for our instruction and admonition. According to the testimony of Jesus Christ Himself and of the men who wrote the Gospels and the Epistles, the Scriptures are verbally inspired; that is, the Holy Ghost gave the words and holy men penned them down.

As we study the Epistle to the Romans, we will notice the exceeding sinfulness of sin; how sin entered; the final wages of sin; and the only hope for the sinner. Then we will see clearly set forth the righteousness of God in Christ Jesus, and our desperate need for His righteousness if we would enter the City of God. We will clearly see that God honors only the righteousness that comes through faith in the finished work of the Lord Jesus Christ, His only begotten Son.

As we come to the closing chapters of the book, we will see clearly set forth the walk of the believers. We will see what the Holy Spirit reveals through Paul concerning our conduct toward each other, and as believers we will learn what true Bible holiness is. We will learn much about the ministry of the Holy Spirit in our heart and life after we become a child of God.

Introduction

Paul told the Ephesian believers: "Ye were sometimes darkness, but now are ye light in the Lord: *walk as children of light*" (Eph. 5:8). Certainly, as we study Romans, we will receive new light, increased light—and if we fail to walk *in* that light, then we will be worse off after studying this marvelous Epistle, than we were before we began the study. If we see these things and know these things, happy will we be if we *do* them; but if we see them and refuse to accept them, if the light is revealed and we refuse to walk in it, then better had we never been exposed to the tremendous spiritual truths of Romans.

Chapter I

1. Paul, a servant of Jesus Christ, called to be an apostle, separated unto the gospel of God,

2. (Which he had promised afore by his prophets in the holy scriptures,)

3. Concerning his Son Jesus Christ our Lord, which was made of the seed of David according to the flesh;

4. And declared to be the Son of God with power, according to the spirit of holiness, by the resurrection from the dead:

5. By whom we have received grace and apostleship, for obedience to the faith among all nations, for his name:

6. Among whom are ye also the called of Jesus Christ:

7. To all that be in Rome, beloved of God, called to be saints: Grace to you and peace from God our Father, and the Lord Jesus Christ.

8. First, I thank my God through Jesus Christ for you all, that your faith is spoken of throughout the whole world.

9. For God is my witness, whom I serve with my spirit in the gospel of his Son, that without ceasing I make mention of you always in my prayers;

10. Making request, if by any means now at length I might have a prosperous journey by the will of God to come unto you.

11. For I long to see you, that I may impart unto you

some spiritual gift, to the end ye may be established;

12. That is, that I may be comforted together with you by the mutual faith both of you and me.

13. Now I would not have you ignorant, brethren, that oftentimes I purposed to come unto you, (but was let hitherto,) that I might have some fruit among you also, even as among other Gentiles.

14. I am debtor both to the Greeks, and to the Barbarians; both to the wise, and to the unwise.

15. So, as much as in me is, I am ready to preach the gospel to you that are at Rome also.

16. For I am not ashamed of the gospel of Christ: for it is the power of God unto salvation to every one that believeth; to the Jew first, and also to the Greek.

17. For therein is the righteousness of God revealed from faith to faith: as it is written, The just shall live by faith.

18. For the wrath of God is revealed from heaven against all ungodliness and unrighteousness of men, who hold the truth in unrighteousness;

19. Because that which may be known of God is manifest in them; for God hath shewed it unto them.

20. For the invisible things of him from the creation of the world are clearly seen, being understood by the things that are made, even his eternal power and Godhead; so that they are without excuse:

21. Because that, when they knew God, they glorified him not as God, neither were thankful; but became vain in their imaginations, and their foolish heart was darkened.

22. Professing themselves to be wise, they became fools,

23. And changed the glory of the uncorruptible God into an image made like to corruptible man, and to birds, and fourfooted beasts, and creeping things.

24. Wherefore God also gave them up to uncleanness

through the lusts of their own hearts, to dishonour their own bodies between themselves:

25. Who changed the truth of God into a lie, and worshipped and served the creature more than the Creator, who is blessed for ever. Amen.

26. For this cause God gave them up unto vile affections: for even their women did change the natural use into that which is against nature:

27. And likewise also the men, leaving the natural use of the woman, burned in their lust one toward another; men with men working that which is unseemly, and receiving in themselves that recompence of their error which was meet.

28. And even as they did not like to retain God in their knowledge, God gave them over to a reprobate mind, to do those things which are not convenient;

29. Being filled with all unrighteousness, fornication, wickedness, covetousness, maliciousness; full of envy, murder, debate, deceit, malignity; whisperers,

30. Backbiters, haters of God, despiteful, proud, boasters, inventors of evil things, disobedient to parents,

31. Without understanding, covenantbreakers, without natural affection, implacable, unmerciful:

32. Who knowing the judgment of God, that they which commit such things are worthy of death, not only do the same, but have pleasure in them that do them.

Verse 1: *"Paul, a servant of Jesus Christ, called to be an apostle, separated unto the Gospel of God."*

The original name of the author of this Epistle was *Saul* (Acts 7:58; 8:1, 3; 9:1-31; 11:25-30; 13:1-9). "Saul" was a Hebrew name, and "Paul" was a Roman name. After Acts 13:9, he is consistently called Paul. Just why his name was changed is not certainly known. It was, however, in accord to the customs of the times.

Paul called himself *"a servant of Jesus Christ."* The meaning of this opening phrase of verse 1 is literally "Paul the bondsman, or the bond-servant." Or, as some outstanding commentators put it, "the bond-slave" of Jesus Christ. You see, Paul had known what it was to be a slave to sin and a slave to Judaism, the religion of his fathers—and he had fought desperately in the defense of Judaism until he met Jesus on the road to Damascus. Also, although Paul was an Israelite, he was also a Roman citizen (Acts 16:37, 38; 22:25-29) and knew much about slavery—and now he has met One he loves so much that it is a joy to be His slave. He becomes the slave, the servant, of the Christ who delivered him from the bondage of corruption and brought to his heart the glorious liberty of the Spirit. Paul therefore opens his letter to the Romans by announcing that he is a servant, a slave, a bond-servant, of the Lord Jesus Christ.

Not only was Paul a servant, but he was *"called to be an apostle."* The word *"called"* means here not merely to be *invited,* but has the sense of *appointment.* It indicated that he had not assumed the office himself, but that he was set apart to it by the authority of Christ Himself. It was important for Paul to state this, for the other apostles had been called, or chosen (Matt. 10:1-4;

14

Luke 6:13-16; John 15:16). Also, since Paul was not
one of those originally appointed, it was necessary
for him to affirm that he had not taken this high
office by himself but had been called by the Lord
Jesus Christ. His appointment to this office he
often vindicated. (Read Romans 11:13; I Corinthians 9:1; II Corinthians 12:12; Galatians 1:12-24;
I Timothy 2:7; and II Timothy 1:11.)

". . . *separated unto the Gospel of God.*" When
Paul (Saul of Tarsus) met Jesus on the Damascus
road just outside the Damascus gate, he fell to the
earth and cried out to the Lord Jesus, asking Him
who He was. He then said, "What wilt thou have
me to do?" (Read Acts 9:1-19.) And from that
moment until his dying day, his whole soul's desire
was to serve Jesus with a fervent spirit, an unselfish heart, and with a body completely dedicated
to God . . . a living sacrifice! He was a servant;
he was an apostle; and he was a specific and
peculiar vessel, separated unto the Gospel of God.
His message was singular: The death, burial, and
resurrection of Jesus Christ . . . and only according
to the Scriptures (I Cor. 15:1-4).

All of the other apostles received their education
at the feet of Jesus. They followed Jesus during
His brief earthly ministry—but Paul, before he
became a believer, was a *persecutor.* Suddenly he
became an apostle by special calling, and when
he began teaching and preaching, he "conferred not
with flesh and blood" (Gal. 1:16). He did not go

down to Jerusalem to meet with the religious dignitaries, to beg their good graces and favors upon his ministry. He knew the Lord Jesus; he had met Him face to face. He had heard His command, and he obeyed with all of his heart. He was a special and a peculiar apostle. He had an experience such as no man before or since had—or ever will have. He was called, ordained, and sent by God—a minister to the Gentiles.

In the New Testament the word "apostle" means "one sent by God and clothed by God with full and complete authority," to speak and to act for the Divine Sender. The New Testament apostle delivered God's message, fresh from God's heart.

Paul set forth, in the very beginning of his letter to the Romans, the fact that he was separated unto the Gospel of God. This man had no difficulty in making clear who he was. He knew his ministry, he knew to whom he was to speak, he knew to whom he belonged, and he knew who he was. He was the Lord's slave, and he was in a peculiar business preaching the Gospel of God—God's good news to hell-deserving sinners. He knew he was a chosen vessel, he knew he was dedicated to a peculiar ministry (Acts 9:15). This ministry was blueprinted and outlined from the very day he was born (Gal. 1:15).

Paul, like many of us, was a long time finding his place in life and in the New Testament Church; but thank God, when he met Jesus on the road to

Damascus, he lost his life that he might find it in Christ. I believe he said every word God ever impressed upon him to say. I believe he preached every sermon he was supposed to preach. I believe he conducted every campaign God intended for him to conduct. I believe his ministry was as nearly perfect as that of any human who ever lived and ministered on this earth. I base that statement on the following words, which Paul wrote to Timothy shortly before his death:

"For I am now ready to be offered, and the time of my departure is at hand. *I have fought a good fight, I have finished my course, I have kept the faith:* Henceforth there is laid up for me a crown of righteousness, which the Lord, the righteous Judge, shall give me at that day: and not to me only, but unto all them also that love His appearing" (II Tim. 4:6-8).

Note these words: "I HAVE FOUGHT A GOOD FIGHT . . . I HAVE FINISHED MY COURSE . . . I HAVE KEPT THE FAITH." To me, that is the perfect testimony. Paul was a good soldier; he fought every battle and fought it well. He did not deviate from the faith one iota, from the day he met Jesus on the Damascus road until the day he closed his eyes in a martyr's death!

Just what does Paul mean by *"the Gospel of God"*? Great commentators down through the ages agree that "the Gospel of God" is the widest possible designation of the whole body of redemption truth concerning the grace that Jesus brought through His sacrificial death, burial, and resurrection for all, because God is no respecter of persons (Rom. 2:11). He is not the God of the Jews only, but He is the God of the Gentiles also (Rom. 3:29). No longer is there a "middle wall of partition" (Eph. 2:14). He removed that barrier, and now it is "whosoever will." That is the Gospel of God: Redemption for all who will come to God by Christ; redemption from all sin through His shed blood; redemption only on the grounds of faith—faith such as even a little child can exercise.

The Gospel of God reveals the doctrine of grace as having to do with our salvation from sin, and the Gospel of God reveals the great promises God makes to us after we are saved by grace. The Gospel of God reveals to us our position in the economy of God, in the Church of the living God, of which Jesus is the Head and the Foundation; we are members of His body, bone of His bone and flesh of His flesh. The Gospel of God clearly sets forth that we, the bride of Christ, are not a continuation of the kingdom for Israel, but are distinctly a new body. The Gospel of God assures us that God has not forgotten Abraham or Israel, nor has God robbed them of their covenant promises; but God will fulfill every promise in every minute detail. To sum it up: *The Gospel of God is the widest possible designation of the whole body of redemption truth.*

Verse 2: *"(Which He had promised afore by His prophets in the holy Scriptures.)"*

The main point in the statement made in this verse is that the Gospel was revealed in fulfillment of the promises which God had made in the Old Testament era, and also in the beginning of the New Testament era. In I Peter 1:10-12 we read:

"Of which salvation the prophets have inquired and searched diligently, who prophesied of the grace that should come unto you: searching what, or what manner of time the Spirit of Christ which was in them did signify, when it testified beforehand the sufferings of Christ, and the glory that should follow. Unto whom it was revealed, that not unto themselves, but unto us they did minister the things, which are now reported unto you by them that have preached the Gospel unto you with the Holy Ghost sent down from heaven; which things the angels desire to look into."

Here in our verse in Romans, Paul declares that he is not about to advance anything new. His doctrines, though hidden in the Old Testament era, were consistent with *"the holy Scriptures"* as penned down by the prophets. The Scriptures were called "holy" because they were inspired by the Holy Ghost: "For the prophecy came not in old time by the will of man: *but holy men of God spake as they were moved by the Holy Ghost"* (II Pet. 1:21).

Verses 3 and 4: *"Concerning His Son Jesus*

Christ our Lord, which was made of the seed of David according to the flesh; and declared to be the Son of God with power, according to the Spirit of holiness, by the resurrection from the dead."

The Person Jesus Christ is the center, the heart, the very substance of the Gospel of God. As the prophets had prophesied, Jesus, *"according to the flesh,"* came through the seed of David; He was a descendant of David. And *"according to the Spirit of holiness"* He was proven to be *"the Son of God with power,"* and this proof came *"by the resurrection from the dead"*—and not only through *His* resurrection, but the fact that He had the power to resurrect *others.*

Jesus, the only begotten SON OF GOD, has accomplished a work; however, it is not the work, but *Himself,* who is the true SUBJECT of the Gospel. He is the heart, the soul, and the very essence of the Gospel. In Romans we have Him presented in a twofold aspect:

First: He is the object of the promises—Son of David according to the flesh.

Second: He is the Son of God in power; and as the Son of God in power, He walked by the Spirit in divine and absolute holiness apart from sin in thought, word, or deed, even though in the midst of sin. He was (and *is*) the Sinless One. Not only was He the Son of David according to the flesh, but He was the Son of *God*—yea, very God in flesh. He proved this by His victorious

20

resurrection from the dead. His resurrection was a public manifestation that He was God's only begotten Son.

What a marvelous demonstration of grace! The whole power of evil—the dreadful door of death which closed upon sinful men, leaving them in the darkness of death to be judged by God's holiness—was broken and destroyed by our Lord. Jesus was willing to step inside this gloomy chamber of death and take upon Himself all the weakness of man in death, and thus absolutely and completely deliver man, whose penalty He had borne in submitting to death. Jesus conquered hell, death, and the grave, and walked out with the keys, victorious over all the power of darkness and hell.

Jesus came into this world on a singular mission —to "taste death for every man" (Heb. 2:9). He personally attacked death—stepped into the very darkness of death, and in His own power He conquered death and walked out of the grave victorious. The Son of God took upon Himself the seed of David after the flesh, and in a body did what the Law had never done—nor ever could have done. Jesus proved that He was God in flesh by His resurrection from the dead.

The resurrection is the hub of the wheel of truth concerning Jesus as very God. All the spokes of truth point to the hub—the resurrection. Had He not conquered death, had He not risen from the dead, then all that He claimed would have been untrue. The greatest bombshell ever to explode in the face of an unbelieving world was the resurrection of the Lord Jesus Christ from the dead. The fact that He arose from the dead proved that He lived a holy, sinless, spotless life, free from any and all iniquity or stain caused by sin.

The message of the resurrection of Jesus changed the world in His day, and it still divides mankind into two groups. Immediately after His resurrection, the Jewish world was divided into two groups. The Jewish leaders declared that the disciples had stolen His body, but the disciples testified that He had risen from the dead. I repeat: The resurrection of the Lord Jesus was and is the greatest bombshell ever to explode in the face of an unbelieving world.

The resurrection of Jesus Christ teaches us that death is not the end. Death is an enemy; but to a believer, death is an exit from a life of sorrow into a life of peace and joy in the presence of Jesus, the One who conquered death.

If Jesus Christ arose from the dead (and we know He did), then His resurrection declares Him to be the world's greatest Teacher. No other teacher who ever lived has ever come back from the dead in a body and appeared to his followers. There have been, and there are, many great religious leaders; but the Lord Jesus Christ is the only Person who died and then did exactly what He told the people in advance that He would do—

that is, the third day He would come back from the dead. *He did just that.*

The resurrection of Jesus Christ is the secret of the power of the New Testament message. The resurrection of Jesus completely transformed the lives of His disciples. These men had fled from Gethsemane, scared out of their wits, scampering into hiding to save their lives. But after the resurrection, they suddenly became "dare-saints"—and even death did not make cowards of these one-time weaklings who now had become instantaneous spiritual giants. Many of these early Christians who lived in the first century and shortly thereafter, were thrown to hungry lions, burned at the stake, severely tortured . . . but they held not their lives dear unto themselves. These early believers challenged the power of heathen kings, and surrendered their life's blood to testify that they had complete, unshakable faith in the Man Christ Jesus.

The resurrection of Jesus Christ still speaks to every sinner on earth. If we believe that Jesus died and rose again, and if we will confess with our mouth as we believe in our heart, the Christ who walked out of the tomb will save us. The verse that changed my life clearly states "That if thou shalt confess with thy mouth the Lord Jesus, and shalt believe in thine heart that God hath raised Him from the dead, *thou shalt be saved*" (Rom. 10:9).

Jesus said, "Come unto me, all ye that labour and are heavy laden, and I will give you rest" (Matt. 11:28). Multiplied millions of men and women, young men and young women, boys and girls, have accepted His invitation, and they can testify that Jesus keeps His word. They came—and He gave rest. The righteous have peace that a dead Christ and a dead religion could not give. The poor heathen who worship idols and gods of stone cannot testify that they have peace within. They live in fear, they die in fear. But those of us who have put our trust in the risen Lord can truthfully say, "For to me to live is Christ, and to die is gain." We can shout the victory over death, hell, and the grave, because we believe in Him who conquered all the power of hell, death, and the grave!

Verse 5: *"By whom we have received grace and apostleship, for obedience to the faith among all nations, for His name."*

"...grace and apostleship...." Some suppose this is a figure of speech by which one thing is expressed in two words, meaning the grace or favor of the apostolic office. But it could mean, and probably does mean, the two things—both grace *and* the apostolic office: grace, the favor of God to Paul's own soul as a personal matter; and the apostolic office as a distinct thing. Paul often speaks of his office as an apostle as a matter

24

of special favor (Rom. 15:15, 16; Gal. 2:9; Eph. 3:7-9).

"... *for obedience to the faith among all nations, for His name.*" Romans is the Epistle of divine life in Christ for all nations, but only on the condition of simple faith. The works of the Law are excluded from this salvation purchased by the death, burial, and resurrection of the Christ of God.

The Gospel according to Paul is the universal Gospel—not a Gospel to the Jew only, but to the whole wide world, a Gospel to the Gentiles and to all nations. The Gospel was from God Himself, but it is from Jesus Christ Himself that Paul received his mission. Jesus was the Head of the work, but He sent forth laborers into the harvest which they were to reap in the world. The object of the mission (and its extent) was *obedience to the faith* (not obedience to the Law) *among all nations*, establishing the authority and the value of the name of Christ. It was *this* name which should prevail and be acknowledged.

The resurrection of Jesus from the dead declared Him to be the Saviour of *all* men—not just the Jews or certain groups. And through the power of His resurrection He provides endless life for all who will believe on His name!

Verses 6 and 7: "*Among whom are ye also the called of Jesus Christ: to all that be in Rome, beloved of God, called to be saints: Grace to you and peace from God our Father, and the Lord Jesus Christ."*

In these verses Paul speaks of the children of God as follows:

1. We are *"the called of Jesus Christ"* (v. 6). Jude speaks of "them that are sanctified by God the Father, and preserved in Jesus Christ, *and called"* (Jude 1). Jesus came into the world "to seek and to save that which was lost" (Luke 19:10). The world is not seeking Christ, but He came to seek the world—"whosoever" among all nations, regardless of color, class, or creed. Christ came to save ALL who will believe.

2. Believers are termed *"beloved of God"* (v. 7), and surely they are that. In his letter to the Colossians, Paul calls them "the elect of God, holy and *beloved"* (Col. 3:12).

3. We are also *"called saints"* (v. 7). (See also I Corinthians 1:2.) Greek authorities tell us that the words "to be" are not in the original manuscript but were supplied by the translators. We are not called *to be* saints—but we *become* saints the moment we believe on Jesus Christ. Let me point out something here that will enrich your life immensely if you will see it and believe it:

We become Christians by receiving the finished work of the Lord Jesus Christ. He shed His blood for the remission of sin. We are *saved* by His shed blood—and there is *no salvation apart from*

His cleansing blood. When we receive Him as our Saviour by faith, when we put our trust in His shed blood, we are justified (Rom. 5:1, 9). When we are justified by faith in His shed blood, we instantaneously become just as just as *Jesus* is just, because He is the One who justifies us. We become just as pure as the blood that covers us. When we receive the Lord Jesus Christ, we are "crucified with Christ," and we are "hid with Christ in God" and sealed by the Holy Spirit "unto the day of redemption."

Will you please turn in your Bible and read carefully the following verses: Romans 5:1; II Corinthians 5:21; Galatians 2:20; Ephesians 4:30; Colossians 1:27; 2:9, 10; 3:3; Hebrews 9:22; and I John 1:7. These verses clearly and unmistakably teach us that salvation is *of the Lord*—entirely of the Lord, totally of the Lord—completely apart from man. Christ is our redemption, our righteousness, our sanctification, our holiness—and when we are in Christ and Christ is in us, in God's eyes we are just as just as Jesus is just, because God the Father sees the Christ who saves us, the precious blood that covers us, and the Holy Spirit who seals us.

We are not saved to *become* saints . . . *we become saints the split second we are saved.* In Christ Jesus our Lord, we are already saints. We are God's holy ones. We are set apart for God. We belong to God—and we are following Him because "as many as are led by the Spirit of God, they are the sons of God" (Rom. 8:14; I Cor. 1:29, 30).

It is true that we are commanded to "work out" our own salvation "with fear and trembling" (Phil. 2:12). We are commanded to present our bodies a living sacrifice unto God (Rom. 12:1). We are commanded to yield our members "as instruments of righteousness unto God" (Rom. 6:13). But God help you to see and understand that *the instant we are saved we are just as saved as we ever will be saved!* We do not become "better saved" the longer we live for Jesus. We *should* become better Christians; we should become *stronger* Christians. But the moment we are born into God's family we are just as much a son of God that split second as we ever will be a son of God. When we receive Jesus, we receive divine life; divine nature becomes ours (II Pet. 1:4)—and if we live for Jesus for fifty years, we will never be any better saved or any more saved than we are the split second we exercise faith in His finished work. I repeat: We are not "going to become" saints; we are saints *already* if we are believers, if we are born again children of God.

"To all that be in Rome . . . ." Paul is addressing the believers in Rome, primarily; but as I have stated previously, these truths are also ours. All Scripture is given by inspiration of God, and all Scripture is profitable to us. It is true that certain

specific sections of the Word of God have to do with specific peoples, such as the *Jew,* the *Gentile,* and the *Church of God* (the body of Christ). But all Scripture is profitable to us as believers, from Genesis 1:1 through the last verse in Revelation.

"Grace to you and peace from God our Father, and the Lord Jesus Christ." These words of greeting are used by Paul in most of his epistles. *Grace* is God's free, unmerited favor toward men, and grace brings *peace* to the heart of the believer. Grace and peace come equally from the Father and from the Lord Jesus Christ.

Verse 8: *"First, I thank my God through Jesus Christ for you all, that your faith is spoken of throughout the whole world."*

"I thank my God through Jesus Christ . . . ." Christ is the Mediator between God and men. He has made the way to God accessible to us, whether it be by prayer or by praise; and it is owing to His mercy and grace that any of our services are acceptable to God.

". . . for you all, that your faith is spoken of throughout the whole world." Paul thanks God first for the faith of the believers in Rome. The readiness with which the Romans embraced the Gospel was so remarkable that it was known everywhere.

Jesus said to His disciples, "Have faith in God" (Mark 11:22). Paul tells us in Hebrews 11:6 that

without faith it is *impossible to please God.* James
tells us that if we lack wisdom we should "ask of
God"—and I certainly believe that we may put
any other need we have in the stead of wisdom.
But James says, ". . . let him ask *in faith,* nothing
wavering" (James 1:5, 6). He goes on to assure us
that if we waver, or doubt, we will not receive
anything from the Lord. God is not concerned
about numbers, or a big show. God is honored
by our *faith* in God's Christ. God *honors* faith,
and faith alone. We will be rewarded for the
works that we do in true faith. "Whatsoever is
not of faith is sin" (Rom. 14:23).

Verse 9: *"For God is my witness, whom I serve
with my spirit in the Gospel of His Son, that
without ceasing I make mention of you always
in my prayers."*

"God is my witness . . . ." Paul was very careful to assure those to whom he wrote, that what
he was saying was witnessed by God and the Holy
Ghost. He always carefully set forth the fact that
he was telling the truth. (Read Romans 9:1; II
Corinthians 1:23; Philippians 1:8; I Thessalonians
2:5, 10; and I Timothy 2:7.)

". . . *that without ceasing I make mention of
you always in my prayers."* Paul admonished the
Christians at Thessalonica, *"Pray without ceasing"* (I Thess. 5:17). Here in Romans he assures
the believers that he *does* pray for them "without

30

ceasing." You see, this man practiced what he preached. He did not preach one thing, and live another. He prayed for the people to whom he ministered.

I believe one of the outstanding sins in the church today is prayerlessness among the saints. *If God's people spent as much time in prayer as they do before their televisions, I am sure we would have a revival that would shake the world!* But a *prayerless* church is a *powerless* church; and by the same token, a prayerless *Christian* is a powerless Christian. And the *preacher* who does not season his message with prayer, cannot hope for God's blessings to follow his message.

Paul was a praying man. One of the most interesting chapters in the Bible on evangelism and soul winning is Acts 16. In that chapter we find recorded three remarkable conversions in the ministry of Paul, and on each occasion, prayer is mentioned as the important factor:

In Acts 16:12-15, Lydia, an outstanding lady of Thyatira, was converted. Paul led her to the knowledge of salvation while attending a prayer meeting. Read the account.

In Acts 16:16-18 Paul led a fortuneteller to Jesus. She gave up her witchcraft and became a disciple of Christ. It was on the way to a prayer meeting that the fortuneteller began to listen to Paul and Silas: "And it came to pass, *as we went to prayer,* a certain damsel possessed with a spirit of divination met us, which brought her masters much gain by soothsaying" (v. 16).

In Acts 16:19-34, we find that because of the conversion of the fortuneteller, Paul and Silas were put in prison. In the prison, Paul and Silas *prayed* —and then they sang. God answered their prayer, sent an earthquake that almost shook the jail down —and a jailor got saved!

Paul prayed—and a dignified lady named Lydia found Christ. Paul prayed—and a poor, fallen witch (practicing witchcraft) was saved. Paul prayed—and a jailor found Christ. Yes, Paul was a praying man.

God help us who name the name of Jesus and profess to be His followers, to pray as we have never prayed before! James says: "... *ye have not, because ye ASK not*. Ye ask, and receive not, because ye ask amiss, that ye may consume it upon your lusts" (James 4:2, 3).

Verse 10: *"Making request, if by any means now at length I might have a prosperous journey by the will of God to come unto you."*

In this verse, Paul simply states that he is requesting prayer that he may have a prosperous journey by God's will in coming to Rome to preach the Gospel to the people there in Rome. *"If by any means"* shows the earnest desire which he had in coming to them, and implies that he had before designed it but had been hindered (see v. 13).

"*. . . by the will of God . . . .*" Paul was saying, "if God by His great mercy and wisdom shall grant me this request of coming to you."

Verses 11 and 12: "*For I long to see you, that I may impart unto you some spiritual gift, to the end ye may be established; that is, that I may be comforted together with you by the mutual faith both of you and me.*"

No doubt there were those who declared that Paul had no desire nor intention of visiting Rome—and also that the Romans were too well informed, much too cultured, entirely too sophisticated and highly educated to accept such a message as Paul preached; namely, "suffering, blood, death, burial, and miraculous resurrection." Those who may have said that he would never preach in Rome did not know the power of the message of the resurrected Lord. Personally, I believe Paul had a burning desire and a deep longing to visit Rome and preach the Gospel, that he might "*impart . . . some spiritual gift*" and help the believers to "*be established.*" He states just that in these verses, and I believe he was sincere.

Verse 13: "*Now I would not have you ignorant, brethren, that oftentimes I purposed to come unto you, (but was let hitherto,) that I might have some fruit among you also, even as among other Gentiles.*"

It seems, according to this verse, that Paul probably had sent a message to Rome on several occasions, to the effect that he would visit the city to witness to the saving grace of Christ. But he had never been able to keep his proposed appointments because of the enemy, the devil. In I Thessalonians 2:18 Paul declares that Satan hindered him from visiting the church in Thessalonica. Again, in Romans 15:22 he refers to the fact that he had been hindered from coming to the church at Rome. It seems the devil did everything in his ungodly power to keep this spiritual giant from preaching the Gospel in the great city of Rome; but in spite of the devil, in spite of all the forces of hell, Paul finally visited Rome!

Paul's desire was *"that I might have some fruit among you"*—or, "that I might be the means of the conversion of sinners and the edification of the church in the city of Rome." Paul's motive did not stem from curiosity or the love of travel, but solely from the desire to be of spiritual help to the people of Rome. Jesus Himself said: ". . . I have chosen you, and ordained you, that ye should go and *bring forth fruit*, and that your fruit should remain . . ." (John 15:16).

Verses 14-17: *"I am debtor both to the Greeks, and to the Barbarians; both to the wise, and to the unwise. So, as much as in me is, I am ready to preach the Gospel to you that are at Rome also.*

For I am not ashamed of the Gospel of Christ: for it is the power of God unto salvation to every one that believeth; to the Jew first, and also to the Greek. For therein is the righteousness of God revealed from faith to faith: as it is written, The just shall live by faith."

There is a marvelous sermon in these verses. I would call the sermon *"The Three 'I Ams' of Paul."*

1. *"I am debtor . . . ."* This does not mean that those whom Paul names had conferred a favor upon him which put him under obligation to return a favor. It means that he was under obligation to preach the Gospel *to all to whom it was possible.* This obligation arose from the mercy and grace God had bestowed upon him in saving him and then calling him to this work. Paul was especially chosen to carry the Gospel to the Gentiles (Acts 9:15; Rom. 11:13).

Just as Paul was a debtor, every true born again child of God is a debtor to those who do not know Christ as Saviour. And if you know God, do not ever forget to thank Him for those who prayed for you, witnessed to you, and helped you find true salvation through hearing the pure Gospel.

2. *"I am ready . . . ."* I wonder just how many of us who name the name of Jesus, who profess to be followers of the Lamb of God, are ready to go where He bids, say what He bids, and do what He commands? If we are ready to follow Jesus,

He will lead us by the still waters and into green pastures, where we can bear much fruit to glorify His precious name! Can you say, "I am ready"? Can you say, "I'll go where you want me to go, dear Lord, over mountain, or plain, or sea. I'll say what you want me to say, dear Lord; I'll be what you want me to be"? If you cannot say that, why not bow your head this very moment and yield yourself entirely and unreservedly to God?

3. *"I am not ashamed . . . ."* The Jews had cast Paul off (Acts 9:22-24) and with the Gentiles had persecuted him and driven him from place to place. He was regarded as "the filth of the world" and "the offscouring of all things" (I Cor. 4:9-13). Men mocked at the message he preached, for it was "foolishness" to them (I Cor. 1:18)—but he was still not ashamed of the Gospel.

So many of us are timid—or perhaps we are just purely *ashamed* of Jesus! God pity us if we are! Do you speak up when you should? Do you speak out for Jesus in the midst of the enemies of Jesus? Are you ashamed of His name? Are you ashamed of the Gospel? God help us not to be ashamed of the Gospel, because it was *the Gospel* that brought light to our poor, blinded minds. It was the Gospel that brought power to transform us from dead sinners to living sons. It is the Gospel that is a lamp to our feet and a light to our pathway.

You and I who name the name of Jesus should

always open the conversation when among people. We should speak out for Jesus. No, I do not mean that we should become an offence by screaming out His name to the top of our voices. I mean we should let the whole wide world and each and every individual with whom we come in contact, know that we belong to Jesus and we are His because we have learned about Him through the precious, pure, powerful Gospel.

According to verse 14, Paul was not a hyper-Calvinist. (Hyper-Calvinist doctrine teaches that some people are elected to heaven and others are elected to hell—and that it is impossible for the *elect* to go to *hell,* and it is just as impossible for those *outside* the elect to be saved and go to heaven.) Paul declared that he was in debt *"to the Greeks, and to the Barbarians; . . . to the wise, and to the unwise."* He believed that Christ died for the sins of the whole wide world. He believed that the Gospel was for *everyone. I believe that, too—and so does every other Bible-believing preacher!* We are in debt to *all* peoples, regardless of their color, class, or creed. We who know the truth of the pure Gospel of grace should not be satisfied until we have done all in our power to preach this message to all people, regardless of who they are.

Paul was *ready* with all of his power and might —*"as much as in me is"* (v. 15). He was ready to spend and be spent in Rome—but only *"to preach the Gospel."* He did not wish to make a name for himself; he had a burning desire to go to Rome to preach the Gospel—and if you want to know what Paul called the Gospel, read I Corinthians 15:1-4. There he clearly outlines his message: *First,* the *death* of Jesus . . . blood. *Second,* the *burial* of Jesus—that is, a dead Christ was taken off of a cross and placed in a tomb, dead. *Third,* the *resurrection* of Jesus. Paul believed in the *literal* resurrection. He did not believe or teach that the resurrection is a myth; he believed in the *bodily resurrection.* His message was *"Christ— crucified, buried, and risen . . .* according to the Scriptures." He preached the pure, unadulterated Gospel. He was not trying to make a name for himself or for a religion. He was interested in making disciples for Jesus.

Paul boldly declared to the Romans, *"I am not ashamed of the Gospel of Christ.* It may cause me persecution. I may suffer . . . I may be stoned, I may be beaten, I may be dragged outside of the city for dead; but I am not ashamed of the Gospel. I want everyone in Rome to know that I believe the Gospel; I preach the Gospel. The reason I am not ashamed of it is, it is the power of God to save everyone who believes. The message is to the Jew first—but it is also to the Greek (or to the Gentile) . . . *whosoever will.* This message is for everyone!"

Many people use the statement *"to the Jew first"*

to lay Jewish missions heavily upon the hearts of people. I believe in Jewish missions. I have been to Israel and have given liberally to Jewish missions. BUT . . . *the Jew had his chance FIRST.* When Jesus came to this earth and called the twelve disciples, He instructed them to go "to the lost sheep of the house of Israel," and He commanded them *not* to go to the Gentiles (Matt. 10:5, 6). To a Gentile woman He said, "I am not sent but unto the lost sheep of the house of Israel" (Matt. 15:24). But in John 1:11 we read, *"He came unto His own, and His own RECEIVED HIM NOT"* . . . they despised and rejected Him.

Pilate led Jesus out on the platform on that memorable day and asked the Jews, "Which prisoner do you desire . . . Jesus, or Barabbas?" And they all shouted in unison, "Barabbas!" Pilate said, "What shall I do then with Jesus?" And they shouted, "Crucify Him! Let His blood be on us and on our children . . . we do not want Him! We want a robber; we want Barabbas! Kill Jesus!"

Yes, the Jew had his chance first. Do not misunderstand me; God saves Jews today, but He saves the Jew exactly as He saves the Gentile. The message today is to the Jew and the Gentile alike. In the Church of the living God there is no difference; the middle wall of partition has been broken down. (Please study carefully Ephesians 2:11-22.)

Paul tells us that the Gospel is *"the power of God unto salvation"*—not the power of God "unto religion" or "good living" or "good works," but "unto *salvation.*" Salvation signifies *saving*—and for one to be saved, he must first be *lost.* The great need today is to get people to see that they are lost, in order that we may be able to get them to come to Christ for salvation.

The words "saved" and "salvation" are not prominent in modern sermons. We hear the words "decision," and "unite with us," and "join the church and become a part of us." Not many invitations are extended for poor wretched, hell-deserving sinners to come and humbly bow upon their knees to receive Jesus Christ as Saviour, to be saved from sin.

Salvation is the great inclusive word of the Gospel. It signifies the acts of redemption, justification, propitiation, forgiveness, sanctification, and glorification. It implies *deliverance, safety, preservation, spiritual healing*, and *soundness.*

Our salvation is in three tenses:

1. In the first place, every born again one *has been* saved from the guilt, the penalty, of sin. (Read Luke 7:50; I Corinthians 1:18; II Corinthians 2:15; Ephesians 2:5, 8; and II Timothy 1:9.)

2. In the second place, every believer is daily *being* saved from the habit (or the dominion) of sin (Rom. 6:14; 8:2; II Corinthians 3:18; Galatians 2:19, 20; Philippians 1:19; 2:12, 13; II Thessalonians 2:13).

3. In the third place, every believer in the future *will be saved* entirely from the very *presence* of sin. (Read Romans 13:11; I Thessalonians 4:13-18; Hebrews 10:14; I Peter 1:5; and I John 3:2.)

Salvation comes by God's grace through faith. It is God's free gift to a hell-deserving sinner, wholly and entirely without works (Rom. 3:27, 28; 4:1-8; 6:23; Eph. 2:8, 9).

Salvation is followed by works; we prove our salvation by our works. We are God's workmanship. (Read Ephesians 2:9, 10 and Titus 3:5-8.) It is true that Paul admonishes us to work out our own salvation with fear and trembling (Phil. 2:12), but beloved, we cannot *work out* our own salvation until we *possess* salvation by faith. Salvation does not come by works, but by faith. When we exercise saving faith, faith automatically works in our heart and life. According to James 2:14-26, faith *without* works is *dead*. If a person testifies that he has faith, and yet he does not do works of righteousness, his testimony is void and vain. We prove our saving faith by our righteous works. Salvation is not OF works, but *salvation WORKS*.

In verses 16 and 17 we find some marvelous truths concerning the Gospel proclaimed by Paul:

The *nature* of the Gospel is *"the power of God."* The Gospel is powerful. Greek scholars tell us that the word "power" here is our word "dynamite." In other words, the Gospel is the dynamite of God which will blast the devil and sin out of human hearts that embrace the Gospel by faith.

The *aim* of the Gospel of God is *"unto salvation,"* and that salvation is from the penalty, the power, and, eventually, the very *presence* of sin.

The *scope* of the Gospel is to each and *"every one that believeth"* the Gospel. Salvation is to the Jew, the Greek, the Barbarian, the wise, the unwise, the bond, the free. No one is barred, no one is shut out, no one is left out . . . *"whosoever will,* let him take the water of life freely" (Rev. 22:17).

The *revelation* of the Gospel is: *"For therein is the righteousness of God revealed from faith to faith."* The Gospel is the only message that reveals to us the sovereignty of God, the holiness of God, the purity of God—yea, *God* is revealed in the Gospel.

The Gospel also reveals to us how, and through what power, the justified live; namely, *"The just shall live BY FAITH."* This statement was true in the Old Testament era (Hab. 2:4) just as surely as it is true in this Day of Grace. The just have always lived by faith. God has always dealt in faith and through faith. By faith *Abel* offered a blood sacrifice. By faith *Enoch* walked with God. By faith *Noah* built an ark. By faith *Abraham* moved out into a strange country, not knowing where he was going—but moving by faith. By faith *Moses* chose to suffer the afflictions of God's people rather than be called Pharaoh's son. (Read Hebrews chapter 11.) From Genesis to Malachi it is *by faith . . . by faith . . . by faith.* I remind you again that Jesus said to His disciples, "Have faith in God" (Mark 11:22). The Gospel reveals to us that we are to live by faith—not by sight, not by might, not by feelings, but by naked faith! Faith believes God simply because God *is* God. Faith accepts the Gospel of God because *God said it*—and if God said it, we can believe it. And if God said it, God is able to do it. "Is there any thing too hard for God?" He is able to do exceeding abundantly above anything that we think or ask in Jesus' name! Thank God for the Gospel.

The devil hates the Gospel and is doing everything in his devilish power to discredit the fundamentals of the faith and to bring Jesus down on the level with man. But the devil will never destroy the Gospel, because God's Word is forever settled in heaven! (Psa. 119:89). The devil cannot touch the Gospel! Hallelujah for the Gospel!

I am not ashamed of the Gospel; I am ready to preach the Gospel; I am ready to defend the Gospel; I am ready to live by the Gospel and to die by the Gospel. I will stand by the Gospel and tell those to whom I minister that we are saved by God's grace, through faith! We are *kept* by faith—and the justified shall *live* by faith!

PART I

THE GUILTY WORLD;
THE WRATH OF GOD REVEALED

The first seventeen verses of Romans chapter 1 comprise the introduction to the Epistle. Beginning with verse 18, and running through chapter 3, verse 20, we have the account of the guilty world and the wrath of God revealed from heaven against all ungodliness and wickedness.

Verse 18: *"For the wrath of God is revealed from heaven against all ungodliness and unrighteousness of men, who hold the truth in unrighteousness."*

Beginning here, sin is brought before us—and we need to *see* sin as it is, for all heresy has its source in wrong or feeble conception of sin. The naked, horrid facts concerning sin are here dragged out and made to stand before the blazing light of God's holiness and His holy wrath against all ungodliness and wickedness, regardless of the form. We need to see the wrath of God poured out—for we cannot fully appreciate the righteousness of God, the tenderness of God, the long-suffering of God, unless we are willing to face the wrath of God. Only they know what it is to be saved, who know what it is to be lost.

God is not a one-sided God. In this day of liberalism and modernism, we hear much about the love of God, the fatherhood of God, and the goodness of God. God *is* a good God—but He is not a one-sided God. "God is love" (I John 4:8)— but God is also "a consuming fire" (Heb. 12:29). The Bible teaches us that God is long-suffering, gentle, kind, and meek; but the Word also teaches us that God is "angry with the wicked every day"! (Psalm 7:11).

In this division of Romans we will learn that (1) all Gentiles are guilty before God; (2) all Jews are guilty before God; and (3) every mouth is stopped before God. In other words—all are in the same boat, there is no difference, all have sinned. Therefore, except a man (any man, *all* men) be born from above, he cannot enter the kingdom of God (John 3:3, 5).

"The wrath of God is revealed from heaven...." There are, then, two revelations from heaven (verses 17 and 18); and until this matter is explained, these revelations only bring terror to guilty man. The last thing any sinner wants to be reminded of is the wrath of God. He has yet to learn the marvel of the Gospel, by which God's righteousness actually becomes our righteousness when we accept Jesus Christ. When we accept Jesus, the wrath of God is lifted, and we become sons; not only sons, but heirs of God and joint-heirs with the Lord Jesus Christ.

Meanwhile, God's wrath is directed *"against all ungodliness and unrighteousness of men, who hold the truth in unrighteousness."* Ungodliness is the absence of conformity to the will of God. When we refuse to conform our will to the will of God, we automatically do those things that are not right in the sight of God. The only person who can live right and righteously, is the person who has been born of the Spirit and who is daily led by the Spirit. The flesh is not willing . . . never has been, nor ever will be. We must submit soul, spirit, and body to God, yielding our members to Him to be directed by the Holy Spirit who abides in the bosom of every child of God (Rom. 8:9, 14, 16; Eph. 4:30; John 3:5).

Since ungodliness is the absence of conformity to the will of God by man, it leads to the practice of unrighteousness as to men's relations with each other. Then, too, they will not heed the facts. They "hold the truth in unrighteousness"; therefore they do things one to another that are not right. The only person who can live in the truth and practice truth is the man who possesses Jesus, THE TRUTH.

The natural heart is "deceitful above all things, and desperately wicked" (Jer. 17:9). Since this is true, the natural heart refuses to face the truth and walk in the truth. This is the universal rule, whether the truth be revealed through the light of nature, or the moral sense, or the preaching of the Gospel. Natural man hates the truth, and "the carnal mind is enmity against God" (Rom. 8:7).

46

I am not saying that every person who is not a born again child of God is a grand rascal. That is not true at all. But let me assure you that regardless of how clean you may live and how upright your dealings with your fellowman may be, you are still living a lie if you know that Jesus died for you and you refuse to submit to that truth. Jesus said, *"I am the Way, the Truth, and the Life: no man cometh unto the Father, but by me"* (John 14:6). If you know that, but refuse to surrender your life to the Lord Jesus who is the Way, the Truth, and the Life, you are branding God a liar!

I know the statement I have made is a hard statement, and if I did not have the Word of God to back it up I would not make such a statement. But since I have clear Scripture to substantiate what I have said, then I say it without hesitation, reservation, or fear.

In I John 5:10 we read: "He that believeth on the Son of God hath the witness in himself: HE THAT BELIEVETH NOT GOD HATH MADE HIM (GOD) A LIAR; BECAUSE HE BELIEVETH NOT THE RECORD THAT GOD GAVE OF HIS SON." According to this verse, if we hear the message that God gave Jesus to die for us, and we know Jesus died on the cross to save us, and, knowing that fact, we refuse to receive Jesus and refuse to conform our will to His will, *we brand God a liar!* Why do I say that? Simply because

God so loved us that He paid sin's debt, and through simple faith in Jesus Christ we are allowed to become God's sons, God's heirs and joint-heirs with Jesus—and if a person hears and *believes* such a message, *he will accept it* . . . because any hell-deserving sinner had rather accept Jesus and go to the Pearly White City of God than to *reject* Jesus and burn in hell forever. The whole thing boils down to the final point that when a sinner hears the Gospel message and refuses to receive it, in the true sense of the word he simply does not BELIEVE the message. I will illustrate:

If someone warns you that a certain bridge is out, as you are rushing down the highway toward that bridge at sixty miles an hour, you will turn your car around and go in the opposite direction if you believe the bridge is actually out. To continue down the road at sixty miles an hour would be to plunge over the embankment into the river and drown. Rational, thinking people do not desire to depart this life by drowning. And I say without hesitation that when you *believe* there is a devil's hell, a roaring flame in the lake of fire, and that sinners go to hell simply for rejecting Jesus . . . when you *really believe* that . . . you will turn to Jesus and receive Him as your personal Saviour. Again I quote: *"He that believeth not God HATH MADE HIM A LIAR; because he believeth not the record that God gave of His Son"* (I John 5:10).

The general idea is that people go to hell because they drink liquor, because they murder, gamble, lie, steal, commit adultery, etc. But the Bible fact is clearly stated in John 3:18: "He that believeth on Him is not condemned: but *he that believeth not is condemned already, because he hath not believed in the name of the only begotten Son of God."* Men are saved by believing on the Lord Jesus Christ from the heart (Rom. 10:10). Men are *condemned* (and those who plunge into hell will do so) because they *refuse* to believe on the Lord Jesus Christ. John 3:18 clearly teaches this solemn fact.

Sinners will not be lost "when" they die . . . sinners are lost this very moment! Every believer is *saved now,* and every *unbeliever* is *condemned* now! In John 3:36 we read: *"He that believeth on the Son HATH EVERLASTING LIFE:* and he that *believeth not* the Son *shall not see life; BUT THE WRATH OF GOD ABIDETH ON HIM."* All unbelievers are guilty before God, and the wrath of God is resting upon them *now.* The reasons are clearly set forth in the following verses:

Verses 19 and 20: *"Because that which may be known of God is manifest in them; for God hath shewed it unto them. For the invisible things of Him from the creation of the world are clearly seen, being understood by the things that are made, even His eternal power and Godhead; so that they are without excuse."*

"That which may be known of God . . ."—or "that which is knowable concerning God." The expression implies that there may be many things concerning God which cannot be known. But there are many things which may be ascertained—such as His existence, many of His attributes, His power, wisdom, and justice. Paul's object was not to say that *everything* pertaining to God could be known by the Romans. We must interpret the expression according to the object which he had in view; that was to show that so much might be known of God as to prove that they had no excuse for their unrighteousness.

"For the invisible things of Him from the creation of the world are clearly seen, being understood by the things that are made . . . ." The Psalmist declares: "The heavens declare the glory of God; and the firmament sheweth His handywork. Day unto day uttereth speech, and night unto night sheweth knowledge. *There is no speech nor language, where their voice is not heard"* (Psalm 19: 1-3). The things of God are clearly seen and understood by all who desire to see and understand.

The heathen are guilty before God whether they are evangelized or unevangelized; that is, ALL are guilty, and in the verses which follow we will clearly see three reasons why we have heathen people. (You must remember that Adam and Eve are the parents of all living. Then, after the Flood, Noah and his righteous family started again to replenish this earth. So somewhere down the line something happened that caused multiplied billions to be on earth today, who have never heard the name of Jesus.)

The heavens and nature clearly teach us two things about God: First, *"His eternal power"*; second, His *"Godhead."* In other words, nature teaches us that there MUST BE a Creator—a Supreme Being, a Master mind—behind the heavens and the creations around us. If He is Creator, then He ought to be worshipped and He is worthy of all worship.

I have been in the jungles of South America, the jungles of Africa. I have been to the peoples who never heard the name of Jesus Christ. I had the privilege of speaking to a group, through an interpreter, in the jungles of Africa; and in that group were some who had never heard the name of Jesus. And yet—those people had their gods. They worshipped gods of stone, wood; some of them worshipped trees, the moon. In other words, all peoples of the earth (regardless of where they live) know that there IS a God—a Supreme Being— somewhere. Therefore, *"they are without excuse."*

There are people who refuse to believe that the heathen are lost. They believe that somehow those who have never heard the Gospel will be permitted to enter heaven. But beloved, if we believe the record given to us in the Word of God, we MUST accept the fact that all who fail to believe on the name of the Lord Jesus Christ cannot enter the kingdom of God. It is true they may never have heard that name . . . but that is not God's fault. Much of the blame lies at the feet of those of us who have been saved and yet have been so lazy we have not carried the Gospel to those people. But it is impossible for *any* person to be saved (or to enter heaven) until he receives the Lord Jesus Christ by faith as his personal Saviour.

Jesus said, *"No man cometh unto the Father, but by me"* (John 14:6). And the Scriptures clearly teach us that "there is *none other name under heaven given among men, whereby we must be saved"* (Acts 4:12). Therefore, I declare that the heathen are lost . . . but I hasten to say that God will deal with the heathen in righteousness. The heathen will be judged according to their opportunities, according to their light. Those of us who live in the land of the Gospel, and reject Jesus, will meet much more severe wrath and judgment than will the heathen who never heard the name of Jesus or had the opportunity to believe on Him as Saviour. You may rest assured that God will deal with the heathen in righteous judgment. But here we have clearly stated in God's Word, God's own declaration concerning the guilt of the heathen world: "THEY ARE WITHOUT EXCUSE."

There is no evolution of man here. According to this truthful statement, man has not "evolved" into a higher being; instead, he has become more degraded all the way. The following verses show us clearly that insofar as the evolution of man is concerned, man without God is *evolution in reverse.* Man has not risen from protoplasm toward the likeness of Almighty God . . . far from it! God Himself tells us in these verses that man has been going downward instead of upward.

In the beginning, man was in perfect fellowship with God, and from that high estate, he fell—and man's fall was complete; that is, man is totally depraved, hopelessly lost, alienated from God . . . unless he believes on the Lord Jesus Christ and receives Him by faith as his personal Saviour. Without God, man is hopeless, helpless, and hell bound; but in Christ, thank God, we are sons and heirs of God.

Gentile World Apostasy

In verses 21 through 32 the apostasy of the Gentile world is set forth in three stages (listing three sins—each progressively worse)—and these are given as sufficient proof that men are indeed without excuse.

Verses 21-24: *"Because that, when they knew God, they glorified Him not as God, neither were thankful; but became vain in their imaginations, and their foolish heart was darkened. Professing themselves to be wise, they became fools, and changed the glory of the uncorruptible God into an*

*image made like to corruptible man, and to birds,
and fourfooted beasts, and creeping things. Wherefore God also gave them up to uncleanness through
the lusts of their own hearts, to dishonour their
own bodies between themselves."*

"Because that, when they knew God . . . ."
Man knew God in the beginning. God created man
in His own image; He breathed into man's nostrils
the breath of life, and man became a living soul
(Gen. 1:27; 2:7).

Let me remind you here of a truth concerning
man: *Man is a trinity;* that is, man is made up of
soul, spirit, and body. The human soul and spirit
are not identical, they are not the same. This is
proven in Hebrews 4:12, which speaks of *"the
dividing asunder* of soul and spirit." Also, the
soul and spirit are distinguished in the burial and
resurrection of the body. According to I Corinthians 15:44, the body is sown a natural body, but
raised a *spiritual* body. To declare therefore that
there is no difference between the soul and spirit
is to declare that there is no difference between the
mortal body and the resurrection body we will
receive when Jesus comes in the Rapture.

If we will search the Scriptures, we will see the
distinction between spirit, soul, and body. The
spirit is the part of man which "knows" or reasons;
it is the *mind:* "For what man *knoweth* the things
of a man, save *the spirit* of man which is in him?

Even so the things of God knoweth no man, but the Spirit of God." This verse clearly teaches that the spirit of man is the part of man that "knows."

The *soul* is the seat of affections, desires, emotions. It is the part of man that loves and hates. When Jesus wept with Mary and Martha concerning their dead brother, He "groaned in the spirit" (John 11:33). But when Jesus prayed in the Garden of Gethsemane, loving the whole world, paying the sin-debt for all sinners, His perspiration became as blood; and He said, "My *soul* is exceeding sorrowful, even unto death" (Matt. 26:38). Jesus was *loving* the whole world as He prayed in the Garden of Gethsemane. He was *thinking* in sorrow with two sisters as He groaned in His spirit.

The *body,* of course, is the house in which the soul and the spirit live. To prove that statement we need only one verse of Scripture—James 2:26: "For as *the body without the spirit is dead,* so faith without works is dead also." You see, when the spirit leaves the body, the body is dead.

It is clear, then, that the body, the spirit, and the soul are not the same. You remember when Jesus died on the cross, He said, "Father, into thy hands I commend my *spirit.*" It was prophesied concerning Jesus, ". . . thou wilt not leave my *soul* in hell, neither wilt thou suffer thine Holy One to see corruption" (Psalm 16:10; Acts 2:27). And we read in John's Gospel that Joseph of Arimathaea and Nicodemus prepared the *body* of Jesus for burial and placed it in Joseph's new tomb (John 19:38-42). Let us see the picture here:

The *body* of Jesus was hanging on the cross, limp and dead. Joseph and Nicodemus removed that body from the cross and placed it in a tomb. But Jesus, before His death, had committed His *spirit* back to the heavenly Father; and it was prophesied that His *soul* would not be left in hell (Hades)—certainly not the torment side of the Old Testament hell, but the Paradise side. Jesus descended into Paradise and announced to the spirits of the Old Testament saints that the sin-debt had been paid, the Lamb had been slain—once, for all, forever. He made this announcement to the saints in the Paradise side of hell, and then He brought all the spirits of the righteous out of the Paradise in the heart of the earth and carried them to the Paradise far above all heavens. (Read Ephesians 4:7-10.)

In Luke 16 we learn that hell, in the Old Testament era, was made up of two compartments. The rich man was on the torment side, and Lazarus was on the Paradise side. (Read Luke 16:19-31.) It was into Paradise, where Lazarus was, that the soul of Jesus entered when He died on the cross.

Yes, man was created in the image of God: man is a trinity—body, soul, and spirit. I have gone into detail to point this out, to show you how man can become "brute beast." Man can go on in sin until he is "past feeling" (Eph. 4:19). Let

56

me assert here and now that the reason for the hideous sex crimes and brutal slayings that are being committed today, is that there are thousands of men walking the streets and back alleys of our cities who have no more feeling for human beings than a dog—and in many cases, they do not have *as much* feeling for their fellow man as one dog has for another! When a person is totally and entirely given up by God, he becomes demented and demons control his every move and desire. Watch these tremendous statements as we study them in these verses.

The First Step Toward Heathenism

As we have already noted, man in the beginning "knew God"—but man failed to maintain himself in this position of grace. When men knew God, *"they glorified Him not as God, neither were thankful."* Then they *"became vain in their imaginations"*; that is, all they could think of and imagine, was vanity, emptiness. (Compare Genesis 6:5.)

"Professing themselves to be wise . . . ." Man is always prone to turn to reason, rather than to God. Preferring "the tree of knowledge" to "the tree of life," the inevitable result is that he became vain and puffed up (I Cor. 8:1). The end of this process is darkness. The way into light is by faith, not by knowledge. Knowledge outlaws God. God is not found by searching, nor by knowledge.

God is not found in a laboratory on a slide under a microscope. God is found through simple faith! So—these people professed themselves to be wise, but *"they became fools."*

They *"changed the glory of the uncorruptible God"*—the great, divine God who created man. The word "uncorruptible" here is applied to God in opposition to man. God is unchanging, indestructible, immortal, and eternal. In all the changes of life, man can come to God in perfect assurance that *He changes not* (Mal. 3:6).

". . . into an image made like to corruptible man . . . ." This does not mean that they literally transmuted God Himself, but that in their views they exchanged Him, or they changed Him as an object of worship, for idols. They produced, of course, no change in the glory of the infinite God; the change was in themselves. They forsook Him of whom they had knowledge (v. 21) and offered to idols the homage which was due Him. They made gods of *"birds, and fourfooted beasts, and creeping things."*

Because they did this, *"God . . . gave them up to uncleanness through the lusts of their own hearts, to dishonour their own bodies between themselves."* This is deeper than mere lusts of the flesh. Flesh has natural desires, which may or may not be yielded to. Notice that when man is delivered from divine restraint, the lusts of his heart plunge him into even deeper bodily uncleanness and bodily vileness. Notice: *God gave them up* to dishonor their bodies between themselves. They yielded their bodies completely and entirely over to lust and to lewd practices between human bodies.

To know that God is love, that God gave Jesus to die on the cross to save sinners, and knowing that, yet refusing to believe on Him and receive Him as God, is to place yourself in the position for God to *give you up* and to allow you to become a brute beast insofar as the practices of your body are concerned. You must remember that God created your body for the specific purpose of indwelling that body with and by the Holy Spirit, the Third Person of the Trinity. *Every believer* is a tabernacle in which God lives, in the Person of the Holy Ghost. Paul said to the Corinthian believers, *"Know ye not that your body is the temple of the Holy Ghost?"* (I Cor. 6:19). So the body is the temple of the Holy Ghost if the body is in the right relationship with God; and if the body is *not* surrendered to God, eventually the demons will take full control of it.

One of the most dangerous sins being committed today by man is having the knowledge of God and yet refusing to surrender his all to God. Man knows what he *should* do, but selfishly he refuses to give to God what rightfully belongs to God and what he knows he should surrender to God; namely, his body, soul, and spirit.

We can see from this passage in Romans that *the first step toward heathenism is to "demote" God to the level of man* (and that is exactly what is going on in the liberal religious circles of our day). These people spoken of in Romans 1:21-24 became so "wise" and so "brainy" they demoted God! But God said they were fools. First of all, these "heathen in the making" changed God's glory into that of corruptible man—and then they went downward a step further and made birds their god. Then they stepped one step further, to the beasts, and then a little lower to "creeping things." Insofar as evolution is concerned, man has always "evolved" downward, not UPward. All you need do to see corruption in action is just allow children to "express" themselves; never suppress, never correct, never instruct them in godliness—and you will see corruption in the making!

Because these people knew God but refused to glorify Him AS God, and step by step they went down, down, *down*, God gave them up to uncleanness through lust, and they dishonored their own bodies.

Here in Romans Paul gives the history and the origin of idolatry. These men knew God, and refused to worship Him—and idolatry naturally followed such living. (The earliest mention of idolatry in the Word of God was in the days of Abraham and his father, according to Joshua 24:2.)

God's call is not to uncleanness, but to holiness

(I Thess. 4:7), and when men do not respond to the call to holiness, uncleanness is just as natural as water running downhill! When men begin to worship the creature instead of God the Creator, then men become slaves to uncleanness "and to iniquity unto iniquity"! (Read Romans 6:19.) What could be more sad than to read concerning man, "Wherefore God gave them up"? So, because of man's actions as recorded in verses 21 through 24 of Romans chapter 1, God gave up their bodies.

Let all who have ears to hear give uttermost attention to what God says about our state by nature. Do not apply the threefold "God gave them up" (Rom. 1:24, 26, 28) to the heathen only, as most do. It will not only fail to help us, but it will seriously harm us to study the awful arraignment of God against human sin, unless we apply it to ourselves, thereby discovering our own state by nature. Christendom is rapidly losing sin-consciousness, which means losing *God*-consciousness—which means *eternal doom*.

The Second Step Toward Heathenism

Verses 25-27: *"Who changed the truth of God into a lie, and worshipped and served the creature more than the Creator, who is blessed forever. Amen. For this cause God gave them up unto vile affections: for even their women did change the natural use into that which is against nature: And likewise also the men, leaving the natural use*

61

of the woman, burned in their lust one toward another; men with men working that which is unseemly, and receiving in themselves that recompense of their error which was meet."

Man's *second step downward* was *changing the truth of God into a lie.* In his original creation, man was chaste; but when he cast God off and refused to worship God *as* God, his animal passions were unchained and therefore took control of his being.

Man changed God's truth into the lie of idolatry; he did not change the lie into a *truth.* (Man in his natural form does not travel up.) He set up his own idol worship. Man is incurably religious, regardless of his color, regardless of his nationality, regardless of his education. He may be wise or he may be ignorant; but wherever you find man, he worships something or someone! Man is created to worship—and worship he will, until he dies. Therefore when a man turns his back on the true God he automatically begins to fashion his own gods.

Men changed the truth of God into a lie *"and worshipped and served the creature more than the Creator . . . ."* They took the truth of God which He gave them, and perverted it to the falsehood of idol worship.

"For this cause God gave them up unto vile affections"—and the verse goes on to say, *"for*

even their women . . . ." Note the word "even."
Woman is the purer and the more modest of the
sexes. God made woman to make this earth a
sweeter place to live; He gave woman to Adam to
make his life more complete. God said, "It is not
good for man to be alone" — so God created the
beautiful, sinless, tender, loving Eve. But now—
since man has changed the truth of God into a lie,
even the women became worse than beastly, and
equalled vile, lustful man in depravity. They
*changed "the natural use into that which is against
nature."*

In this verse God is not speaking of natural and
normal appetites of the body, or even the *abuse* of
these—adultery or harlotry. He is here describing
that state of *unnatural* appetites in which all
normal instincts are left behind—and it is signifi-
cant, as originally the *woman* took the lead in sin,
so *here.*

The corruption that came into the blood of the
human race by the fall of Adam did not show
itself instantaneously. The early families and
tribes of the world were not beastly in their sex
practices and in their actions one toward another
in the body. God kept them pure. They called on
the Lord, according to Genesis 4:26. Whatever
morality there is in the world is not due to human
nature but to the restraining power of God.

As men began to multiply upon the earth, they
became wise and resourceful. They forgot God—

and made their own gods. Therefore, since they changed God's truth into the lie of idolatry, *God gave them up.*

Verse 27 is sordid and despicable, to state it mildly—yet we must face it. And do not forget—*you* live in a tabernacle that is capable of committing any sin ever committed by any mortal, and do not deny that fact! I quote: *"FOR FROM WITHIN, out of the HEART OF MEN, proceed evil thoughts, adulteries, fornications, murders, thefts, covetousness, wickedness, deceit, lasciviousness, an evil eye, blasphemy, pride, foolishness: ALL THESE EVIL THINGS COME FROM WITHIN, AND DEFILE THE MAN"* (Mark 7:21-23).

You may not appreciate this—but if your heart is not permeated and controlled by the Holy Spirit, that little "machine" in your bosom, from whence come "the issues of life" (Prov. 4:23), makes you capable of committing any sordid, despicable, lustful, beastly, inhuman sin that any other human has ever committed—yes, even these described in Romans 1:27.

This verse is a commentary on the sin of Sodom, and which from that is called *sodomy.* Read Genesis 19, and you will read what was going on in Sodom when God declared that the stench of the city had reached His nostrils and He decided the only thing to do was to burn it to an ash heap— and God did just that! Romans 1:27 describes men who become so sinful and so lustful that they forget the woman and turn to other men and commit wholesale the sin of sodomy.

"... *receiving in themselves that recompence of their error which was meet.*" The meaning of this is, that the effect of such base and unnatural passions was to enfeeble the body, to produce premature old age, disease, decay, and an early death. That this is the effect of the indulgence of licentious passions is amply proved by the history of man. God has not changed His mind about this sin, although in this day men are seeking to make it legal and instead of hanging their heads in shame are publicizing their vile affections.

When men forget God, their affections become vile; and the further men go from God, the more degraded and vile their affections become. Instead of loving the things that are wholesome and pure, they love the things that are vile and unclean. Human nature is destined to rot, unless the Holy Spirit occupies the throne of the heart. The Holy Spirit leads into paths of right living, and only He can keep us from the cesspools of iniquity and sin.

The Third Step Toward Heathenism

Verses 28-32: "*And even as they did not like to retain God in their knowledge, God gave them over to a reprobate mind, to do those things which are not convenient; being filled with all unrighteousness, fornication, wickedness, covetousness, maliciousness; full of envy, murder, debate, deceit, malignity; whisperers, backbiters, haters of God, despiteful, proud, boasters, inventors of evil things, disobedient to parents, without understanding, covenantbreakers, without natural affection, implacable, unmerciful: Who knowing the judgment of God, that they which commit such things are worthy of death, not only do the same, but have pleasure in them that do them."*

Man's *third step* toward heathenism was: *"they did not like to retain God in their knowledge."* This was the true source of their crimes. They did not *choose* to acknowledge God. It was not because they *could not,* but because they chose to *forsake* Him and follow their own passions and lust. To "retain God" means to *think* of Him or to serve and adore Him.

Please notice: The chapter closes with a statement that assures us that these people had been exposed to the truth and knew that God is God, that God is righteousness, and that God is a God of judgment. They KNEW God would judge the wicked—but in spite of their knowledge they continued in their ungodliness and their sordid living, knowing that people who do those things are worthy of death. They not only did them, but they had *great pleasure* in them that did them! They made sport of men and women who practiced lust in the most sordid fashion.

This section (verses 21 through 32) begins and

ends with the same truth: that is, these people knew God but refused to glorify Him AS God, and they did not even like to keep God in their thinking. Do not forget—Solomon, the man of wisdom, said concerning man, *"As he thinketh in his heart, SO IS HE"* (Prov. 23:7). These people thought on lust, worldly wisdom, getting ahead socially, financially, and from the standpoint of the flesh, refusing to allow God to occupy their mind, their heart, and their body. Therefore:

1. God gave them up to uncleanness as having to do with their bodies.

2. Because they changed God's truth into a lie, God gave them up to wicked, dirty, vile, despicable affections; that is, instead of loving the natural, they loved the unnatural. Instead of practicing the natural, they practiced that which is unnatural.

3. They did not like to retain God in their knowledge; therefore God gave them over to a dull mind (a mind void of judgment). Their mind became so calloused that they took joy in doing things which they knew were against God's will.

"God gave them over to a reprobate mind, to do those things which are not convenient"—those things which are not fit or proper, which are disgraceful and shameful; those things which are named in the rest of the chapter. When a person refuses to let God occupy his mind, it follows that *unrighteousness* will occupy it. The mind is never idle; the mind is alive; the mind is always in

operation; and if we are not thinking good, we are thinking evil. If we are not thinking right, we are thinking wrong.

"Being filled . . . ." That is, the things which are specified were common or abounded among them. This is a strong phrase, denoting that these things were so often practiced that it might be said they were *FULL of them.* When a person refuses to let God occupy his mind, the devil automatically *fills* it with *unrighteousness, fornication,* all kinds of *wickedness, covetousness, maliciousness, envy, murder, deceit, malignity.* Men become *whisperers, backbiters* — and eventually they become *HATERS OF GOD.*

When men refuse to let God occupy their mind, they are *despiteful,* they become *proud,* they *boast,* they *invent evil things,* and children become *disobedient to parents.* Men are *without understanding,* they *break covenants,* they are *without natural affection,* they are *implacable* and *unmerciful.*

"Implacable" means "they cannot be pacified; or, having a nature that cannot be satisfied." I wonder if the truth of that word really soaks in. Can we face it? We are living in an age when people cannot be still. They rush . . . they run . . . they seek . . . they go here and there — but they are never satisfied. The home has become a place to change clothes and prepare for the next club meeting or the next trip . . . never satisfied. "Godliness with contentment is great gain"; but today we have a civilization that cannot be satisfied . . . implacable.

And certainly our civilization is very *unmerciful*. Today in America, you cannot pick up a newspaper of any size without seeing "murder" on the front page. We are living in a day when men are very unmerciful. The reason? They do not like to retain God in their knowledge!

Let us notice verse 32 again: *"Who knowing the judgment of God, that they which commit such things are worthy of death, not only do the same, but have pleasure in them that do them."* Here we are confronted with three terrible realities:

1. They have complete inner knowledge from God, that their ways deserve and must have divine condemnation and judgment.

2. They persist in their practices despite the witness of conscience.

3. They are in a fellowship of evil with other evildoers. In other words, they not only do these things, but are also in agreement with others who so act.

What a description of this world of sinners, this race alienated from the life of God—at enmity with Him, and at strife with one another . . . but all in hellish UNITY OF EVIL!

To summarize: There are *three sins* that will write "Doomed!" across your record and "Eternal Damnation" across your soul, if you practice them:

1. If you know God, and refuse to glorify Him

AS God—that is, you know there is a God, and that He is a God of mercy, love, and tenderness, yet you refuse to receive Him, serve Him, and live for Him—you invite God to give up your body to demons, lust, sin, and ruin.

2. To know the truth of God, to know the Bible is the Word of God, and yet refuse to believe what it says, is to brand God a liar (I John 5:10). To know that God's Word invites you to repent, believe and be saved ... and then refuse to do that ... is to cause God to give you up to vile affections. You will no longer love the things you should love; you will love lust and ungodliness. Your love will become sordid. You will find yourself seeking the base things of life, the despicable things of life. Your mind will be in the gutter.

3. If you refuse to allow God to occupy your thinking, if you refuse to keep God in your mind, your mind will become dull, reprobate. The demons will take charge of your mind, and you will become a demon-possessed maniac. You will practice things that are wrong. You will indulge in fornication, wickedness, and all the other things that are catalogued in Romans 1:29-31.

When God gives up the body, the heart, and the mind, my friend, you are just as sure for hell as it is sure there IS a hell! When God gives up the body, demons take control of its members. When God gives up the heart (the seat of affections, love, emotion), the heart becomes vile, sordid

—and demons order for you the things you will love. When God gives up the mind, it becomes dead and dull—for after demons conquer the body and the heart, they permeate the mind . . . and God has no way of entering your life! The body is given up to uncleanness. The heart is given up to vile affections; and the mind is given over to dull, dead, unrighteousness and wicked thinking. Therefore, the Spirit of God cannot speak to your mind through the Word. The Spirit of God cannot reach your heart through the message of the Gospel. If the Spirit of God cannot enter your mind and cause you to think rightly about God and His Word, saving faith can never penetrate your heart and the Holy Spirit can never occupy your body. Thus, if you are given up—body, heart, and spirit— you are given up to be damned in the lake of fire!

Dear reader, if you are practicing these three sins, for your own sake may this be the day you bow your head and solemnly call on God to deliver you from the terrible sins that will cause God to give you up forever!

Chapter II

1. Therefore thou art inexcusable, O man, whosoever thou art that judgest: for wherein thou judgest another, thou condemnest thyself; for thou that judgest doest the same things.

2. But we are sure that the judgment of God is according to truth against them which commit such things.

3. And thinkest thou this, O man, that judgest them which do such things, and doest the same, that thou shalt escape the judgment of God?

4. Or despisest thou the riches of his goodness and forbearance and longsuffering; not knowing that the goodness of God leadeth thee to repentance?

5. But after thy hardness and impenitent heart treasurest up unto thyself wrath against the day of wrath and revelation of the righteous judgment of God;

6. Who will render to every man according to his deeds:

7. To them who by patient continuance in well doing seek for glory and honour and immortality, eternal life:

8. But unto them that are contentious, and do not obey the truth, but obey unrighteousness, indignation and wrath,

9. Tribulation and anguish, upon every soul of man that doeth evil, of the Jew first, and also of the Gentile;

10. But glory, honour, and peace, to every man that worketh good, to the Jew first, and also to the Gentile:

11. For there is no respect of persons with God.

12. For as many as have sinned without law shall also perish without law: and as many as have sinned in the law shall be judged by the law;

13. (For not the hearers of the law are just before God, but the doers of the law shall be justified.

14. For when the Gentiles, which have not the law, do by nature the things contained in the law, these, having not the law, are a law unto themselves:

15. Which shew the work of the law written in their hearts, their conscience also bearing witness, and their thoughts the mean while accusing or else excusing one another;)

16. In the day when God shall judge the secrets of men by Jesus Christ according to my gospel.

17. Behold, thou art called a Jew, and restest in the law, and makest thy boast of God,

18. And knowest his will, and approvest the things that are more excellent, being instructed out of the law;

19. And art confident that thou thyself art a guide of the blind, a light of them which are in darkness,

20. An instructor of the foolish, a teacher of babes, which hast the form of knowledge and of the truth in the law.

21. Thou therefore which teachest another, teachest thou not thyself? thou that preachest a man should not steal, dost thou steal?

22. Thou that sayest a man should not commit adultery, dost thou commit adultery? thou that abhorrest idols, dost thou commit sacrilege?

23. Thou that makest thy boast of the law, through breaking the law dishonourest thou God?

24. For the name of God is blasphemed among the Gentiles through you, as it is written.

25. For circumcision verily profiteth, if thou keep the law: but if thou be a breaker of the law, thy circumcision is made uncircumcision.

26. Therefore if the uncircumcision keep the righteousness of the law, shall not his uncircumcision be counted for circumcision?

27. And shall not uncircumcision which is by nature, if it fulfil the law, judge thee, who by the letter and circumcision dost transgress the law?

28. For he is not a Jew, which is one outwardly; neither is that circumcision, which is outward in the flesh:

29. But he is a Jew, which is one inwardly; and circumcision is that of the heart, in the spirit, and not in the letter; whose praise is not of men, but of God.

Verse 1: *"Therefore thou art inexcusable, O man, whosoever thou art that judgest: for wherein thou judgest another, thou condemnest thyself; for thou that judgest doest the same things."*

"Therefore" means "for that reason; because of that; to that end; consequently; hence." Therefore—"because of the preceding, the following is true."

". . . thou art inexcusable, O man . . . ." In chapter 1, we learned that the Gentiles were "without excuse," and here in the very first verse of chapter 2, the same indictment is brought against the Jew.

". . . whosoever thou art that judgest . . . ." The Jews were the people who "judged" and pronounced all Gentiles to be born in sin and therefore under condemnation, and classified them as "dogs." Doubtless there were also proud and censorious men among the Gentiles, to whom the

rebuke might apply; but it is very doubtful that Paul had them in mind when he said, "THERE-FORE thou art inexcusable, O man, whosoever thou art that judgest."

"*. . . for wherein thou judgest another, thou condemnest thyself; for thou that judgest doest the same things.*" Read verses 17 through 23 of this chapter, and you will note the same charge is implied in a direct statement to the Jews. Paul is pointing out here that regardless of the nationality—Jew, Gentile, or "whosoever"—they are all under sin; all are in the same spiritual category.

It was easy to prove the Gentile a sinner in Paul's day. The Gentile claimed nothing for himself. His immorality was well known and was witnessed by all. Paul had only to point to the facts concerning the Gentile and his wickedness.

But in the case of his own brethren, the Jews, it was quite different. The Jew had a divinely given system of religion, and he observed the letter of the Law—which was never better observed than when Paul wrote. The Jew as a son of Abraham considered himself righteous *by* the Law. But the Apostle affirms here that the Jews were no less guilty than the Gentiles, and that they needed the same salvation. While they excused themselves on grounds that they possessed the Law and the oracles of God, they were inexcusable in their sins. They had light and yet committed the same wickedness. If the *Gentiles* were without excuse in their sins, much more would the Jew who condemned them be without excuse on the same ground. However, to convince the Jew that he was a sinner was no easier than it is to convince tens of thousands of Gentiles today that baptism and church membership will not save them!

Paul's one aim was to drive home the fact that the Gospel is the power of God unto salvation—and ONLY the Gospel is the power of God unto salvation. The Gospel is nothing of which to be ashamed, regardless of whether you be Jew or Gentile. Paul was preaching and pointing out that if Judaism could save men, then the Gospel was not necessary; but if Judaism could not save men, if the Law could not make men righteous, then we find the righteousness of God revealed in the Gospel which is the power of God unto salvation to everyone that believeth—to the Jew first, and also to the Gentile.

Verse 2: *"But we are sure that the judgment of God is according to truth against them which commit such things."*

In the first sixteen verses of this chapter, we have the *four principles of God's judgment* clearly set forth:

1. It is *"according to truth"* (v. 2).
2. It is *"to every man according to his deeds"* (v. 6).
3. It is with *"no respect of persons"* (v. 11).

77

4. It is *"according to my (Paul's) Gospel"* (v. 16).

Here in verse 2 Paul says, *"We are sure that the judgment of God is according to truth . . . ."* I like those words. Many times on the radio and in my meetings, in my books and booklets, I have made the statement that you may rest assured you will get what is coming to you from the hand of Almighty God. Saint or sinner will be judged in righteousness and truth by a holy God. This is the first of the four principles laid down in this chapter as to the judgment of God.

The Jew had no right to suppose that because he knew the will of God (v. 18) he was safe from judgment. *Jesus* told the Jews on one occasion: "If any man hear my words, and believe not, I judge him not: for I came not to judge the world, but to save the world. *He that rejecteth me, and receiveth not my words, hath one that judgeth him: THE WORD THAT I HAVE SPOKEN, the same shall judge him in the last day"* (John 12:47, 48).

". . . against them which commit such things" — that is, the crimes enumerated in chapter 1. Paul is not to be understood as affirming that each and every individual among the Jews was guilty of the specific crimes charged on the Gentiles, but that they were *as a people* inclined to the same things. Even if they were externally moral, they might be guilty of cherishing evil thoughts in their hearts, and thus be guilty of the offence (Matt. 5:28).

Paul is pointing out that if we know the Word of God, and if we know the things of God, yet we refuse to obey His Word and practice the things we know to be right, then by our self-willed action we bring God's condemnation and judgment down upon us. Jew or Gentile, God does not wink at wickedness or pass lightly over sins.

Verse 3: *"And thinkest thou this, O man, that judgest them which do such things, and doest the same, that thou shalt escape the judgment of God?"*

This is an appeal to their common sense, to their deep and instinctive conviction of what was wrong or right. If *they* condemned men for these offences (chapter 1), how much more would a holy and righteous God be likely to pronounce judgment on them.

It was no doubt a prevalent belief among the Jews that, provided they adhered to the rituals of their religion and observed the ceremonial law, God would not judge them with the same severity as He would the idolatrous Gentiles. But Paul is showing them that crime is crime, evil is evil, wherever committed—and those who profess to be "people of God" have no license to sin. In short, Paul is asking the Jews if they think they can judge others for doing the same things they themselves practice—and then themselves escape the judgment of God.

The Jew was proud of his religion, proud of the

fathers, proud of the temple and the rituals—yet he lived just as ungodly as those whom he pronounced to hell. The Apostle is sternly rebuking him, and reminding him that he cannot do these things and get away with them just because he is a Jew, for God is holy and He "will not at all acquit the wicked" (Nahum 1:3). God cannot look on sin (Hab. 1:13)—and "The soul that sinneth, it shall die" (Ezek. 18:20).

Verse 4: *"Or despisest thou the riches of His goodness and forbearance and longsuffering; not knowing that the goodness of God leadeth thee to repentance?"*

Paul asks, *"Despisest thou the riches of His goodness . . . ?"* The Jews did not make proper use of God's goodness; they did not regard it as fitted to lead them to repentance. They derived a practical impression that because God had not come forth in judgment and cut them off, but had continued to follow them with blessings, they were safe from judgment and God did not regard them as sinners. (Compare Luke 13:1-5.)

". . . and forbearance"—or holding in His hand of judgment; holding in or restraining His indignation; or forbearing to manifest His displeasure against sin.

". . . and longsuffering." This word denotes God's slowness to anger, or His allowing His people to long commit sin without punishing them.

(Read II Peter 3:9; Psalm 86:15; and Nehemiah 9:17.)

"*. . . not knowing that the goodness of God leadeth thee to repentance?*" Paul asks the Jews, "Do you despise the riches of God's goodness? Do you despise God's longsuffering? Do you not know that God's goodness leads you to repentance?" In other words, he is reminding his own people of God's goodness to the nation of Israel. No people ever lived on God's earth to whom God showed more kindness or to whom He gave more blessings. Paul is reminding his people that God's goodness to them should lead them to repent.

God will do everything in His power to bring you to Himself, by being good to you. There is no man who has not seen repeated proofs of His goodness and mercy. Yet sin is a stubborn and amazing evil; men still resist God's goodness and make their way down to hell through all the proofs of God's love. If you are not saved, why not give your heart to Jesus because of His goodness? Do not force God to deal with you in severity.

Verse 5: "*But after thy hardness and impenitent heart treasurest up unto thyself wrath against the day of wrath and revelation of the righteous judgment of God.*"

"*After thy hardness and impenitent heart . . .*" — a heart which is not affected with sorrow for sin, in view of the goodness and mercy of God.

". . . treasurest up unto thyself wrath against the day of wrath"—the day when God shall show or execute His wrath against sinners—*"and revelation of the righteous judgment of God."* Here we learn that the punishment of the wicked will be just. It will be a righteous judgment because God Himself will render the judgment.

What Paul is saying is this: You face the goodness of God, you recognize that God gives the sunshine and the rain, health and strength, food and raiment; but in spite of the light you have, you still keep on rebelling against God. You are piling up, heaping up, damnation and wrath against yourself at the time when you stand before God to be judged.

Verse 6: *"Who will render to every man according to his deeds."*

This is the *second principle* of the judgment of God: *"to every man according to his deeds."* If you think that all sinners die and go to hell and that is the end of it, you are in total spiritual ignorance concerning God's judgment and the perdition of ungodly men. Every wicked person will be tormented in hell according to the extent of his or her wickedness. Every person who dies in unbelief and wakes up in hell will suffer damnation and torment in intensity according to the light rejected, the opportunities turned down, and the goodness of God ignored. The heathen who has never heard the name of Jesus, who roams the jungles naked and feeds his children to the crocodiles, will not suffer the same intensity of damnation as will the person in America who has heard the Gospel but refused it. God will deal with the heathen in righteousness and in justice.

Jesus clearly taught, while here on earth, that those who know right and refuse to DO right will be beaten with many stripes, but that the person who never knew, never heard, and in ignorance committed things worthy of stripes, will be beaten with *few* stripes (Luke 12:42-48).

If you are a sinner, you are making the intensity of the hell you will suffer, by the wickedness you are practicing. Men are lost and separated from God because of *unbelief*, and every unbeliever will open his or her eyes in hell—but those who go to hell will not all suffer the same agony IN hell. There is no fact in the Bible that is more clearly taught than the fact I have just stated.

Again and again throughout the New Testament we are reminded that when we stand before God we will be rewarded *according to our deeds*. We are *saved* by *believing on the Lord Jesus Christ*. There is not one single, solitary thing a person can do to save himself, or to *help* God save him. When he realizes he is lost, and receives Jesus by faith, Jesus saves him; but the *reward* he receives in heaven will be determined by faithful stewardship (I Cor. 3:11-15). We will be rewarded for the deeds

done in our body (II Cor. 5:10). Each and every
believer will be rewarded individually for his faithful stewardship—or, if he has been unfaithful in
stewardship he will see his works burned.

The same principle of judgment is true concerning the wicked. In Revelation 20:11-15 we
have a very clear, understandable picture of the
judgment of the wicked. We see a great white
throne set, and "Him that sat on it." The peoples
judged are the wicked . . . not one believer will be
judged at the great white throne. The dead, small
and great, appear before God; and then the books
are opened. After the books (plural) are opened,
a *book* (singular) is opened. The BOOK is *the
book of life*—but the dead are judged out of the
things "which were written in the BOOKS, *according to their works.*" I see no reason for anyone to misunderstand that statement.

Every *believer* has his or her name in the book
of life. The names of *unbelievers* are *not* in the
book; so the book of life is there just in case some
person would argue with God in the same fashion
Satan argues with Michael, the archangel . . . just
in case there might be some person there who
talks back to God and says, "Now you wait a
minute! I was a good church member . . . I was
a good Baptist, Methodist, Presbyterian, Catholic,
Lutheran . . . ." Then God will simply open *the
book* and show that person that his name is not
there. Only those whose names are written in the

Lamb's book of life will enter heaven (Rev. 21:27). So *the book* is there to shut mouths . . . the *books* are there to determine the degree of damnation the wicked will undergo.

You mark this, and mark it well: Every word you utter, everything you do, every thought you have had, every place you have gone, is on record. Jesus said, "But I say unto you, That every idle word that men shall speak, they shall give an account thereof in the day of judgment" (Matt. 12:36).

If you want to get rid of the wicked thoughts and deeds, come to Jesus, trust His blood; and when your wickedness is put under the blood of Jesus, God sees it no more. I say this humbly and very reverently: God cannot see your sins under the blood of Jesus—but if you stand before God lost, you will be rewarded according to the wicked deeds, the wicked thoughts, and the wickedness you have practiced. You are treasuring up wrath that will be brought out against you in the day of judgment if you know the goodness of God and yet you refuse to serve God.

Verses 7-9: *"To them who by patient continuance in well doing seek for glory and honour and immortality, eternal life: but unto them that are contentious, and do not obey the truth, but obey unrighteousness, indignation and wrath, tribulation and anguish, upon every soul of man that doeth evil, of the Jew first, and also of the Gentile."*

The *"patient continuance in well doing"* in verse 7 is not at all set forth as the means of their procuring eternal life. It is a description of those to whom God *does* render life eternal. "Well doing" is subjection to and obedience to the light God has vouchsafed.

". . . them that are contentious . . . ." This expression (v. 8) usually denotes those who are of a quarrelsome disposition, and generally has reference to controversies among men. But here it denotes a disposition toward God, and is of the same signification as being rebellious, or as opposing God. It is those who contend with the Almighty, who resist His claims, who rebel against His laws and refuse to submit to His requirements which He has made known.

Paul is simply explaining in these verses what I have tried to drive home to your heart: Those who are patient, who seek to live for God and to glorify Him, will inherit immortality and *"eternal life"*; but those who are contentious, who *refuse to* *"obey the truth,"* and who *follow "unrighteousness,"* will receive *"indignation and wrath, tribulation and anguish"*—which will come first to the Jew because he was first to receive the goodness, the mercy, and the long-suffering of God. Jesus said, "Unto whomsoever much is given, of him shall be much required" (Luke 12:48)—and certainly much has been given to the Jew. His damnation will be in accordance with the light he refused and the opportunities he ignored. But God's judgment will be *"upon EVERY soul of man that doeth evil, of the Jew first, and also of the Gentile."*

Verse 10: *"But glory, honour, and peace, to every man that worketh good, to the Jew first, and also to the Gentile."*

To all who accept Jesus, follow the truth and live for God, God will give *"glory, honour, and peace . . . to the Jew first* (the promises are first to the Jew), *and also to the Gentile."* You remember this—and never doubt it: God cannot do wrong. If God did wrong, He would not be God. God is righteous in all of His acts, and He cannot be tempted with evil (James 1:13).

God made promises to faithful Abraham. Abraham believed and obeyed God, and God made a perpetual covenant with Abraham. God will *keep* that covenant and fulfill every promise He made to faithful Abraham. And because of the faithfulness of Abraham, God will keep His covenant with the *descendants* of Abraham; therefore the blessings are *first* to the *Jew*.

"Salvation is *of the Jews"* (John 4:22). Salvation came to us through the seed of David; therefore, since to the Jew was given the covenant of God and the oracles of God, the blessing is to the Jew first . . . but also to the Gentiles.

Verse 11:   *"For there is no respect of persons with God."*

This is the *third principle* of the judgment of God. God will show no respect of persons in the blessing. A born again Gentile has just as great blessing from God as a born again Jew. Of course, God has made specific earthly promises to the nation Israel, and He has also made specific promises to the Gentile bride, the Church. But in the true analysis, God will reward all men righteously, for God is no respecter of men. Just because a Jew is a Jew, his judgment will not be lightened — nor will his reward be increased. God will be just as righteous in judging the Gentile as He is in judging the Jew; His judgment will be strictly impartial. The Gentiles who sinned without the Law must perish, for "the wages of sin is death" — and the *Jews* who sinned *under* the Law must perish, "for the wages of sin is death" (Rom. 6:23). What the Spirit by the Apostle is showing is that apart from the Gospel of the grace of God *no one* could be saved, either Gentile or Jew. Paul is paving the way for the Gospel.

The hyper-Calvinists must of necessity skip over Romans 2:11, because they preach from their pulpits and on the radio that God saves only the elect, the chosen, and all others must be damned because they do not belong to "the elect." But I am so glad the Holy Spirit gave us this verse, telling us that God is no respecter of persons.

God so loved the *world* that He gave the only Son He had, that "whosoever"—Jew, Gentile, white, colored, rich, poor, educated, uneducated . . . *whosoever*—might be saved! If you go to hell, it will not be God's will; it will be your choice.

In connection with verse 11, please read Deuteronomy 10:17; Ezekiel 18:20; Romans 3:29, 30, and 10:12, 13. You will see in these Scriptures that God's judgment will be strictly impartial.

Verses 12 and 13: *"For as many as have sinned without law shall also perish without law: and as many as have sinned in the law shall be judged by the law; (for not the hearers of the law are just before God, but the doers of the law shall be justified."*

"For . . . ." This is to give a reason for what he had just said, or to show on what principles God would treat man, so as not to be a respecter of persons.

". . . as many as have sinned . . . ." This includes *all*. The Apostle does not say that this is applicable to a few only, or to pagan wickedness only. This is a sweeping universal statement including *all*, or "whosoever." *"Without law"* evidently means without the written law, as Paul immediately says (in verse 14) that they had the law of *nature*. *". . . shall also perish without law"*—that is, they shall not be judged by a law which they did not have.

89

The Jews had sinned *"in the law"*; that is, they had the revealed Word of God and they prided themselves much on its possession—and yet they sinned. They, then, would be *"judged by the law"*—by the light they had. They—*"the hearers of the law"* (v. 13)—could not be justified, for they had not *done* the Law. In other words, simply hearing the Law is not meeting all of its requirements. If they expected to be saved by the Law, it would require something more than just *hearing*.

Verses 14 and 15: *"For when the Gentiles, which have not the law, do by nature the things contained in the law, these, having not the law, are a law unto themselves: which shew the work of the law written in their hearts, their conscience also bearing witness, and their thoughts the mean while accusing or else excusing one another)."*

When the Gentiles, not having the Law—that is, the Law as an external revelation from God—*"do by nature the things contained in the law . . . ."* This does not mean they are fulfilling the claims of the Law, for they do not *have* it—but that they are unconsciously aware, as moral beings, of what is right or wrong. These men, then, though not having the Law, *"are a law unto themselves."*

"Which shew the work of the law written in their hearts . . . ." God is describing how He has constituted all men: there is a "work" within them, making them morally conscious. Here note

that it is not *the Law* written in their hearts; it is the "work" that is written by God in the constitution of these men, thereby making them morally conscious. To repeat then—God here in these verses declares that there is a righteous "work" divinely written in men's hearts, from which they cannot escape, because *"their conscience" agrees* with it. The Law of Moses has not been written in the hearts of the Gentiles, but a divine "work" is present in all men. (Note that verses 13-15 are a parenthetical explanation of verse 12.)

Verse 16: *"In the day when God shall judge the secrets of men by Jesus Christ according to my Gospel."*

Both Gentiles (who have "sinned *without* law") and Jews (who have "sinned *in* the law") shall be judged *"in the day when God shall judge the secrets of men."* And who could stand in such a day as that?—"the day of wrath and revelation of the righteous judgment of God" (v. 5). Only the righteous will enter the Celestial City—and the righteous are righteous only because their *Lord* is righteous (I Cor. 1:30; II Cor. 5:21). A person must be righteous to enter the heaven where there is no *un*righteousness, nor anything that defiles, "neither whatsoever worketh abomination, or maketh a lie" (Rev. 21:27). Without holiness no man shall see God (Heb. 12:14)—and holiness and righteousness are ours only through the Lord Jesus Christ.

"... *by Jesus Christ* ...." In Acts 17:31 we read: "He hath appointed a day, in the which He will judge the world in RIGHTEOUSNESS *by that Man whom He hath ordained;* whereof He hath given assurance unto all men, in that He hath raised Him from the dead." And the only people who will appear righteous before Him are those who have believed with the heart the doctrine delivered by the Lord Jesus Christ. (Please read carefully II John, verses 8 through 11.)

"... *according to my Gospel.*" Here we have the *fourth principle* of God's judgment as laid down in this second chapter of Romans. Thank God—not "according to the Law of Moses," for "by the deeds of the law there shall no flesh be justified" (Rom. 3:20). I am glad we will be judged according to the Gospel of the marvelous grace of God—not according to the Law.

Except for the Gospel purchased by the precious blood of Jesus Christ, brought down to man by the only begotten Son of God, entrusted to holy men whom God called, ordained, and sent to preach the Gospel, not one of us could stand before God's holiness and righteousness in that great day. For this reason Paul shouted out: *"I am not ashamed of the Gospel* ... for it is the power of God unto salvation ... for therein is the righteousness of of God revealed from faith to faith: as it is written, The just shall live by faith" (Rom. 1:16, 17).

Paul is sternly and solemnly driving home the

Bible fact that all have sinned and come short of the glory of God, there is none righteous (no, not one); there is not a just man upon the earth that doeth good and sinneth not. If we say we have no sin, we deceive ourselves, and the truth is not in us. If we say we have not sinned, we make God a liar. And we must face the solemn fact that man is hopeless, helpless, and hell-bound without Christ; but *in* Christ we are righteous, we are redeemed, and we are ready to stand before Him in that great judgment morning. "Nothing in my hand I bring; simply to Thy cross I cling"! Paul's message was singular: The death, burial, and resurrection of the Lord Jesus Christ—the only hope of salvation.

The Jew Is Condemned by the Law

Verse 17: *"Behold, thou art called a Jew, and restest in the law, and makest thy boast of God."*

"Jew" was the name by which the Hebrews were generally known, and it is clear they regarded it as a name of honor and valued themselves on it (see Galatians 2:15). It came to represent all the special favors of their religion.

The name originally denoted one belonging to the tribe or to the kingdom of Judah (II Kings 16:6; 25:25). (It was from the tribe of Judah the Messiah was to be born. See Genesis 49:8, 10; Hebrews 7:14; and Revelation 5:5.) In the days of Rehoboam, the kingdom of Israel was divided, and the ten northern tribes became known as *Israel*. The tribes of Judah and Benjamin, in the south, made up the kingdom of *Judah*. As punishment for sin and idolatry, the ten northern tribes were carried into captivity and scattered among the nations. Eventually the tribes of Judah and Benjamin were carried captive into Babylon, from whence a remnant later returned to Jerusalem (under Ezra and Nehemiah). The meaning of the word "Jew" was then extended and applied to anyone of the Hebrew race who returned from the captivity—and finally it included anyone of that race throughout the world.

"*. . . and restest in the law . . . .*" The Jew leaned upon and relied upon the Law for acceptance or favor. "The Law" here means probably the whole Mosaic economy.

"*. . . and makest thy boast of God.*" The Jew felt himself superior to all other nations and despised them, because he had the Law of God. It is true the Law was given to Israel and that God had declared Himself to be their God, but this was not reason for boasting (especially since they did not keep the Law). Instead of boasting they should have felt gratitude for the mercies and favors God had bestowed upon them.

The implication in this verse is that one might be *called* a Jew, and yet not BE a Jew. (I might add that today one may be called a *Christian*—and yet not *be* a true Christian.) Here Paul is proving that the so-called Jew is just as helpless a sinner as the Gentile, in spite of all his Jewish boasting. He rested in the Law, but at the same time he failed to recognize the Law as an instruction in righteousness: "All Scripture is given by inspiration of God, and is profitable for doctrine, for reproof, for correction, for instruction in righteousness: that the man of God may be perfect, throughly furnished unto all good works" (II Tim. 3:16, 17).

Verses 18-20: *"And knowest His will, and approvest the things that are more excellent, being instructed out of the law; and art confident that thou thyself art a guide of the blind, a light of them which are in darkness, an instructor of the foolish, a teacher of babes, which hast the form of knowledge and of the truth in the law."*

The Jew made his boast of God; and yet he forgot that God is a just God, and that He is the God of the just. The Jew *knew God's will* (v. 18), but it never occurred to him that he should *obey* God's will. This knowledge he obtained from the Scriptures. He was a student of Old Testament Scriptures, and he was able to *approve the things that were "more excellent"* — and yet, even though he was *"instructed out of the law,"* he did not use his wisdom to guide the blind (the Gentile) out of darkness into the light. The Jew looked upon himself as *"an instructor of the foolish, a teacher of babes,"* having *"the form of knowledge and of the*

95

truth in the law" (v. 20). Here we have a complete picture of what the Jew thought of himself—but what *God* thought of him was altogether another matter.

In these verses Paul concedes to the Jews all that they claim. They had the form of knowledge in the Law—but the Apostle is prepared with truth and force to convict them of their deep depravity in sinning against the superior light and privileges which God had conferred on them. The Holy Spirit is here proving the Jew a lost sinner... just as lost as the Gentile "dog."

Verses 21-24: *"Thou therefore which teachest another, teachest thou not thyself? Thou that preachest a man should not steal, dost thou steal? Thou that sayest a man should not commit adultery, dost thou commit adultery? Thou that abhorrest idols, dost thou commit sacrilege? Thou that makest thy boast of the law, through breaking the law dishonourest thou God? For the name of God is blasphemed among the Gentiles through you, as it is written."*

He who teaches another is expected to be learned himself. Evidently the Jews had not thought of that. You see, these Jews were always ready to instruct and correct and teach others—but they were not willing to be taught themselves.

"... dost thou steal? ... dost thou commit adultery? ... dost thou commit sacrilege?" I believe

Paul introduces and names these sins to make the inconsistency of their conduct more apparent. We expect a man to set an example of what he means by his public instructions.

Paul continues by asking, *"... through breaking the law dishonourest thou God? For the name of God is blasphemed among the Gentiles through you, as it is written."* Because of the inconsistent conduct of the Jews, the name of God was blasphemed among the Gentiles. (Read Isaiah 52:5; Ezekiel 36:19-23; and II Samuel 12:13, 14.)

Verses 25-27: *"For circumcision verily profiteth, if thou keep the law: but if thou be a breaker of the law, thy circumcision is made uncircumcision. Therefore if the uncircumcision keep the righteousness of the law, shall not his uncircumcision be counted for circumcision? And shall not uncircumcision which is by nature, if it fulfil the law, judge thee, who by the letter and circumcision dost transgress the law?"*

Paul is attempting to show the Jews that man looks on the outward appearance, but God looks on the heart—and as he so clearly states later in this Epistle, "with the *heart* we believe unto righteousness." It is not the outward show, but the inward possession, that matters with God.

"For circumcision verily profiteth, if thou keep the law . . . ." There is a big, mountainous "IF" here in verse 25—an *important* "if." The Jew

must learn that circumcision in itself could not and does not save. "*. . . but if thou be a breaker of the law, thy circumcision is made uncircumcision.*" Paul is saying that Jewish circumcision, which was the mark of that nation's separation to God (the sign of God's covenant with His people), was good only if one was really separated to God; but that if not, the Jew was really an uncircumcised one. He was thus judged by those who, wholly outside circumcision, feared God and walked with Him (verses 26 and 27).

But to this the Jew replied that circumcision was a necessary and important factor in their religion. Paul did not deny the truth of their statement; but his argument was that when a man has truth and purity in the *heart,* even though he may not have gone through the rituals of Judaism, that man is far better off in the sight of God than the man who goes through formalities and yet inwardly does not possess true spiritual circumcision of the heart. Paul is driving home to the Jewish people the fact that the Law does not save, the Law does not justify: "Knowing that *a man is not justified by the works of the law, but by the faith of Jesus Christ,* even we have believed in Jesus Christ, that we might be justified by the faith of Christ, and not by the works of the law: for *by the works of the law shall no flesh be justified*" (Gal. 2:16). ". . . the letter killeth"—but the Spirit brings life eternal (II Cor. 3:6). Therefore those who keep the

Law *without* circumcision judge and condemn the Jew who has the letter of the Law and still transgresses the Law.

Verses 28 and 29: *"For he is not a Jew, which is one outwardly; neither is that circumcision, which is outward in the flesh: But he is a Jew, which is one inwardly; and circumcision is that of the heart, in the spirit, and not in the letter; whose praise is not of men, but of God."*

In these verses Paul argues that *"he is not a Jew, which is one outwardly."* This summing up should be connected with verse 17, where he said, "Behold, thou art called a Jew." One could be called a Jew outwardly, but being a Jew outwardly did not make him a son of God nor a son of Abraham in the faith. He who is merely descended from Abraham, is circumcised, and only externally conforms to the Law, does not possess the true character and manifest the true spirit contemplated by the separation of the Jewish people. Their separation required much more.

"But he is a Jew, which is one inwardly . . . ." Here Paul is getting down to the heart of the matter. We read in Psalm 51:6, "Behold, thou desirest truth in the inward parts." Circumcision, as practiced in the days of the Apostle, was merely an outward act. The Jews could have observed *all* the external rites of Judaism, and yet not have known the Lord God Almighty in the heart. *True*

circumcision *"is that of the heart, in the spirit, and not in the letter."* Paul told the Philippians, "We are the circumcision, which worship God in the spirit, and rejoice in Christ Jesus, and have no confidence in the flesh" (Phil. 3:3). Such people have *"praise... not of men, but of God."*

Later in this Epistle (ch. 10), Paul speaks of the "zeal" of his people—but he declares they are zealous "without knowledge." He declares they are ignorant of God's righteousness, and they go about to establish their own righteousness through rituals and practices of Judaism; and doing this, they will not submit themselves unto the righteousness of God, which is Christ (I Cor. 1:30).

The remarks which are made here in chapter 2 respecting the Jews are also strictly applicable to professing Christians—and we may learn that the Lord observes the *heart,* the "inner man" . . . not the outward show, or the fleshly demonstrations, but the inward possession of the Holy Spirit. We are living in the day when we preachers need to drive home the solid fact that it is not tradition, dogma, denomination, rituals or religious practices that make us children of God. We must be born of the Spirit, washed in the blood, saved by grace through faith—minus rituals.

Baptism does not save. Baptism should be observed by *saved people;* we should follow Christ in baptism when we have believed on Him, when we have received Him as our Saviour by faith—

but if we are baptized ONLY, then we are just as lost as lost can be. Water does not wash away sins. *Observing the Lord's Supper* does not save us. *Joining the local assembly* does not make a Christian of us. All of these things are good when practiced by believers ... but one may practice *all* of these rituals and ordinances, and yet not be saved!

In all the years of my ministry I have found that the most difficult thing for me to do is to persuade people that to be saved they must receive the Lord Jesus Christ by *faith,* and *faith alone!* People want to *do* something ... they want to *practice* something ... they want to *give* something ... they want to *live* something. But God's redemption is a *gift.* Christ died for us while we were yet sinners, and the only way any poor sinner can become a son of God is by receiving the Lord Jesus Christ (John 1:12). We are saved by God's grace. God's grace becomes ours by faith—not by works, but by faith! Faith to become a child of God comes by hearing the Word of God. (Please read Ephesians 2:8, 9; Romans 10:9, 10, 17; John 3:5; 5:24; and I Peter 1:23.)

We cannot *save* ourselves, and neither can we help God *keep* us saved. We are kept by the same power that saves us: "Whatsoever is born of God overcometh the world: and *this is the victory that overcometh the world, even our faith*" (I John 5:4). (Read also I Peter 1:5.)

Chapter III

1. What advantage then hath the Jew? or what profit is there of circumcision?

2. Much every way: chiefly, because that unto them were committed the oracles of God.

3. For what if some did not believe? shall their unbelief make the faith of God without effect?

4. God forbid: yea, let God be true, but every man a liar; as it is written, That thou mightest be justified in thy sayings, and mightest overcome when thou art judged.

5. But if our unrighteousness commend the righteousness of God, what shall we say? Is God unrighteous who taketh vengeance? (I speak as a man)

6. God forbid: for then how shall God judge the world?

7. For if the truth of God hath more abounded through my lie unto his glory; why yet am I also judged as a sinner?

8. And not rather, (as we be slanderously reported, and as some affirm that we say,) Let us do evil, that good may come? whose damnation is just.

9. What then? are we better than they? No, in no wise: for we have before proved both Jews and Gentiles, that they are all under sin;

10. As it is written, There is none righteous, no, not one:

11. There is none that understandeth, there is none that seeketh after God.

12. They are all gone out of the way, they are together become unprofitable; there is none that doeth good, no, not one.

13. Their throat is an open sepulchre; with their tongues they have used deceit; the poison of asps is under their lips:

14. Whose mouth is full of cursing and bitterness:

15. Their feet are swift to shed blood:

16. Destruction and misery are in their ways:

17. And the way of peace have they not known:

18. There is no fear of God before their eyes.

19. Now we know that what things soever the law saith, it saith to them who are under the law: that every mouth may be stopped, and all the world may become guilty before God.

20. Therefore by the deeds of the law there shall no flesh be justified in his sight: for by the law is the knowledge of sin.

21. But now the righteousness of God without the law is manifested, being witnessed by the law and the prophets;

22. Even the righteousness of God which is by faith of Jesus Christ unto all and upon all them that believe: for there is no difference:

23. For all have sinned, and come short of the glory of God;

24. Being justified freely by his grace through the redemption that is in Christ Jesus:

25. Whom God hath set forth to be a propitiation through faith in his blood, to declare his righteousness for the remission of sins that are past, through the forbearance of God;

26. To declare, I say, at this time his righteousness: that he might be just, and the justifier of him which believeth in Jesus.

27. Where is boasting then? It is excluded. By what law? of works? Nay: but by the law of faith.

28. Therefore we conclude that a man is justified by faith without the deeds of the law.

29. Is he the God of the Jews only? is he not also of the Gentiles? Yes, of the Gentiles also:

30. Seeing it is one God, which shall justify the circumcision by faith, and uncircumcision through faith.

31. Do we then make void the law through faith? God forbid: yea, we establish the law.

The Advantage of the Jew
Works Greater Condemnation

In chapter 3 we learn the fact stated earlier in this study: The advantage of the Jew works his greater condemnation, since he has had glorious and golden opportunities provided by Jehovah God, who called out Abraham and made the covenant with him and his seed through perpetual generations. Since the Jew has been blessed of God in so many outstanding ways, his condemnation is heavier and greater because of the opportunities and advantages he has turned down.

Verses 1 and 2: *"What advantage then hath the Jew? or what profit is there of circumcision? Much every way: chiefly, because that unto them were committed the oracles of God."*

The design of the first part of this chapter is to answer some of the objections which a Jew might offer to the statements made in chapter 2.

Here Paul asks and answers a question. The question is: *"What advantage is there in being a Jew, and what profit is there in circumcision,* if circumcision does not save and if God does not bestow special favor upon the Jew?" Paul answers the question by saying, *"Much every way: chiefly, because that unto them were committed the oracles of God."* That is, they possessed the holy Scriptures. God had entrusted to them the oracles of God—or that which was *spoken* by God, particularly the divine promises. To possess these was, of course, a great honor. But Paul does not let his people forget that the greater the honor bestowed, the weightier the responsibility.

Verses 3 and 4: *"For what if some did not believe? Shall their unbelief make the faith of God without effect? God forbid: yea, let God be true, but every man a liar; as it is written, That thou mightest be justified in thy sayings, and mightest overcome when thou art judged."*

"What if some did not believe? . . ." What Paul is saying here is simply this: "What if some did not believe? Shall their faithlessness destroy God's faithfulness? Does their unbelief render the faithfulness of God ineffectual?" The meaning of the objection is that, the fact supposed (that the Jews would become unfaithful and be lost)—would this imply that God had failed to keep His promises to the nation or that He had made promises

which the result showed He could not keep? Paul cries out, *"God forbid!* Let no one ever think such a thing!"

Then Paul thunders out: *"Yea, LET GOD BE TRUE, BUT EVERY MAN A LIAR!"* Let God be esteemed true and faithful, whatever consequences may follow. This is the first principle the Jew should recognize, and it should be so now. We should believe God to be a God of truth regardless of the consequences that may follow. This is a definite statement and demands that every opinion, every doctrine, should be abandoned if it implies that God is false.

Questions are daily asked—"What about the virgin birth? This bishop...this professor...this preacher...tell us that the virgin birth is a myth— a scientific impossibility. What about it?" My answer: "LET GOD BE TRUE, BUT EVERY MAN A LIAR." Others ask, "What about this Gospel that is preached—'You must be washed in the blood...you must be born again...you must repent.' Our pastor teaches us that joining the church and living a good life are all that is necessary in this enlightened age. What about it?" My answer: "LET GOT BE TRUE, BUT EVERY MAN A LIAR."

Regardless of what men may say about the virgin birth, the blood atonement, the verbal in- spiration of the Scriptures, the fact of original sin, the necessity of the new birth, the imperativeness of being washed in the blood, *the truth is in God's Word!* This blessed Book was here before they were, and it will be here when they are dead: *"For ever, O Lord, thy Word is settled in heaven"* (Psalm 119:89). Any man who adds to the Word of God, or takes from it, will burn in hell for doing it, regardless of who he is.

Jesus said, "Except a man be born again, he cannot see the kingdom of God" (John 3:3). Jesus said, "Except ye repent, ye shall all likewise perish" (Luke 13:3,5). Jesus said, "And ye will not come to me, that ye might have life" (John 5:40). John declares, "The blood of Jesus Christ cleanseth us from all sin" (I John 1:7). Paul preached that without the shedding of blood there is no remission of sin (Heb. 9:22). Peter declared that we are "not redeemed with corruptible things, as silver and gold . . . but with the precious blood of Christ . . ." (I Pet. 1:18,19).

It is blood—or hell. It is the new birth—or damnation. It is the virgin birth—or eternal ruin. Jesus was virgin-born. He lived on earth in a body of flesh. He was tempted in all points as we are, yet was without sin. He died on the cross, shed His blood, that we might have salvation. He was buried, and on the third day He rose again bodily; and He ascended back to the Father. Today there is "one Mediator between God and men, the Man Christ Jesus" (I Tim. 2:5).

If you are not born again, if you are not washed

in the blood, if you are not saved by grace, you are lost and on the road to hell. I say again: "LET GOD BE TRUE, BUT EVERY MAN A LIAR." Regardless of what preachers preach or teachers teach; regardless of what you read that preachers and teachers have written, BELIEVE THE WORD OF GOD. You must RECEIVE the Word of God, LIVE by the Word of God, and DIE by the Word of God . . . IF you hope to make heaven your home.

Many false prophets are in the land, who deny the virgin birth, the bodily resurrection, the blood atonement; but Jesus warned concerning these "wolves in sheep's clothing": "Beware of false prophets, which come to you in sheep's clothing, but inwardly they are ravening wolves" (Matt. 7:15). *Paul* warned about false teachers (II Cor. 11:13-15); and *John* warned, *"Try* the spirits, and see if they be of God." (See I John 4:1-3.) Therefore, if you are a victim of confusion, God did not do it! I Peter 2:6 teaches us that believers cannot be confounded and confused. If you are confused, *the devil did it.* God is not the author of confusion; He is the Author of unity, peace, and "joy unspeakable and full of glory"!

If you do not know that you are born again just as surely as you know you are alive and breathing, I pray you will call on God right now and let Him save your poor, lost soul. "Let God be true, but every man a liar."

". . . as it is written, That thou mightest be justified in thy sayings, and mightest overcome when thou art judged." Paul quotes here from Psalm 51:4. Of all the quotations ever made, this is the most beautiful and most appropriate here. David was overwhelmed with grief, he saw his crime to be awful, he feared God's righteousness—yet he never questioned God. He firmly believed that God was always RIGHT. David saw that God was justified in His condemnation of his sin.

This should be the sentiment of every born again child of God . . . that is, let God be justified in everything He does. The ways of God are always right; God's ways cannot be wrong, because He is God. He is righteous; He is faithful; and God cannot do wrong.

Verses 5 and 6: *"But if our unrighteousness commend the righteousness of God, what shall we say? Is God unrighteous who taketh vengeance? (I speak as a man) God forbid: for then how shall God judge the world?"*

The issue raised here is simply this: If God's holiness and righteousness are made manifest by man's *un*righteousness, then God does wrong when He takes vengeance on man because of his unrighteousness. A question often asked by sinners is this: If the character of God—His holiness, His purity—is shown as a result of man's sin, how can God punish that sin? Paul asks *(speaking "as a man"),*

110

"Is God unrighteous who taketh vengeance?" But the Holy Spirit answers, through Paul: *"GOD FOR-BID! for then how shall God judge the world?"* Paul probably had in mind the truth declared in Genesis 18:25, where Abraham puts the question to Jehovah God: "Shall not the Judge of all the earth do right?" (Read also Acts 17:31.) What a terrible calamity it would be if God should ever do wrong! But God cannot do wrong; God *will* not do wrong; it is *impossible* for God to do wrong. "Let God be true"—let every man be wrong!

Verses 7 and 8: *"For if the truth of God hath more abounded through my lie unto His glory; why yet am I also judged as a sinner? And not rather, (as we be slanderously reported, and as some affirm that we say,) Let us do evil, that good may come? whose damnation is just."*

". . . why yet am I also judged as a sinner?" The objection continues, and the point now is that *"if the truth of God"* (and we know that Jesus said, "I AM the Truth") has been made more manifest and exceeding glorious by the *un*truthful-ness of sinful men, then men ought not to be condemned or brought into judgment; they should be *commended,* instead. If that be the case, it would be far better to go on in evil for the Lord's sake. Paul continues by saying, "Yes, some have *slanderously reported* that I (Paul) have advocated that men follow this course of conduct; in other

111

words, *'Let us do evil, that good may come.'*"

But Paul vehemently repudiates this teaching. He denies that he ever suggested such a principle or such a rule of conduct; and now, with one mighty stroke of the pen, Paul brings the whole objection to its logical and absurd conclusion. What he says is simply: "If sin enhances the glory of God, and is therefore no longer guilt (or wrong), then the more we sin, the brighter God's grace will be! If that be true, let us do all the evil we can— for the more sin we commit, the more evil we do, the more praise we bring to His name." But Paul clearly states that he has been *slandered* by those who reported that he believed and taught such a doctrine. And thus he has come around in a most skillful fashion to the assertion with which he began against the Jew, in chapter 2, verse 1: "Thou art inexcusable, O man, whosoever thou art that judgest: for wherein thou judgest another, thou condemnest thyself . . . ."

"*. . . whose damnation is just.*" Very emphatically Paul declares that those who accused him of teaching the doctrine of "doing evil that good may come" were *deserving* of God's punishment. In other words, God is justified in permitting such people to burn in hell. Thus in strong language he silences the objection and teaches as a great fundamental law, that evil is *not* to be done that good may come; that is, whatever is evil is not to be done under pretense that good will come from it.

Paul the Apostle was a preacher of pure grace. He taught that God's grace is greater than all of our sins—"where sin abounded, grace did much more abound" (Rom. 5:20). The Apostle had learned that God's grace is sufficient, it matters not what the need may be. The Judaizers and legalizers hated and persecuted Paul for preaching pure grace. So it is today: There are those who hate God's ministers who preach pure grace minus works.

Let me make this statement here—and I trust you will weigh and study the statement before you condemn it: The righteous, godly, sinless, blameless, and holy life of Jesus could never have saved us. It was not His sinless life, but *His shed blood,* that brought salvation. In other words, if Jesus were on earth today, His sinlessness would only bring to light our sinfulness. If we at our best were placed alongside Jesus, His pure, sinless, holy life would magnify the blackness of our sinfulness.

God's grace was brought down to man in Christ Jesus, but He did not come here to set an example or to live a good life; He came here to lay His life down, that we might be saved (John 10:15-18). He came here with His eye on the cross. Every step He made, every act and motive of His life, was directed to the cross. He came to die on the cross, that we through His death might be saved: "We see *Jesus, who was made a little lower than the angels for the suffering of death,* crowned with glory and honour; *that He BY THE GRACE OF GOD should taste death for every man"* (Heb. 2:9). What a tremendous verse! By faith we see Jesus— He who was made "a little lower than the angels." The angels are "ministering spirits" (Heb. 1:14); but Jesus took a body of flesh—a body a little *lower* than the angels. He took that body for a singular purpose—the suffering of death; and in a body of flesh on the cross, He "tasted death for every man." In other words, Jesus left the bosom of the Father, and in one gigantic step He stepped to the womb of the virgin. He was born of a virgin, born to die on the cross. All hell could not stop Him, because it was on the cross that He paid sin's debt and purchased salvation for hell-deserving men—but on the other side of death He was crowned with glory and honor, and sat down at the right hand of God the Father (Heb. 1:3).

"BY GRACE are ye saved through faith; and that not of yourselves: it is the gift of God" (Eph. 2:8).

"NOT by works of righteousness which we have done, but *according to His mercy He saved us,* by the washing of regeneration, and renewing of the Holy Ghost" (Titus 3:5).

All the World Guilty Before God

Verse 9: *"What then? are we better than they? No, in no wise: for we have before proved both*

Jews and Gentiles, that they are all under sin."

Here Paul continues the argument by asking, *"Are we better than they?"* That is, are the Jews better than the Gentiles? The essence of the question is simply this: "Have we Jews an excuse? Is there any excuse left? Is there any escape from the final verdict of the universal guilt of all men?"

Then Paul thunders back, *"No, in no wise: for we have before proved both Jews and Gentiles, that they are ALL under sin."* The answer is given in plain, understandable words: "No! There is no excuse left; there is no escape from the fact of universal guilt! ALL are guilty. There is no one excluded from the guilt; ALL are included."

Verses 10-12: *"As it is written, There is none righteous, no, not one: There is none that understandeth, there is none that seeketh after God. They are all gone out of the way, they are together become unprofitable; there is none that doeth good, no, not one."*

"As it is written . . . ." In these verses Paul uses a quotation from the Old Testament to prove what he has just stated in verse 9. (Read Psalms 14:1-3 and 53:1-3.) It is God's Word that proves the sweeping declaration that the whole human race is doomed. Not even one single solitary individual can stand before God on his own merit and hope for God to pardon his iniquity and accept him into the family of heaven . . . not one!

Notice the six facts stated here in these verses:

1. *There is none righteous—no, not one.*
2. *There is none that understandeth.*
3. *There is none that seeketh after God.*
4. *They are all gone out of the way.*
5. *They are together become unprofitable.*
6. *There is none that doeth good—no, not one.*

According to these verses, all men are totally depraved. All men possess a darkened intelligence; and all men possess deadened emotions—that is, all men who have not been born again. Isaiah says: *"ALL we like sheep have gone astray;* we have turned every one to his own way; and the Lord hath laid on Him the iniquity of us ALL" (Isaiah 53:6). This verse begins with the word "all" and ends with the word "all." We are *all* in the same boat. We are all in the same category. We are all totally depraved, hopelessly lost, dead in sin—until we hear the Gospel, receive the Gospel, and trust the Christ who IS the Gospel.

Jesus brought down to man the Gospel that is the power of God unto salvation: "In the beginning was the Word, and the Word was with God, and the Word was God. . . . And *the Word was made flesh, and dwelt among us,* (and we beheld His glory, the glory as of the only begotten of the Father,) full of grace and truth" (John 1:1, 14). Jesus was the Gospel wrapped up in flesh. He brought the message of salvation . . . yea, He WAS salvation, brought down to man. Until we accept

Him as our personal Saviour, we are ALL unrighteous; we are ALL darkened in our thinking . . . we cannot *think* right about God until we accept Jesus.

We do not seek God . . . *God* is seeking *us*. Jesus came to seek and to save the lost—but we poor, lost sinners do not seek Christ until we hear and believe the Gospel; then the Holy Ghost, through the Gospel, draws us (John 6:44). *All* men have gone astray. There is no man righteous, no, not one, until that man receives the righteousness of God, which is Christ Jesus our Lord (I Cor. 1:30).

What a picture we have seen of human character! Now what about human *conduct?* Verses 13 through 18 present to us a sordid, despicable picture of the unregenerate. If you know someone who is proud of his goodness, and he boasts that he does not need this blood-bought salvation, let him hear verses 13 through 18 of this third chapter of Romans!

Verse 13:   *"Their throat is an open sepulchre; with their tongues they have used deceit; the poison of asps is under their lips."*

In this verse it is said of unbelievers, *"Their throat is an open sepulchre . . . ."* This terrible picture in words is taken from Psalm 5:9 and Psalm 140:3. The words here deal with man's mouth— and what the mouth speaks is "out of the abundance of the heart" (Matt. 12:34). This description given in Romans 3:13-18 is of unregenerate men, as already pointed out—men whose hearts are deceitful and desperately wicked. The words we speak testify what is in our heart; they are an important part of our conduct. Some men speak lies and blasphemy; filthy words and dirty language make up their conversation. Such men need to be born again.

An *"open sepulchre"* is a shallow grave that contains a body over which no dirt has been thrown. The hot sun beats down upon that dead body. Naturally, deterioration sets in, and the flesh worms begin their work. As from an open sepulchre there rises an offensive odor, and pestilence which endangers the health of others, so from the mouths of vile persons there proceed poisonous and dangerous words.

". . . with their tongues they have used deceit . . . ." James tells us about the tongue. He declares:

"In many things we offend all. If any man offend not in word, the same is a perfect man, and able also to bridle the whole body. Behold, we put bits in the horses' mouths, that they may obey us; and we turn about their whole body. Behold also the ships, which though they be so great, and are driven of fierce winds, yet are they turned about with a very small helm, whithersoever the governor listeth.

"Even so the tongue is a little member, and

boasteth great things. Behold, how great a matter a little fire kindleth! *And the tongue is a fire, a world of iniquity: so is the tongue among our members, that it defileth the whole body, and setteth on fire the course of nature; and it is set on fire of hell.*

"For every kind of beasts, and of birds, and of serpents, and of things in the sea, is tamed, and hath been tamed of mankind: *but THE TONGUE CAN NO MAN TAME; IT IS AN UNRULY EVIL, FULL OF DEADLY POISON.* Therewith bless we God, even the Father; and therewith curse we men, which are made after the similitude of God. Out of the same mouth proceedeth blessing and cursing. My brethren, *these things ought not so to be*" (James 3:2-10).

So we see that James agrees with Paul concerning the throat, the tongue, and the lips: the throat... an open grave; the tongue... very deceitful, full of deadly poison—and *"the poison of asps is under their lips."*

The asp is a species of serpent whose poison is of such active operation that it kills almost the instant that it penetrates, and that without remedy. The meaning here is that, as the poison of the asp is rapid, certain, spreading quickly through the system and producing death, so the words of a slanderer are deadly, quickly destroying the reputation and happiness of man. Lives have been wrecked, homes have been separated, and suicides have been the result of lying tongues. That small portion of the anatomy called the tongue can sow more discord in sixty seconds than a lifetime can cure! Just remember—your tongue, in the hands of the devil and energized by demons, can cause unhappiness and irreparable damage in the lives of your fellow men. If you cannot tell the truth, *be sure to keep your mouth shut!*

Every *believer* should pray with the Psalmist, *"Set a watch, O Lord, before my mouth; keep the door of my lips. . . . Let the words of my mouth, and the meditation of my heart, be acceptable in thy sight, O Lord, my strength, and my Redeemer"* (Psalms 141:3; 19:14). Christian, if you have never done this, bow your head and ask God to sanctify your tongue NOW.

Verse 14: *"Whose mouth is full of cursing and bitterness."*

This is taken from Psalm 10:7, where we read: "His mouth is full of cursing and deceit and fraud: under his tongue is mischief and vanity." The Apostle has not quoted this literally, but has given the sense.

Cursing is reproachful and blasphemous language; it is the cheapest ticket to hell which the devil has—and a man or woman who will blaspheme God is a *coward*. You would not use God's name in vain if He were standing face to face with you! I solemnly warn you that if you are a blasphemer, you will go to hell just as sure as the sun rises—for a *saved* man does not curse. Quiting cursing will not save you, but one who is saved will not curse. James asks, "Doth a fountain send forth at the same place sweet water and bitter?" (James 3:11). And Jesus said: "Every good tree bringeth forth *good fruit;* but a corrupt tree bringeth forth *evil* fruit. *A good tree cannot bring forth evil fruit,* neither can a corrupt tree bring forth good fruit" (Matt. 7:17, 18).

"Bitterness" denotes severity, cruelty, harshness; reproachful and malicious words.

Verses 15-17: *"Their feet are swift to shed blood: destruction and misery are in their ways: and the way of peace have they not known."*

The quotation in these verses is taken from Isaiah 59:7, 8, which reads as follows:

"Their feet run to evil, and they make haste to shed innocent blood: their thoughts are thoughts of iniquity; wasting and destruction are in their paths. The way of peace they know not; and there is no judgment in their goings: they have made them crooked paths: whosoever goeth therein shall not know peace."

We have discussed the throat, the tongue, the lips, the mouth . . . and now *the feet.* The expression *"their feet are swift"* denotes the eagerness of men *"to shed blood"*—to commit crime. They thirsted for the blood of the innocent and

121

hasted to shed it, to gratify their malice or to satisfy their vengeance. (However, one does not need to shed blood to be a murderer, for we read in I John 3:15: *"Whosoever hateth his brother* is a murderer . . . ."*)

"Destruction and misery are in their ways"— that is, they cause the ruin of the happiness and the reputation of others. The tendency of their conduct is to destroy the peace of all with whom they come in contact. The reason destruction and misery are in their ways is given in verse 17: *"And the way of peace have they not known."* They do not know the way of peace, they do not know God.

Verse 18: *"There is no fear of God before their eyes."*

"Fear of God" denotes *reverence* for God. They have no reverence for the character, authority, or truth of God which would restrain them from crime. We were told in chapter 1, verse 21: "When they knew God, they glorified Him not as God, neither were thankful"—and it was because of this they departed from God. The only thing that will be effective in restraining man from crime will be a regard to the honor and law of God.

Let me make a statement here that needs to be made from every pulpit in America at least one time each Sunday: *There is no such thing as true repentance apart from Godly fear.* A person will not truly repent of sin until he truly fears God—

and one of the reasons for the predicament we are in today as a nation is that the preachers have outlawed preaching that creates fear of God. The average person does not want to be told that God is angry with the wicked every day, and that God is a "consuming fire." He wants to hear "the fatherhood of God, the brotherhood of man, everyone is good and no one is bad." I repeat: Until a sinner fears God, that sinner will never truly repent and believe God.

Verse 19: *"Now we know that what things soever the law saith, it saith to them who are under the law: that every mouth may be stopped, and all the world may become guilty before God."*

Here Paul declares that *what the law says,* it says *"to them who are under the law."* The Apostle makes this remark in order to prevent the Jew from evading the force of his conclusion. He had presented proofs from their own acknowledged laws, from writings given expressly *for* them, and which they admitted were divinely inspired. These proofs they could not evade.

". . . that every mouth may be stopped . . . ." Paul is driving home the fact that the Law is a "mouth stopper," not a "heart opener." The Law never saved anyone, nor could it ever save anyone. What the Law could not do in that it was weak through the flesh, God did in Jesus in the flesh. The Law is a "mouth stopper." The Law cries

123

out, *"The whole world* is *guilty before God."* ALL deserve hell. ALL are unrighteous.

God has not *destroyed* the Law . . . *we* are not destroying the Law; but thank God we are not *under* law—*we are under grace* (Rom. 6:14). This is not the age of the Law; this is the dispensation of the grace of God. It matters not how hard you try to keep the commandments, commandment-keeping has never saved anyone and commandment-keeping will not save you, because you cannot keep the commandments.

Verse 20: *"Therefore by the deeds of the law there shall no flesh be justified in His sight: for by the law is the knowledge of sin."*

The conclusion is that the whole world is guilty before God *because "no flesh"* is *justified "by the deeds of the law."* Judged by their own merits, as to their deeds, Gentile and Jew alike are guilty. This is the end of the matter! God has spoken, and He is the righteous Judge of all the world. God did not give the Law to save men. The Law never has saved a man, and the Law never *will* save men—*"for by the law is the knowledge of sin."*

If you want to know the truth concerning Christianity and the Law, you can learn the truth by reading Romans 10:4 and believing it: *"For Christ is THE END OF THE LAW for righteousness TO EVERY ONE THAT BELIEVETH."* This does not mean that Jesus destroyed the Law. In Matthew 5:17 Jesus tells us that He did not come to destroy the Law, nor did He come to destroy the prophets; He came to *fulfill* the Law—and He did exactly that. He fulfilled every jot and every tittle of the Law. He satisfied the demands of God's holiness and purity. In the closing hours of His earthly ministry He said, "I have glorified thee on the earth: I HAVE FINISHED THE WORK WHICH THOU GAVEST ME TO DO" (John 17:4). Again, just before He bowed His head on His pulseless breast, He cried out from the cross, "IT IS FINISHED!" (John 19:30).

I am not trying to do away with the Law, for the Law is holy, it is righteous. God has not changed His mind about the Law. He thunders out, "The soul that sinneth, it shall die!" (Ezek. 18:20). God said that, and He means exactly that; but *Jesus took our place!* And now in this Dispensation of Grace, when God looks at those of us who are believers, He does not see us . . . He sees the precious blood that covers our heart. In Christ we are righteous. In Christ we are holy. Out of Christ we are helpless, hopeless, and hell bound. (Please read I Corinthians 1:29, 30 and II Corinthians 5:21.)

Jesus did for us what we never could have done for ourselves. Jesus did for us what man *never would have* done for himself, even if he *could* have. Let me give you Scripture to prove this statement:

In John 1:11-13 we read: "He came unto His own, and His own received Him not. But as many as received Him, to them gave He power to become the sons of God, even to them that believe on His name: Which were born, NOT OF BLOOD, NOR OF THE WILL OF THE FLESH, NOR OF THE WILL OF MAN, BUT OF GOD!" Verse 12 of this portion of Scripture tells us that God gives the power . . . God furnishes the power when we believe; but "how shall they believe in Him of whom they have not heard? and how shall they hear without a preacher? and how shall they preach, except they be sent?" (Read Romans 10: 13-17.)

God sent the Word down to us in Jesus—the Word of God *in flesh* (John 1:1, 14). We hear the Gospel (I Cor. 15:1-4). The Gospel convicts of sin; the Gospel draws men to God. Therefore, we receive the power to be born into God's family through the power of the Gospel (Rom. 1:16). We do not become a child of God through man's blood, regardless of how aristocratic that blood may be. We do not become a child of God through the will of the flesh, and we do not become a child of God through the will of man . . . *"but of God."*

No man except Jesus has ever been willing to do *exactly* and *all* that God commanded. You will remember that in the Garden of Gethsemane when Jesus saw "the cup" He prayed, "Father, if it be possible, let this cup pass. Nevertheless, NOT

MY WILL, but thine, be done." Jesus is the only Man who ever satisfied God. He is the only Man who was ever willing for God to command every minute detail of His life, His words, His actions. *Adam* was not willing to follow God's command. *Noah, Abraham, Moses, David . . . all* men have failed God; but *Jesus* did in the flesh what the Law never could have done, what *man* never could have done. Jesus willingly took our place and paid sin's debt. He paid the ransom note, and we can go free if we will believe on Him who took our place.

These verses bring us to the end of the Holy Spirit's indictment against the world. As for the Gentile, in chapter 1 he is declared guilty and "without excuse." As for the Jew, the Law settled the matter concerning him: "It speaketh to them that are under the law." The result is, *every mouth is stopped* and the whole world (Jew and Gentile) is declared guilty before a holy God!

This ends the first of the main divisions of the Book of Romans, and in these verses we see that sin has done its deadly work. Man is hopelessly lost and undone, grievously guilty before a holy God; and unless grace finds a way out, there is no hope for any man, Jew or Gentile. Through the Law comes only the knowledge of sin; the Law cannot save. Through the Law there never could be salvation; but thanks be unto God, HE found a way. JESUS is the Way, the Truth, and the Life. He is the Door, He IS salvation. Without Him all men are hopelessly lost. The only way you or I will ever stand before God guiltless and hear Him say, "Enter thou into the joys of thy Lord," will be through the merit of Jesus, not by our righteousnesses (Isaiah 64:6).

"NOT by works of righteousness which we have done, but ACCORDING TO HIS MERCY He saved us, by the washing of regeneration, and renewing of the Holy Ghost" (Titus 3:5).

PART II

THE RIGHTEOUSNESS OF GOD

In Romans 3:21 we begin the second main division of the Epistle to the Romans. Here Paul teaches that justification is by faith in the crucified Christ. We will see clearly as we study, that the crucified Christ is the only remedy for sin. Without the shedding of blood there is no remission; without the shedding of blood there is no covering. The cross of Jesus is the heart of redemption, and without His shed blood there could be no justification from sin. We are justified by faith in the finished work of the Lamb of God, slain "from the foundation of the world" (I Pet. 1:18-23; Rev. 13:8).

In our studies thus far, we have seen that sin ruined man, rendering him utterly unable to help himself. Man was guilty... every man *without exception* was guilty. He could do nothing to make himself acceptable to a holy God. Judged by his own works, he found only condemnation. The Holy Spirit, through the pen of Paul, declared the Gentiles guilty because "when they knew God, they glorified Him not as God, neither were thankful . . . who changed the truth of God into a lie." As a result, God gave them up to gross idolatry and indescribable, horrible immorality. The terrible picture of the Gentile in Romans 1 is given to show just how weak—and how *depraved*—man is without God.

The Jew was as guilty as the Gentile, because he had a more complete revelation of God than the Gentile had; but even though, through the Law, he had the knowledge of sin, he continued in his self-righteousness, judging others while himself committing the same sins. The Jew, then, must find himself in the same position as did the Apostle Paul when he cried out, "O wretched man that I am! Who shall deliver me . . . ?" (Rom. 7:24).

The spiritual situation in Jewry had become worse and worse, instead of better, since the days of the prophets. Israel had "turned away backward." Justice seemed to have been forgotten. Truth was trampled underfoot:

"Judgment is turned away backward, and justice standeth afar off: for truth is fallen in the street, and equity cannot enter. Yea, truth faileth; and he that departeth from evil maketh himself a prey: and the Lord saw it, and it displeased Him that there was no judgment. And He saw that there was no man, and wondered that there was no intercessor: therefore *HIS ARM brought salvation unto Him; and HIS RIGHTEOUSNESS, it sustained Him*" (Isaiah 59:14-16).

Job 33:24 tells us that it was God who was gracious to man, and delivered him from going down to the pit. It was God who found a ransom.   Jehovah God, without sacrificing His own holiness and righteousness (which would have been impossible), found a way to bestow righteousness upon unrighteous men: "To wit, that *God was in Christ, reconciling the world unto Himself,* not imputing their trespasses unto them; and hath committed unto us the word of reconciliation. . . . *For He* (Jehovah) *hath made Him* (Jesus) *to be sin for us, who* (Jesus) *knew no sin; that we might be made the righteousness of God in Him* (Jesus)" (II Cor. 5:19, 21).

In these verses we learn clearly that God was in Christ. Jesus was the God-Man; He was God, and He was man. Jehovah God made Jesus (who knew no sin) to be sin for us, that we in Jesus might be made the righteousness of God. This may be difficult for some to accept, but it is truth. It is not tainted with error. I say boldly that when you or I are covered by the blood of Jesus, we are just as pure in God's eyes as the blood that covers us! We are righteous *in Christ: "There is therefore now NO CONDEMNATION to them which are IN CHRIST JESUS . . . ."* (Rom. 8:1). We are "justified freely by His grace through the redemption that is *in Christ Jesus"* (Rom. 3:24).

I repeat: God found a way. Only God could have provided that way. Now, in Christ, we can be saved and can become righteous. God saves us when we believe on His Son; but never forget the reason God saves us: *". . . God FOR CHRIST'S SAKE hath forgiven you"* (Eph. 4:32).

Verse 21: *"But now the righteousness of God*

without the law is manifested, being witnessed by the law and the prophets."

"*The righteousness of God*" is totally and entirely *"without the law."* It is totally apart from our works, regardless of how good our works may be. The righteousness of God is not the changing of the character of the believer; the righteousness of God is Christ Himself! He alone fully met, in our stead, the demands of the Law. He is "the END of the law for righteousness to every one that believeth" (Rom. 10:4).

James 2:23 says: ". . . Abraham believed God, and it was *imputed* unto him for righteousness." By *imputation* we become righteous—that is, by the act of God whereby He *accounts* righteousness to the believer in Christ. Christ is *"made unto us* righteousness" (I Cor. 1:30). Every believer in Christ is now by grace shrouded under the blessed righteousness of God, which the Law from Mount Sinai could never have furnished. (Read carefully Romans 3:26; 4:5, 6; and Philippians 3:9.)

". . . *being witnessed by the law and the prophets."* Paul was not giving a *new* doctrine. This righteousness was found in the Old Testament, the Jews' own sacred writings. But although the Law *testifies* to the righteousness of God, Paul declares that Gospel righteousness is *apart from* the Law.

The righteousness revealed in the Gospel in the New Testament is not contrary to the Old

Testament Scriptures and prophecies. The Old Testament Scriptures teach the righteousness that saves and has saved ever since God wrapped Adam in the skins provided by innocent substitutes; that is, God condemned the fig leaves that covered the naked bodies of Adam and Eve, and God provided coats of skins—at the expense of the blood of innocent animals. Therefore, the righteousness of God has always provided man's covering. Man could not—and man *cannot*—provide a covering that is acceptable unto God.

Every person in God's Paradise today is there *by grace;* and every person who ever *will* enter the Celestial City will enter by grace—the unmerited favor of God—and not by works. Throughout the Old Testament era, men looked TO Calvary —that is, they looked forward to the day God's Lamb would be slain once, for all, forever. All Old Testament saints were saved by looking forward to the shed blood of Christ, and the blood of the innocent animals slain in the Old Testament era pointed to the blood of THE Lamb which God Himself would provide. In this Day of Grace, we look BACK to Calvary. We know that Jesus died on the cross; we know that He finished God's demand concerning our salvation—and by faith we look back to Calvary. All sinners are saved alike. There is one God, one Father, one Saviour, one salvation, one redemption—and apart from the righteousness of God which is in Christ Jesus our

Lord, no man will be able to stand in the presence of a holy God.

Verses 22 and 23: *"Even the righteousness of God which is by faith of Jesus Christ unto all and upon all them that believe: for there is no difference: for all have sinned, and come short of the glory of God."*

"The righteousness of God" is God's own righteousness; it is *"Christ in you,* the hope of glory" (Col. 1:27)—and if Jesus is not in you, you are not righteous in God's sight. God's righteousness comes only through Christ—it is *"by faith of Jesus Christ unto all and upon all them that BELIEVE."* Righteousness becomes ours by faith in Jesus Christ, Jesus becomes ours by believing—and ALL must believe, *"for there is no difference."* The Jew, the Gentile, the wicked and the moral—ALL must believe.

The righteousness and the holiness that Almighty God requires, the Son of God *became . . .* even in flesh. The Holy Spirit enlightens us of the truth of why Jesus came into the world and what He accomplished while here: "The Son of man came *. . . to give His life a ransom for many"* (Matt. 20:28). But more—we *"walk* in the Spirit" (Gal. 5:16), and we are *taught* by the Spirit (I John 2:20, 27).

The only way we can become a recipient of God's righteousness and holiness is by faith in the finished work of the Lord Jesus Christ. All that God Almighty commands, all that He demands, and all that He approves, is found *in Himself*— and *Christ* was *God in flesh: "God was in Christ,* reconciling the world unto Himself . . ." (II Cor. 5:18, 19). To the believers in the Colossian church, Paul said: *"In HIM* (Christ) *dwelleth all the fulness of the Godhead bodily. And ye are complete in Him . . ."* (Col. 2:9, 10).

You remember in the very outset of this Epistle, Paul declared that the Gospel is "the power of God unto salvation to every one that believeth; to the Jew first, and also to the Greek." Then he goes on to say, "For therein is the righteousness of God revealed from faith to faith: as it is written, The just shall live by faith" (Rom. 1:16, 17). The point is: God's righteousness is not by works, but *by faith* in the finished work of the Lord Jesus Christ.

"For all have sinned . . . ." All men need to be saved, because all have sinned. This has been fully established in the discussion in these chapters. Earlier in this study I referred you to Isaiah 53:6: *"ALL we like sheep have gone astray;* we have turned every one to his own way; and the Lord hath laid on Him the iniquity of us *all."* Memorize this verse.

ALL have *"come short of the glory of God."* "The glory of God" here probably means Jesus Christ Himself as God's standard—*"the brightness of His glory"* (Heb. 1:3)—and surely all have "come short of the glory of God" in this sense.

In Titus 2:11 Paul says, "For the grace of God that bringeth salvation hath appeared to all men." A universal need must be met by a universal remedy; therefore, it had to be a sovereign God who was able to provide a salvation for all . . . because all have sinned, and with God there is no distinction. Since God is holy and righteous and perfect, He cannot approve anything short of perfection, holiness, and righteousness. No man can merit perfect holiness and perfect righteousness; therefore, it is imperative that all who enter the City of God receive the righteousness of God—Jesus Christ, His only begotten Son.

Verses 24-26: *"Being justified freely by His grace through the redemption that is in Christ Jesus: whom God hath set forth to be a propitiation through faith in His blood, to declare His righteousness for the remission of sins that are past, through the forbearance of God; to declare, I say, at this time His righteousness: that He might be just, and the justifier of him which believeth in Jesus."*

"Being justified" is being treated as if righteous. The Apostle has shown that men could not be regarded righteous on any merit of their own, or by personal obedience to the Law. He now affirms that if they are so treated as righteous it has to be by *favor*—*"by His grace"*—and as a matter not of

their right, but of *gift—"freely."* This is the essence of the Gospel. There is no distinction as to the remedy for man's sin . . . ALL must be redeemed alike—*"through the redemption that is in Christ Jesus."*

We have been seeing something of the *power* of the Gospel, but we now come to its *description.* The Gospel is the *good news of salvation,* and of this salvation we learn *seven things* in verses 24-26:

1. Salvation is free (v. 24). Salvation is without cost and without price. The sinner is justified (or pronounced righteous) by God when he *receives Jesus,* who paid the price (John 1:12,13). The sinner comes "without money and without price" (Isaiah 55:1).

2. Salvation is by and through grace, the unmerited favor of God (v. 24). There is not one single, solitary thing that any sinner can do or give to merit salvation. It is *God's gift* to a hell-deserving sinner.

3. Salvation is by and through the redemptive work of the Lord Jesus Christ: ". . . *through the redemption that is in Christ Jesus: whom God hath set forth to be a propitiation . . ."* (vv. 24, 25). We have redemption through Jesus Christ. "Redemption" means "to buy back"; one Bible scholar has said, "A buying-off, by means of a price paid" (Alford). Jesus bought us back at the tremendous price of His shed blood. All men belong to God by creation—the devil never created a man, nor could he *ever* create a man—but only those who are *saved* belong to God by *redemption*. Jesus *bought back* everything Adam sold to the devil in the Garden of Eden.

"Propitiation" is an important word. "The word is used in the Greek translation of the Old Testament, in the sense of an atonement or reconciliation. It refers to the act of getting rid of sin which has come between God and man" (Wuest). "'Propitiation' is the equivalent of 'the mercy seat'" (Alford).

In the ark of the covenant were the tablets of the ten commandments (Deut. 10:1-5), which had been violated by Israel. On the great day of atonement, when the high priest sprinkled the sacrificial blood upon the golden cover of the ark (Lev. 16:14), it became a place of *mercy* and ceased to be a place of *judgment*. Thus our Lord Jesus Christ is both the Mercy Seat and the Sacrifice (the propitiation), whereby mercy is offered to a sinner by faith.

4. Salvation is for those who believe: "through faith" (v. 25). Only believers have salvation. You can be a church member and not be saved. You can embrace "religion" and not be saved. Those who have salvation received that salvation through faith. The only possible way for any person, regardless of who he is, to come into possession of salvation is by simple faith: *"Believe* on the Lord Jesus Christ, and thou shalt be saved" (Acts 16:31).

5. *Salvation is based upon the shedding of blood:* ". . . through faith *in His blood"* (v. 25). It was by the blood of atonement on the mercy seat—the offering of a bullock on the great day of atonement—that the reconciliation was effected in the Old Testament era. Our salvation is also by blood atonement—but it is *by His* (Christ's) *own blood.*

Recently some outstanding theologians have publicly bragged that they do not believe in the virgin birth, the bodily resurrection, or the blood atonement of our Lord. But let me say that according to the infallible, eternal, unchangeable, forever-settled Word of God, *without the shedding of blood there is no remission of sin* (Heb. 9:22). And I boldly state without reservation, hesitation, or apology, that any person who reads these lines and denies the blood atonement will burn in hell just as surely as you breathe. No person—Jew or Gentile—will ever step inside God's Celestial City unless he is covered by the blood . . . *HIS blood.*

6. *Salvation is retrospective in its effect:* "*. . . to declare His righteousness for the remission of sins that are past. . ."* (v. 25)—or "to show His righteousness because of the passing over of *the sins done aforetime"* (Wuest). In Acts 17:30 Paul speaks of a time when God "winked at" ignorance; but no longer is that true. It was this "passing over" of sins before the cross in the sense that God saved sinners without having their sins paid for,

thus bestowing mercy without having justice satisfied—which would make God appear as having condoned sin—that had to be set right in the eyes of men. The matter was always right in *God's* eyes, because He knew Jesus would die on the cross. But the cross had to come, for a righteous God could not pass by sin. The sin-debt had to be paid.

Jesus died for the sins of Adam just as much as He died for your sins and mine. The blood shed by the Lamb of God on the cross made good all of the offerings of the Old Testament era—even the covering that God placed on Adam and Eve in the Garden. The shed blood of the innocent animals (to provide coats of skins for Adam and Eve) pointed to the blood of the Lamb of God, to be shed in the fullness of time on Calvary. As I have said previously in this series, the blood shed by the priest in the Old Testament era *pointed to Calvary*—and if Jesus had never come, if He had not died on the cross, all of the offerings in the Old Testament era would have been void and vain. But He *did* come, and by His *own blood* He made good all the offerings offered in the Old Testament era for sins.

7. *Salvation is also prospective in its effect:* ". . . *that He might be just, and the justifier of him which believeth in Jesus*" (v. 26). The cross took care of all the sins of the Old Testament era and also declares a believing sinner in this Day of

Grace is saved not only by the *mercy* of God, but by the *righteousness* of God—for his salvation rests upon the fact that his sins have been paid for and justice maintained. Thus God is *just* and at the same time the One who justifies the believing sinner.

One commentator says it this way: "Whom God hath set forth as a propitiatory covering, through faith in His blood, for the showing forth of His righteousness, by reason of the passing-by of the previously committed sins, in the forbearance of God—with a view to a showing forth of His righteousness in the present season, that He might be righteous even when declaring righteous him that hath faith in Jesus" (Rotherham).

Paul is not merely repeating here what he said in verse 25, but he is adding something new. That is to say, the work of Christ on the cross not only had in view those who had sinned in the days and the centuries on the other side of the cross, but it also had in mind those who would live even until the consummation of all things, including you and me.

In verses 25 and 26 we have the victory of the Gospel, the triumph of the Gospel. God Himself is justified even though He justifies sinful men. These verses testify to God's righteousness as to *the past,* they testify to God's righteousness *in this present time;* and they testify to God's righteousness in that He is just and yet He justifies the

sinner who on his own merit could never be righteous.   Yes, this is far beyond man's reason, and
certainly we stagger at such tremendous truth.   We
have a wonderful salvation, provided by a wonderful Saviour—but this wonderful Saviour became
ours only because of *God's grace* (Heb. 2:9).

Verse 27:   *"Where is boasting then?   It is excluded.   By what law? of works?   Nay: but by
the law of faith."*

"Where is boasting then?   It is excluded."   The
Gospel excludes all human boasting.   Man has
nothing of which to boast.   If we received our just
reward, what we deserve, we would be screaming
in hell today for one drop of water to cool our
parching tongue.   In I Corinthians 1:26-31 you will
hear this spiritual giant, Paul, crying out again
that no flesh should glory in the presence of God
Almighty.   In Romans 4:2 he said, "If *Abraham*
were justified by works, he hath whereof to glory;
but not before God."   It is only in Jesus that God
accepts us, because *in Jesus* God has given us
wisdom, righteousness, sanctification, and redemption.   There is no boasting.   Men *dare not* boast.
In the words of Paul, *"By the grace of God* I am
what I am" (I Cor. 15:10).

"By what law?   of works?"—that is, the Law
which commands works and on which the Jews
relied.   If they had kept the Law and were thereby
justified, they would have had grounds for boasting

as being justified by their own merits.   But they could not and did not keep the Law.

"Nay: but by the law of faith."   Boasting is excluded not on the principle of *works* but on the principle of *faith.* Paul told the Ephesian believers: *"By grace are ye saved THROUGH FAITH; and that not of yourselves: it is the gift of God: NOT OF WORKS, lest any man should BOAST"* (Eph. 2:8, 9).

Verse 28: *"Therefore we conclude that a man is justified by faith without the deeds of the law."*

To me this verse is a clear, simple conclusion— and anyone who does not see the truth of the verse is "willingly ignorant."   Paul says, *"Therefore"*— as a result of the previous truths set forth—*"we conclude that a man"*—all who are justified, that is—*"is justified by faith . . . ."*   There is no other way.

". . . without the deeds of the law." This does not mean that God has destroyed His law, or done away with the Law.   It does not mean that we who preach this doctrine are trying to destroy or do away with God's law.   The fact clearly set forth is that "Christ is the end of the law for righteousness to every one that believeth" (Rom. 10:4).   It is NOT the Law, but the righteousness of God in Christ Jesus, that justifies a man; and it is totally and entirely apart from works.   Man has always recoiled at being left out of salvation;

but there is not one single, solitary thing you can do to save yourself, or to *help* God save you. You MUST believe "with the heart" unto righteousness (Rom. 10:10); and if you do not believe with the heart, you are hopelessly lost.

Justification and righteousness are Siamese twins in Scripture; you cannot separate them. The believing sinner is justified because Christ bore his sins on the cross, and the justified sinner has been made righteous because he is in Christ Jesus, who is "made unto us... righteousness" (I Cor. 1:30; II Cor. 5:21). Justification originates in the grace of God (Rom. 3:24; Titus 3:4,5). Justification is through the redemptive work of Christ, who fulfilled the Law—every jot and every tittle (Matt. 5:17,18). Justification is by faith, and not by works (Rom. 3:28-30; 4:5; 5:1; Gal. 2:16; 3:8,24). The believer, justified by faith in the finished work of the Lord Jesus Christ, now has nothing laid to his charge (Rom. 8:1,33,34).

God is a righteous God, and therefore He will mete out righteousness and justice to all men—to the Jew and to the Gentile. Since God is righteous, He could not, He would not, provide justification for some, and exclude others.

Verses 29 and 30: *"Is He the God of the Jews only? Is He not also of the Gentiles? Yes, of the Gentiles also: seeing it is one God, which shall justify the circumcision by faith, and uncircumcision through faith."*

You will notice many times in Romans, Paul asks questions and then answers them. He asks here, *"Is God the God of the Jews only?"* Then he answers by saying, *"Is He not also of the Gentiles? Yes, of the Gentiles also."* In other words, God is the God of both the Jew and the Gentile. The Gentiles did not have the Law; it was given to the Jews only. If, therefore, God justified men by the Law, the Gentiles would automatically be shut out; but this was utterly and absolutely impossible because God is the God of the Gentiles also.

"... seeing it is one God, which shall justify the circumcision by faith, and uncircumcision through faith." In these verses Paul shows that as all alike had sinned—both Jews and Gentiles—and as the plan of salvation by faith was adapted to *sinners,* so God could save all on the same terms—"by faith." Since there is one true God, there can be but one means of justification. A righteous judge could not render decisions that would contradict each other. If all are guilty (and according to the Scriptures all ARE guilty), a righteous God could not decide to save the Jew to whom He had given the Law, and damn the Gentile who did not have the Law. God is righteous; He is the God who "so loved the world, that He gave His only begotten Son, that *whosoever* believeth in Him should not perish, but have everlasting life." God loved *the world,* and God's plan of redemption

145

includes everyone and excludes no one, in spite of the teaching of the hyper-Calvinists. It is not God's will that *any* perish, but that *all* come to repentance (II Pet. 3:9). All who come to God will be received; not one will be excluded (Matt. 11:28-30; John 6:37). *"Whosoever will,* let him take the water of life freely" (Rev. 22:17).

Verse 31: *"Do we then make void the law through faith? God forbid: yea, we establish the law."*

In this verse, the question is raised, "If salvation is by grace and not through the Law, then is the Law made void?" In other words, "Is the Law done away with, or destroyed? Do we render the Law vain and useless? Do we destroy its moral obligation?" Paul thunders back: *"GOD FORBID!"* And he goes on to say, *"Yea, we ESTABLISH the law."* Paul is saying that rather than making God's law of none effect, faith *establishes* it.

Dr. Scofield says: "The sinner establishes the Law in its right use and honour by confessing his guilt, and acknowledging that by it he is justly condemned. Christ, on the sinner's behalf, establishes the Law by enduring its penalty, death."

Moffett's translation gives us the following in verses 27-31:

"Then where is the boasting? Shut out. By what kind of law? The law of deeds? No, by a

law of faith. For we reckon that a man is justified by faith apart from the deeds of the law.
What! Is God only the God of the Jews? Is He
not also the God of the Gentiles? Assuredly,
of the Gentiles also, seeing that it is one God
who shall justify the circumcision in consequence
of faith, and the uncircumcision through the same
faith. Then, through faith do we annul the law?
God forbid! We uphold the law."

The theme of chapter 4 is to prove that this
is true—where Paul shows that saints like Abraham
under the old dispensation were saved by faith.

Chapter IV

1. What shall we say then that Abraham our father, as pertaining to the flesh, hath found?

2. For if Abraham were justified by works, he hath whereof to glory; but not before God.

3. For what saith the scripture? Abraham believed God, and it was counted unto him for righteousness.

4. Now to him that worketh is the reward not reckoned of grace, but of debt.

5. But to him that worketh not, but believeth on him that justifieth the ungodly, his faith is counted for righteousness.

6. Even as David also describeth the blessedness of the man, unto whom God imputeth righteousness without works,

7. Saying, Blessed are they whose iniquities are forgiven, and whose sins are covered.

8. Blessed is the man to whom the Lord will not impute sin.

9. Cometh this blessedness then upon the circumcision only, or upon the uncircumcision also? for we say that faith was reckoned to Abraham for righteousness.

10. How was it then reckoned? when he was in circumcision, or in uncircumcision? Not in circumcision, but in uncircumcision.

11. And he received the sign of circumcision, a seal of

the righteousness of the faith which he had yet being uncircumcised: that he might be the father of all them that believe, though they be not circumcised; that righteousness might be imputed unto them also:

12. And the father of circumcision to them who are not of the circumcision only, but who also walk in the steps of that faith of our father Abraham, which he had being yet uncircumcised.

13. For the promise, that he should be the heir of the world, was not to Abraham, or to his seed, through the law, but through the righteousness of faith.

14. For if they which are of the law be heirs, faith is made void, and the promise made of none effect:

15. Because the law worketh wrath: for where no law is, there is no transgression.

16. Therefore it is of faith, that it might be by grace; to the end the promise might be sure to all the seed; not to that only which is of the law, but to that also which is of the faith of Abraham; who is the father of us all;

17. (As it is written, I have made thee a father of many nations,) before him whom he believed, even God, who quickeneth the dead, and calleth those things which be not as though they were.

18. Who against hope believed in hope, that he might become the father of many nations; according to that which was spoken, So shall thy seed be.

19. And being not weak in faith, he considered not his own body now dead, when he was about an hundred years old, neither yet the deadness of Sarah's womb:

20. He staggered not at the promise of God through unbelief; but was strong in faith, giving glory to God;

21. And being fully persuaded that, what he had promised, he was able also to perform.

22. And therefore it was imputed to him for righteousness.

23. Now it was not written for his sake alone, that it was imputed to him;

24. But for us also, to whom it shall be imputed, if we believe on him that raised up Jesus our Lord from the dead;

25. Who was delivered for our offences, and was raised again for our justification.

Justification by Faith Illustrated and Defined

Chapter 4 begins with the revelation that Gospel righteousness—or New Testament righteousness, righteousness by faith minus law—is not contrary to the Old Testament righteousness, or the Old Testament teaching concerning God's righteousness.

Verse 1: *"What shall we say then that Abraham our father, as pertaining to the flesh, hath found?"*

The question is, What do you make of Abraham, with the theory just described in chapter 3? Was Abraham justified by anything which *pertained "to the flesh"*?

The whole case of the present argument is not to disprove the privilege of the Jew (which was established in chapters 2 and 3), but to show that the father and head of the race was himself justified *not* by works but by *faith*. What then did Abraham the father gain, and how did he gain it?

Verse 2: *"For if Abraham were justified by works, he hath whereof to glory; but not before God."*

If Abraham was *"justified by works,"* or on the grounds of his own merits, *he would have reason "to glory,"* or to boast. The inquiry then is whether or not there was to be found any statement in Abraham's record of a reason for self-praise or self-glorying.

Paul hurries on to say, through the leading of the Holy Spirit: *"BUT NOT BEFORE GOD."* The statement "before God" is the key that unlocks the seeming conflict between the teaching of Paul and the teaching of James (James 2:14-26). *James* is speaking of justification *in the sight of men; Paul* is speaking of justification *before Almighty God.* That no flesh is justified by works "in the sight of God" is Paul's Gospel truth, while James points out that the man of faith *shows* his faith *by his works.* True faith, saving faith, is visible only to the eye of Almighty God; but saving faith manifests itself by works. Faith which only God can see justifies the unbeliever in God's sight; but works testify to the eyes of men that we are believers and have exercised faith in God. We *prove* our faith by our works.

James says, "Faith without works is *dead.*" A man who is born again may not do much, he may not make a big show; but if he is truly saved he is alive unto God, and there will be some movement or activity on his part to prove that he is alive unto God. The man who testifies with the mouth that he has faith in God, and yet he never does anything to prove that faith, has put a big question mark around his profession in the eyes of his fellow men. Only God can see the heart, and only God knows who has saving faith and who does not exercise saving faith; WE know only by their fruits and by their works. There is no conflict between the teaching of Paul and the teaching of James. Paul is speaking concerning faith before God; James is speaking concerning faith that produces works that can be seen by our fellow men.

Verse 3: *"For what saith the Scripture? Abraham believed God, and it was counted unto him for righteousness."*

"For what saith the Scripture?" Paul relied on the Scriptures. (Read I Corinthians 15:1-4.) He did not deviate from the pure Word of God; he preached the Gospel "according to the Scriptures." According to the Scriptures, *"Abraham believed God, and it was counted unto him for righteousness."* (See Genesis 15:6.) Abraham was reckoned righteous because he trusted God to perform His promise. In other words, Abraham placed himself in such an attitude of trust in acceptance of the promise of God's blessings, it made it possible for God to bestow righteousness upon him.

"It was counted" means "put to one's account." Thus God put to Abraham's account *righteousness*. The actual payment had not been made; Jesus had not yet died—but in God's eyes Abraham possessed righteousness because "Abraham believed God." This is righteousness by faith, and not by works. It is "by-faith" righteousness that saves, not righteousness by works—because all of our righteous works add up to no better than filthy rags in God's sight (Isaiah 64:6).

It took many years for Abraham's faith to prove itself in outward demonstration, but God knew what the outcome would be; He knew from the very moment Abraham believed. Oh, yes, I believe in the sovereignty of God. I cannot explain it, but God knows the end from the beginning, and He knew exactly what would happen to Abraham. By means of faith—or *on account of* faith—God's righteousness is imputed to the sinner; so God made Abraham righteous "on account of" the merit of his faith.

In Genesis 12:1-3, God commanded Abraham to get up and get out, leave his country and his kindred, and go to a land that God would show him. God did not give him a road map, He did not give him any names. He simply said, "Get up and get out"—and Abraham got up and "departed, as the Lord had spoken unto him . . ." (Gen. 12:4).

God told Abraham that in him would all families of the earth be blessed and that his seed would be as the stars of heaven (Gen. 12:3; 15:5). But he had no son (Isaac had not been born)—and yet, *Abraham believed God.* He believed that he would be partaker of the blessing, and he was honored and justified through faith in God. God spoke, Abraham believed it, and God marked it down to him as righteousness. Read carefully John 5:24 and you will learn that sinners are saved by hearing the Word of God and believing on the Lamb of God whom God sent. Abraham heard God's Word, believed God's Word, obeyed God's Word, acted upon God's Word, and his faith in God saved him. He became "the father of the faithful."

Verse 4: *"Now to him that worketh is the reward not reckoned of grace, but of debt."*

A worker has his wage given to him as a debt due, not as a favor. It is no favor to pay a man what he has earned . . . it is a debt due him. So, says the Apostle, it would be if a man were justified by his works. He would have a claim on God; it would be God's *duty* to justify him. This doctrine of works cannot be true (Rom. 11:6).

We have all sinned; there is none righteous; we have all gone astray. Who would dare stand and announce to his neighbors, "I have never committed a sin!" Since "the wages of sin is death," and since all have sinned, then all deserve hell. Therefore if we want God to pay us what we are due, then we will receive the singular paycheck— *death* (Rom. 6:23). No, we are not justified by works; we are not saved by works. We are saved by pure grace, the gift of God: *"NOT by works of righteousness which we have done,* but according to His *mercy* He saved us, by the washing of regeneration, and renewing of the Holy Ghost" (Titus 3:5).

Verse 5: *"But to him that worketh not, but believeth on Him that justifieth the ungodly, his faith is counted for righteousness."*

Justification is offered by God — not to the worker, not to the striver, not to the endurer — *but to the believer,* the one who *"believeth on Him that justifieth the ungodly."* Yes, salvation works, and we are commanded to work out our own salvation with fear and trembling; but you cannot work out your own salvation until you *possess* salvation by faith. We are "created in Christ Jesus *unto good works"* (Eph. 2:10), but salvation is not the reward of works; it is the gift of God through faith — *"to him that worketh not, but BELIEVETH . . . ."* Thank God, grace saves, even to the uttermost, all who will come to God by Christ Jesus.

Verses 6-8: *"Even as David also describeth the blessedness of the man, unto whom God imputeth righteousness without works, saying, Blessed are they whose iniquities are forgiven, and whose sins are covered. Blessed is the man to whom the Lord will not impute sin."*

This quotation from Psalm 32:1, 2 is offered by Paul as further proof that the Gospel righteousness "by faith" which he is preaching does not contradict what David and the Old Testament prophets preached and taught. David was an Old Testament saint, and he declared his justification was by faith. David *"describeth the blessedness of the man, unto whom God imputeth righteousness without works."* He said, *"Blessed are they whose iniquities are forgiven, and whose sins are covered. Blessed* (or happy) *is the man to whom the Lord will not impute sin."* To *impute* is "to put on one's account; to credit him with; to put on deposit." David had the same wonderful, happy salvation that we have; and according to his own testimony, his righteousness was not earned, but *imputed* by Almighty God through the faith David exercised in God.

Justification Is Apart from Ordinances and Apart from the Law

Verses 9-12: *"Cometh this blessedness then upon the circumcision only, or upon the uncircumcision also? for we say that faith was reckoned to Abraham for righteousness. How was it then reckoned? when he was in circumcision, or in uncircumcision? Not in circumcision, but in uncircumcision. And he received the sign of circumcision, a seal of the righteousness of the faith which he had yet being uncircumcised: that he might be the father of all them that believe, though they be not circumcised; that righteousness might be imputed unto them also: and the father of circumcision to them who are not of the circumcision only, but who also walk in the steps of that faith of our father Abraham, which he had being yet uncircumcised."*

In these verses we learn that justification in the Old Testament, as well as in the New Testament, is totally and entirely independent of ordinances, rituals, or works. With this fact established, a new question now confronts Paul: If the rite of circumcision did not confer justification, what was its purpose? What did it accomplish?

The rite, instead of *conferring* righteousness, *confirmed* what Abraham *already had,* in that it was a *"sign"* and *"a seal"* of it. Circumcision attested the validity of Abraham's faith. Therefore justification in the Old Testament era was not a reward for circumcision. Abraham was justified years before he was circumcised. In Genesis 15:1-6 God confirmed His promise to Abraham, and verse 6 says: "And he believed in the Lord; and He counted it to him for righteousness." This was before Ishmael was born, and therefore about fourteen years before he and Ishmael were circumcised. (See Genesis 17:23-26.) Thus he is *"the father of all them that believe,"* whether they be Jews or Gentiles. "So then they which be of faith are blessed with faithful Abraham" (Gal. 3:9).

Religions that magnify works—that command (or demand) that the sinner "do something" to *be* saved, "do something" to *keep* saved, or add his or her good works and deeds to the grace of God—are growing by leaps and bounds all over America. They are trying to mix law and grace. They say, "Grace! Grace!" and then add their rituals, dogmas, doctrines, and traditions to the marvelous grace of God. But justification comes *through God's grace*. God provides justification in Christ, and *Christ in you* is "the hope of glory" (Col. 1:27) . . . the ONLY hope of your entering glory.

Verse 13: *"For the promise, that he should be the heir of the world, was not to Abraham, or to his seed, through the law, but through the righteousness of faith."*

This verse clearly teaches that justification in the Old Testament, as well as in the New Testament, is totally independent of the Law that was given to Moses on Mount Sinai. *Abraham never had the Law*—and *without* the Law Abraham was justified. Abraham was saved by *promise*. The Law came four hundred and thirty years afterward. When God gave the Law on Mount Sinai, He did not make void the older covenant, the covenant of promise. The Law simply *added to* the promise, and that only until "the seed of the woman" to whom the promise was made, should come. He, having come, the Law (which was a "schoolmaster" to bring us unto Him) is now done away. (Please read carefully Romans 10:4; II Corinthians 3:6-18; and Galatians 3:19-29.)

"The promise" was not *"through the law, but through the righteousness of faith."* The two covenants cannot be mingled together. They are fundamental principles in the sharpest contrast.

Verse 14: *"For if they which are of the law be heirs, faith is made void, and the promise made of none effect."*

If the inheritance is to be earned by obedience to the Law, *"faith is made void . . . ."* Paul told the Galatians: *". . . if righteousness come by the law, then Christ is dead in vain. . . . Christ is become of no effect unto you, whosoever of you are justified by the law . . ."* (Gal. 2:21; 5:4). If man could give perfect obedience to God's law, if by nature he had within him the ability to live *a perfect life* by that law, then he would have no need of a Saviour, no need of the blood of Jesus or the regenerating power of the Holy Spirit.

". . . and the promise made of none effect." In Galatians 3:18 we read, "For if the inheritance be of the law, it is no more of promise: but God gave it to Abraham by promise." God's promises in the Abrahamic Covenant were based upon pure grace; there were no conditions attached to them. The fulfillment of the promises did not depend upon anything Abraham did or did not do, nor upon anything his *seed* did or promised to do.

God's covenant with faithful Abraham has been confirmed, and the Law cannot set it aside or

160

make it "of none effect": "The covenant, that was confirmed before of God in Christ, *the law, which was four hundred and thirty years after, cannot disannul, that it should make the promise of none effect*" (Gal. 3:17).

Verses 15 and 16: *"Because the law worketh wrath: for where no law is, there is no transgression. Therefore it is of faith, that it might be by grace; to the end the promise might be sure to all the seed; not to that only which is of the law, but to that also which is of the faith of Abraham; who is the father of us all."*

"The law worketh WRATH"—not salvation. *"Therefore it is of faith, that it might be by grace . . . ."* On no other basis could grace manifest itself. Even if men were justified by law, it would be by their own merit and not grace. Now justification is of mere unmerited favor, *"to the end the promise might be sure to all the seed"*—not only to the Jew, who had the Law, but to all who had the same faith as Abraham, *"who is the father of us all."*

When works enter in, grace is excluded and becomes void. If it is works, it is not grace; and if it is grace, it is no more works (Rom. 11:6).

Verses 17-22: *"(As it is written, I have made thee a father of many nations,) before Him whom he believed, even God, who quickeneth the dead, and calleth those things which be not as though they were. Who against hope believed in hope, that he might become the father of many nations; according to that which was spoken, So shall thy seed be. And being not weak in faith, he considered not his own body now dead, when he was about an hundred years old, neither yet the deadness of Sarah's womb: he staggered not at the promise of God through unbelief; but was strong in faith, giving glory to God; and being fully persuaded that, what He had promised, He was able also to perform. And therefore it was imputed to him for righteousness."*

"As it is written . . . ." Here Paul quotes from Genesis 17:4, 5: "As for me, behold, my covenant is with thee, and *thou shalt be a father of many nations.* Neither shall thy name any more be called Abram, but thy name shall be Abraham; for *a father of many nations* have I made thee."

"Who against hope"—that is, all apparent or usual ground for hope—*"believed in hope . . . ."* God gave Abraham a promise which was definitely opposed to nature; but because *God made* the promise, Abraham *"considered not his own body now dead . . . neither yet the deadness of Sarah's womb."* He did not *stagger "at the promise of God through unbelief"*—but he was *"STRONG IN FAITH . . . ."*

"And being fully persuaded . . . ." Abraham

was thoroughly and entirely convinced that God was *able to perform* the humanly impossible. HE BELIEVED GOD; and because he believed God, *"it was imputed* (or reckoned) *to him for righteousness."*

Verses 13 through 22 clearly teach that we are justified through faith, and not by works . . . that justification is totally and entirely apart from the Law. These verses clearly teach that Abraham was not justified by anything he did, but by *believing God.*

Verses 23-25: *"Now it was not written for his sake alone, that it was imputed to him; but for us also, to whom it shall be imputed, if we believe on Him that raised up Jesus our Lord from the dead; who was delivered for our offences, and was raised again for our justification."*

The fact that Abraham's faith was "imputed to him for righteousness" was not written *"for his sake alone,"* but for our sake also. The Old Testament and the New Testament are in perfect accord. They do not contradict each other; they agree in every minute detail. To the Old Testament saint, faith was reckoned for righteousness . . . and not only to the Old Testament saint, but also to us, *"to whom it shall be imputed, if we believe on Him that raised up Jesus our Lord from the dead."*

When we believe that God delivered Jesus from death and the grave through the miracle of the resurrection (the greatest bombshell ever to explode in the face of an unbelieving world), we are saved (Rom. 10:9, 10). But please notice: Verse 25 is added. Why did the Holy Spirit add verse 25? The answer: To show that the faith that saves is not faith in the *act* of the resurrection, but in its *import*. He who is justified and made righteous must believe from the heart—not only that Jesus died, was buried, and rose again—but that *HE DIED "FOR OUR OFFENCES."*

Let me try to state clearly, in an understandable way, what I am trying to get across to you: It is not enough to believe that "God so loved the world" that He gave Jesus to die on the cross. It is not enough to believe that Jesus died on the cross, that He was buried and rose again. We must believe that God loved us, and *in spite of our sins and offences* He loved us enough to permit Jesus, the sinless One, to die for wretched, miserable sinners like you and me. We must believe it was *for US—for OUR sins—*that He died.

Paul has been pointing out, in these first chapters of Romans, that *"all have sinned, and come short of the glory of God"*—the Jew, the Gentile— and it was for the "offences" of men that Jesus died and rose again. Sin was so exceeding sinful that nothing but the blood of Jesus could atone for sin—and His death *does* atone for sin and the offences of man; therefore, no works of the Law can find any place or part in our justification.

He who believes in the resurrection of Jesus Christ must first believe that his own personal offences sent the Lord Jesus Christ to the rugged cross and the terrible death He died there. He who believes in the resurrection unto the salvation of the soul must believe that Jesus was the all-sufficient, satisfying Sacrifice for sin. Real, true, Holy Ghost conviction of sin makes possible such believing.

Jesus went to the cross for our offences. He died for our sins "according to the Scriptures." He was buried—but thank God, death could not hold Him! He was raised from the dead the third day, "according to the Scriptures." Heart belief in the death, burial, and resurrection of the Lord Jesus "for our offences" brings salvation. I repeat for emphasis: Such faith, such belief, comes only when there is a deep conviction of sin, and godly fear and godly sorrow in the heart. I do not believe there has ever been a case of genuine conversion that was not preceded by godly fear and true Bible repentance.

This religious mockery today which has outlawed repentance and has substituted hand-shaking and card-signing is no good. It is a counterfeit and a side-track of the devil. Jesus clearly taught, *"Except ye repent*, ye shall all likewise *perish"* (Luke 13:3, 5).

We are saved by grace through faith, and that not of ourselves; it is the gift of God. But before any person will receive this gift of God he must first recognize and face the fact of sin—*personal* sin, personal offences. He must believe with the heart that Jesus went to the cross for his individual sins.   Until he believes this as an individual, he will never accept Christ's death, His sacrifice, His blood, as the atonement for his sins and as the ground for his justification.

"*. . . and was raised again for our justification.*" The fact that Jesus walked out of the tomb is everlasting proof of His sufficiency in atoning for our sins.   The resurrection from the dead proved that He holds the keys of death, hell, and the grave.   The wages of sin is death; but Jesus personally conquered all the forces of hell.   In the personal conflict with the devil, sin, and all the forces of the underworld, Jesus captured the keys; and now He holds the keys to death, hell, and the grave (Rev. 1:18).

Chapter V

1. Therefore being justified by faith, we have peace with God through our Lord Jesus Christ:

2. By whom also we have access by faith into this grace wherein we stand, and rejoice in hope of the glory of God.

3. And not only so, but we glory in tribulations also: knowing that tribulation worketh patience;

4. And patience, experience; and experience, hope:

5. And hope maketh not ashamed; because the love of God is shed abroad in our hearts by the Holy Ghost which is given unto us.

6. For when we were yet without strength, in due time Christ died for the ungodly.

7. For scarcely for a righteous man will one die: yet peradventure for a good man some would even dare to die.

8. But God commendeth his love toward us, in that, while we were yet sinners, Christ died for us.

9. Much more then, being now justified by his blood, we shall be saved from wrath through him.

10. For if, when we were enemies, we were reconciled to God by the death of his Son, much more, being reconciled, we shall be saved by his life.

11. And not only so, but we also joy in God through our Lord Jesus Christ, by whom we have now received the atonement.

12. Wherefore, as by one man sin entered into the world,

and death by sin; and so death passed upon all men, for that all have sinned:

13. (For until the law sin was in the world: but sin is not imputed when there is no law.

14. Nevertheless death reigned from Adam to Moses, even over them that had not sinned after the similitude of Adam's transgression, who is the figure of him that was to come.

15. But not as the offence, so also is the free gift. For if through the offence of one many be dead, much more the grace of God, and the gift by grace, which is by one man, Jesus Christ, hath abounded unto many.

16. And not as it was by one that sinned, so is the gift: for the judgment was by one to condemnation, but the free gift is of many offences unto justification.

17. For if by one man's offence death reigned by one; much more they which receive abundance of grace and of the gift of righteousness shall reign in life by one, Jesus Christ.)

18. Therefore as by the offence of one judgment came upon all men to condemnation; even so by the righteousness of one the free gift came upon all men unto justification of life.

19. For as by one man's disobedience many were made sinners, so by the obedience of one shall many be made righteous.

20. Moreover the law entered, that the offence might abound. But where sin abounded, grace did much more abound:

21. That as sin hath reigned unto death, even so might grace reign through righteousness unto eternal life by Jesus Christ our Lord.

Seven Results of Justification

The righteousness imputed to us by Almighty

God through Jesus Christ His Son brings the seven results I want us to see in verses 1 through 11:

1. We have peace with God (v. 1).
2. We have access into grace (v. 2).
3. We rejoice in hope of the glory of God (v. 2).
4. We glory in tribulations (v. 3).
5. God's love is shed abroad in our hearts (v. 5).
6. The Holy Ghost is given to us (v. 5).
7. We joy in God (v. 11).

Verse 1: *"Therefore being justified by faith, we have peace with God through our Lord Jesus Christ."*

1.

". . . we have peace with God . . . ." The word *"therefore"* reaches back to the contents of chapter 4: *"Therefore being justified"* — not by works (4:1-8), not by ordinances (4:9-12), not by obedience to the Law (4:13-22) — but *"by faith, we have peace . . . ."* The first three never give peace, but faith does.

". . . through our Lord Jesus Christ." Christ Jesus Himself *"is our peace"* (Eph. 2:14). It will be a happy day when you accept the fact that all God has to offer you is in Christ Jesus. *"Ye are complete in Him"* (Col. 2:10). Jesus is our salvation, He is our righteousness, He is our holiness, He is our sanctification, He is our redemption, He is our victory, He is our peace, He is our assurance, He is our keeper. In Christ we have all things.

169

When Adam sinned, the whole human race was subject to sin and death. The peace between man and God was broken; but the second Adam (Christ) purchased peace through His shed blood. Therefore the justified have peace with God; His wrath (Rom. 1:18) no longer threatens them, and they are accepted in Christ. It is not a change of tranquility in their feelings which is indicated, but in God's relation to them.

Jesus appears to the Father in our stead. Jesus said: "Whosoever therefore shall confess me before men, him will I confess also before my Father which is in heaven" (Matt. 10:32). Paul emphatically states a Bible fact: "There is one God, and one Mediator between God and men, the Man Christ Jesus" (I Tim. 2:5). Therefore, when we know the Lord Jesus Christ as our personal Saviour, He is our peace. He pleads our case to the heavenly Father (I John 2:1,2). When we stand before God, Jesus will stand by our side to confess us as His child.

Verse 2: *"By whom also we have access by faith into this grace wherein we stand, and rejoice in hope of the glory of God."*

2.

". . . we have access by faith into this grace wherein we stand . . . ." The word *"access"* means literally "a way in." Jesus clothes the believing sinner with Himself and His righteousness, cleanses

170

him in His own precious blood, and brings him into the unlimited favor and infinite grace of God the Father. All men, apart from Jesus Christ, are shut out from God's presence; and there is no way for man to approach God and hope to gain an audience with Him, except through the Lord Jesus Christ. Jesus said, *"I am the Door: by me* if any man enter in, he shall be saved, and shall go in and out, and find pasture" (John 10:9). Again, to Thomas He said, *"I am the Way, the Truth, and the Life: no man cometh unto the Father, but by me"* (John 14:6).

By Him "we have access by faith." A standing in grace is now conferred upon the believer. The Gospel has been preached to him, which he has received and wherein he *stands* (I Cor. 15:1). His standing before God is the standing of Christ Himself. We who are saved have been "accepted *in the Beloved"* (Eph. 1:6). Positionally, we "are dead, and (our) life is hid *with Christ in God"* (Col. 3:3). *In Jesus* we are righteous and holy (II Cor. 5:21).

"But for how long? *'Have'* is perfect in tense (in Greek). The translation reads, 'through whom we have our permanent entree by faith into this unmerited favor in which we have been placed, and that permanently'" *(Wuest).*

3.

We "rejoice in hope of the glory of God." The unregenerate sinner has no joy in the prospective

171

glory of God; but to the believer it is given to "rejoice in hope" of that glory. The believer, knowing the peace of God because Jesus has "made peace through the blood of His cross" (Col. 1:20), has the right to "rejoice in hope" because Jesus has opened for him a way into God's presence, fellowship, and peace. To know that *now* we sit together in heavenly places in Christ Jesus, to know that our lives are hid with Christ in God, is certainly "joy unspeakable and full of glory" (I Pet. 1:8).

Verses 3-5: *"And not only so, but we glory in tribulations also: knowing that tribulation worketh patience; and patience, experience; and experience, hope: and hope maketh not ashamed; because the love of God is shed abroad in our hearts by the Holy Ghost which is given unto us."*

4.

". . . *we glory in tribulations also."* We as believers do not glory only in the fact that we are saved and know we are bound for heaven; but we rejoice *in tribulation, "knowing that tribulation worketh patience; and patience, experience; and experience, hope: and hope maketh not ashamed"* —a hope that never brings disappointment, a hope that is sure that "all things work together for good to them that love God, to them who are the called according to His purpose" (Rom. 8:28). I am afraid that a person who throws up his hands and quits at the first trial or tribulation that comes after he professes to be saved, has never been truly born again.

Jesus said, *"In the world ye shall have tribulation: but be of good cheer; I have overcome the world"* (John 16:33). Paul tells us, "There hath no temptation taken you but such as is common to man: but God is faithful, who will not suffer you to be tempted above that ye are able; but will with the temptation also make a way to escape, that ye may be able to bear it" (I Cor. 10:13). Paul tells us again, "We are more than conquerors through Him that loved us" (Rom. 8:37). With promises such as these, we who are truly born again do not shudder or quit when we are tried. The true believer rejoices in tribulation and trials. If we suffer with Christ, we will reign with Him; but if we deny Him, He will deny us (II Tim. 2:12).

5.

". . . the love of God is shed abroad in our hearts . . . ." The love of God referred to in this verse is not our love for God, but it is God's own love as it pours forth from His great heart through our heart. The indwelling love of God is proof that we are saved. Love is the very essence of salvation:

"Beloved, let us love one another: for love is of God; and *every one that loveth is born of God, and knoweth God.* He that loveth not knoweth not

God; for God is love. . . . *If we love one another, God dwelleth in us, and His love is perfected in us.* . . . And we have known and believed the love that God hath to us. God is love; *and he that dwelleth in love dwelleth in God, and God in him"* (I John 4:7, 8, 12, 16).

6.

". . . the Holy Ghost . . . is given unto us." God not only puts His *love* in our heart when we are saved, but God Himself dwells in us in the Person of *the Holy Spirit* (Rom. 8:9). Any person who does not possess God's Holy Spirit is not a child of God! Never let any preacher, teacher, or anyone else tell you that you can be saved apart from the Holy Spirit. We are *born* of the Spirit (John 3:5). We *possess* the Spirit (Rom. 8:9). We are *led* by the Spirit (Rom. 8:14). We are *assured* by the Spirit (Rom. 8:16). We are *sealed* by the Holy Spirit (Eph. 4:30). We are *filled* with the Spirit (Eph. 5:18).

Love is the *fruit* of the Spirit (Gal. 5:22). We know He lives in us because of the presence of God's love in our heart. When we cannot love people because of their wicked, evil ways or their hateful manners, if we are willing to submit completely and unreservedly to the love of God, God will love them through us in spite of our weakness through the flesh. *"It is God* which worketh in you both to will and to do of His good pleasure" (Phil. 2:13). If you know someone you cannot love, are you willing to allow God to love that person through you? If you are, God will work a miracle in your life.

There is nothing more clearly taught in the New Testament than the fact that the Holy Spirit is given to every believer and that He dwells in the heart of every child of God (I Cor. 6:19; Rom. 8:9).

The steps leading up to the seventh result of justification (v. 11) are found in verses 6 through 10:

Verses 6-8: *"For when we were yet without strength, in due time Christ died for the ungodly. For scarcely for a righteous man will one die: yet peradventure for a good man some would even dare to die. But God commendeth His love toward us, in that, while we were yet sinners, Christ died for us."*

Almighty God, because of His great love for His enemies, gave His only begotten Son to *die* for His enemies. When sinners were *"yet without strength"*—in the condition in which they were powerless for good—He died for them.

"For scarcely for a righteous man will one die . . . ." The meaning of this verse and the following is, to illustrate the great love of God by comparing it with what *man* was willing to do. For "a righteous man," the man who conforms to the Law, one would "scarcely" die. And it is an unusual occurrence, an event which is all that we can hope for from the highest human love and

the purest friendship, that one would be willing to die for *"a good man."*

"But God commendeth His love toward us...." *"But GOD"*—what a sharp contrast . . . the difference of earth and heaven—*gave His Son to die for "sinners"!* His love has no parallel among men. It is *divine*. What men can "scarcely" (with difficulty, hardly) do for the *good*, God has done abundantly, willingly, and lovingly for the vile and the despicable.

Verses 9 and 10:   *"Much more then, being now justified by His blood, we shall be saved from wrath through Him. For if, when we were enemies, we were reconciled to God by the death of His Son, much more, being reconciled, we shall be saved by His life."*

"Much more then" shall these enemies of God, *"now justified"* by the shed blood of Jesus, be kept safe through Christ from the wrath to come; because, having reconciled us to Himself when we were His enemies, He surely will preserve us who have become His friends:

"And you, that were sometime alienated and enemies in your mind by wicked works, yet now hath He reconciled in the body of His flesh through death, to present you holy and unblameable and unreproveable in His sight" (Col. 1:21, 22).

". . . we shall be saved by His life." Christ, who died for our sins, who died in order that we

might be saved, now lives at the right hand of God the Father to *keep* us saved: *"Wherefore He is able also to save them TO THE UTTERMOST that come unto God by Him, seeing He ever liveth to make intercession for them"* (Heb. 7:25). We are "kept by the power of God through faith . . ." (I Pet. 1:5).

We dare not doubt God's great love toward us, for Christ Jesus died for us while we were yet "without strength" and while we were yet poor, ungodly enemies of God. Paul has declared in these verses (6-10) that it might be possible to find someone to die for a good man—but Jesus did not die for *good* men; He died for *sinners*. And since He died for the ungodly, that is unmistakable proof of God's love for us.

Therefore, it stands to reason that since we are justified by the blood of Jesus Christ, we shall be kept safe in Christ from the wrath to come. Since we who were the enemies of God have been reconciled to God through the death of the Lord Jesus, we shall, by Christ's life at God's right hand, be kept safe from the onslaughts of the devil—from the devil himself, who would damn us. In other words, BECAUSE JESUS LIVES, WE LIVE ALSO. Our life now is His life within us—as Paul told the Galatians: "I am crucified with Christ: nevertheless *I live; yet not I, but CHRIST LIVETH IN ME:* and the life which I now live in the flesh I live by the faith of the Son of God, who loved

177

me, and *GAVE HIMSELF FOR ME"* (Gal. 2:20).

Verse 11: *"And not only so, but we also joy in God through our Lord Jesus Christ, by whom we have now received the atonement."*

7.

". . . we also joy in God . . . ." In a word, the believer has been brought into a new state of reconciliation, and it is made evident that God will keep him in this state. Therefore we "joy (or rejoice) in God." Notice the words I have just quoted: "We also joy IN GOD." The believer not only enjoys the blessings *of* God, but the believer positionally is actually IN God (Col. 3:3). Being reconciled to God changes the relationship between God and ourselves. Before becoming believers, we were enemies with God; but having been reconciled, we now *joy in God*—and this joy in God is ours *"through our Lord Jesus Christ, by whom we have now received the atonement* (the reconciliation)."

Always keep in mind "THROUGH OUR LORD JESUS CHRIST, BY WHOM WE HAVE NOW RECEIVED THE ATONEMENT." All we are, all we have, all we enjoy as a believer, all we ever hope to be, all we ever hope to have, is as a result of His death on the cross. Therefore, if when we were hateful to God, God loved us, will God now, since we have been made recipients of His grace, change His mind about us? Will God, who loved

us when we were enemies, provide His salvation
for us—and then forget to give us the grace, power,
and strength to overcome the world, the flesh, and
the devil? Will God support us in our trials, shield
us in our temptations, pour His love through our
hearts, abide in our bosoms in the Person of the
Holy Ghost—and then leave us to fight our own
battles and to preserve our own faith?

He who promised cannot be untrue nor unfaithful. He promised to go with us all the way, even
to the end, through the valley of the shadow of
death—and finally to stand with us and confess us
to God the Father! With such a glorious salvation
in the Lord Jesus Christ, abiding in us in the
Person of the Holy Ghost, we cannot lose. *In
Christ* we cannot fail, we cannot lose; *without*
Christ we cannot *win!* Salvation is by faith in
the finished work of the Lord Jesus Christ. Salvation is receiving the Lord Jesus Christ into the
heart. Salvation is depending upon the promise
laid down in the Word of God: *"As many as
received Him, to them gave He power to become
the sons of God, even to them that believe on His
name:* which were born, not of blood, nor of the
will of the flesh, nor of the will of man, but of
God" (John 1:12, 13).

PART III

SANCTIFICATION:
INDWELLING SIN—THE GOSPEL REMEDY

Part III of Romans deals with Bible sanctification . . . how to deal with indwelling sin, and the Gospel remedy for ALL sin. Through Adam's sin, all are sinners; and therefore all die because of sin, apart from Christ. We shall see set forth the all-inclusive aspect of the redemptive work of Christ in His death on the cross. Adam and Christ are brought into contrast to show the effect of Adam's sin on the one hand, and the effect of Christ's atoning death on the other.

Verses 12-14: *"Wherefore, as by one man sin entered into the world, and death by sin; and so death passed upon all men, for that all have sinned: for until the law sin was in the world: but sin is not imputed when there is no law. Nevertheless death reigned from Adam to Moses, even over them that had not sinned after the similitude of Adam's transgression, who is the figure of Him that was to come."*

The argument set forth in these verses is that *when Adam sinned, all mankind sinned in him.* This fact is proven in the fact that *physical death was common in all men "from Adam to Moses."* Irresponsible persons—including infants and the insane—died (as well as all others). These could not have died as a result of any sin of their own—and as death is the result of sin, Paul shows in this passage that death was the outgrowth of their sin when they were yet in Adam's loins. (A similar argument is found in Hebrews 7:9, 10, where it is declared that Levi *paid tithes* to Melchisedec *in Abraham,* "for he was yet in the loins of his father, when Melchisedec met him.")

Before he had begotten a single child, Adam fell into sin; and as a result, his nature became sinful and corrupt and death dealing—and his offspring (which, of course, includes the whole human race) has inherited from him the poison of his fallen nature and the seeds of his death. This fact is unfolded in verses 13 through 17.

Sin was in the world *before* the Law was given on Mount Sinai. Therefore men could not have died as a result of sin through the breaking of the Law; but men died, nevertheless. WHY did they die, if death is the penalty of our sinful acts? There was no written law to transgress—and yet, *"death reigned . . . even over them that had not sinned after the similitude* (or likeness) *of Adam's transgression."*

Adam transgressed *God's* law when he sinned; please notice I said "God's law." Of course, it is true that the Law of Moses is God's law; but there is a difference between the Law of Moses as such, and God's *commandments* throughout the Bible. (The New Testament is full of commandments; for instance, in I John 2:15 we read, "Love not the world, neither the things that are in the world. If any man love the world, the love of the Father is not in him." That is a direct command: *"Love not the world."*) Adam transgressed God's command. God had clearly instructed Adam what to do and what not to do; He commanded Adam to eat freely of all the trees of the Garden—EX-CEPT the tree of the knowledge of good and evil. God said, "For in the day thou eatest thereof, thou shalt surely die" (Gen. 2:15-17).

Adam ate the forbidden fruit; he transgressed God's command, God's law—and he reaped the penalty . . . he died. He died spiritually the moment he ate; he was cut off for the time being from the life of God. His eyes were opened, and he saw his nakedness. He was afraid, and he set about to correct his error through the labor of his own hands and the wisdom of his own brain. But God condemned the covering Adam's wisdom and hands provided, and God provided a *blood* covering—skins taken at the expense of the blood of innocent animals. Not only did Adam die spiritually the moment he ate—but eventually he died physically because he transgressed God's law. If Adam had not sinned, he would be alive today.

Adam's descendants lived and multiplied through the centuries from Adam to Moses . . . and even though they were not under law, they died. This shows that the descendants of Adam died because they had all sinned against the law of God in the act of Adam while they were yet in his loins—*"who is the figure of Him that was to come."*

Verse 15: *"But not as the offence, so also is the free gift. For if through the offence of one many be dead, much more the grace of God, and the gift by grace, which is by one Man, Jesus Christ, hath abounded unto many."*

"But not as the offence (the fall of Adam) . . . ."* This is a point of contrast between the effect of the sin of Adam and the work of Christ. God created Adam a free moral agent, with the right to choose. God placed him in a garden of perfection and instructed him what to do and what not to do. Adam willfully sinned; his sin was the result of willful disobedience on his own part.

". . . so also is the free gift." The gift is not in its nature and effect like the offence. The "free gift" refers to the grace bestowed in the Gospel of Christ. God provided the remedy; He promised the seed of the woman that would bruise the head of the serpent (Gen. 3:15). God did not promise Jesus because of divine obligation but because of "His great love wherewith He loved us" (Eph. 2:4).

"For if through the offence of one many be dead . . . ." This simply states that through Adam's transgression "many" were dead. I am sure that someone who reads these lines will object by saying, "Why should I suffer, why should I burn

in hell for Adam's mistake and his disobedience to God's command?'' You will not! If you burn in hell, it will be your own choice; it will not be because of Adam's transgression.

"*. . . much more the grace of God, and the gift by grace, which is by one Man, Jesus Christ, hath abounded unto many.*" God Almighty has provided a way of escape . . . a remedy. God gave the best heaven had, and all you need do to miss hell is to accept the finished work of the Lord Jesus Christ on the cross. Receive Him, and God will do the rest (John 1:12, 13).

Verses 16-18: "*And not as it was by one that sinned, so is the gift: for the judgment was by one to condemnation, but the free gift is of many offences unto justification. For if by one man's offence death reigned by one; much more they which receive abundance of grace and of the gift of righteousness shall reign in life by One, Jesus Christ. Therefore as by the offence of one judgment came upon all men to condemnation; even so by the righteousness of One the free gift came upon all men unto justification of life.*"

The contrast in verse 16 is that of source: Out of the source of one sin (Adam's), God's judgment fell, resulting in the condemnation of all. Out of the source of many transgressions, God's grace, a free gift of salvation, came, resulting in justification.

In verse 17 it is declared again that Adam's sin is the source of death among men, as was proved in verses 12 through 14. Then we read, *"... much more they which receive abundance of grace and of the gift of righteousness shall reign in life by One, Jesus Christ."* Paul's argument has now reached its point: If the relation to Adam brought death, the relation to Christ, formed by receiving the "abundance of grace" in Him, will more surely issue life. If death in Adam is certain, life in Christ is more so.

The truth of these tremendous verses is simply this: God's free Gift—namely, His only begotten Son the Lord Jesus Christ—immeasurably outweighs the transgression of man. If, through the transgression of the first Adam, all men die—"much more" through the obedience and the perfect, sinless righteousness and holiness of the second Adam, many shall be made alive (or brought back from the dead).

All sinners are spiritually dead. This truth is clearly taught in the New Testament: "And you hath He quickened, *who were dead in trespasses and sins*" (Eph. 2:1). Again, "She that liveth in pleasure is *dead while she liveth*" (I Tim. 5:6). Therefore, all sinners are dead; but through the obedience of Jesus Christ the grace of God has been brought down to all men. And through His obedience and finished work, the Father (yes, the Triune God) can be just and yet justify the most ungodly man who ever lived, when that man exercises faith in the Lord Jesus Christ.

In Adam all are sinners, all die; but all are invited to come to Jesus Christ, and *in Him* all have *life*. If Jesus delays His coming, one day I will die physically. The reason? My dad died. The reason my daddy died? His dad died—and so we could go on, back to Adam. But *spiritually* I have *everlasting life* because I possess Jesus Christ (I John 3:1-3; 5:11-13). He abides in my bosom *now* in the Person of the Holy Spirit and the divine nature of Almighty God (Rom. 8:9; II Pet. 1:4). The reason I have everlasting life is not because I am good, or righteous, or holy, or pure . . . or, if it could be, sinless. I have everlasting life because I possess Jesus Christ. By faith He lives in my heart.

Verses 19-21: *"For as by one man's disobedience many were made sinners, so by the obedience of One shall many be made righteous. Moreover the law entered, that the offence might abound. But where sin abounded, grace did much more abound: that as sin hath reigned unto death, even so might grace reign through righteousness unto eternal life by Jesus Christ our Lord."*

Wuest translates these verses as follows:

"For just as through the disobedience of the one man the many were constituted sinners, thus also through the obedience of the One, the many will be constituted righteous. Moreover, law entered in alongside in order that the transgression might be augmented. But where the sin was augmented, the grace superabounded with more added to that, in order that just as the aforementioned sin reigned as king in the sphere of death, thus also the aforementioned grace might reign as king through righteousness, resulting in eternal life through Jesus Christ our Lord."

This passage clearly teaches us that in spite of the Bible fact that men are "by nature the children of wrath" (Eph. 2:1-3), God has set another fact into operation; that is, by His grace, through the Lord Jesus Christ and His death on the cross, He (Jesus, the only begotten Son) "tasted death for every man" (Heb. 2:9). Therefore, if in Adam's sin all men are sinners and death moved upon all men through Adam's sin, it is also true that in Christ's death on the cross, many—yea, ALL who will come to God by Christ Jesus—can be made righteous through His shed blood.

I feel in my heart that anyone desiring to see this tremendous truth can see it. Jesus Christ did on the cross—in a body like yours and mine—what we never could have done for ourselves. He did for us what the *Law* never could have done. He took our place. And when we accept Him by faith, God looks upon us as being just as just as Jesus is just, just as righteous as Jesus is righteous, and just as holy as Jesus is holy. When we are covered by His blood and hid with Christ in God, God does not see our sinful nature, but He sees the blood that covers us and the divine nature that indwells us.

"Moreover the law entered, that the offence might abound. . . ." (Read Galatians 3:19.) The Law was added to the Abrahamic Covenant because through the Law we see more clearly the exceeding sinfulness of sin. And of course the Law was given only temporarily, until the Seed (that is, Christ) should come and pay the sin-debt in full. In other words, the Law was given to magnify the exceeding sinfulness of sin: *". . . that sin by the commandment might become exceeding sinful"* (Rom. 7:13).

"But where sin abounded, grace did much more abound." In spite of the exceeding sinfulness of sin, God's remedy was at hand and the sin-debt was paid in full through the blood of Jesus Christ and God's marvelous grace. One translator puts it this way: "Where sin increased, grace has overflowed."

This portion of Romans is very important, so let me give you a brief outline of what I have tried to point out and what the Word of God clearly teaches in this passage:

1. Death is universal (vv. 12-14). All men die—sinless infants, good moral people, religious people, wicked people—ALL die, regardless.

2. Since death is universal and affects all, there

must be a universal cause. There is: The answer is *universal sin* (v. 12). Adam's sin caused many to be "made sinners" (v. 19). By the offence of one man (Adam), judgment and death came upon all men (v. 18).

3. From Adam to Moses, death reigned (v. 14). There was no law between Adam and Moses; therefore men did not die because of personal guilt. Where there is no law, personal guilt is not imputed (v. 13). Therefore, from Genesis 4:7 to Exodus 29:14 the sin offering is not mentioned one time. Since "death reigned from Adam to Moses," it stands to reason that it was due to the universal sinful state—or the universal sinful nature of man. That state is declared to be *our inheritance* from father Adam.

The moral state of fallen, sinful man is clearly described in the Word of God. Let me give you just a few references. Please read them, for space will not permit me to print them here: Genesis 6:5; I Kings 8:46; Psalm 14:1-3; Jeremiah 17:9; Mark 7:20-23; Romans 1:21-32; 3:9-19; I Corinthians 2:14; Galatians 5:19-21; Ephesians 2:1-3; and Colossians 1:21.

Chapter VI

1. What shall we say then? Shall we continue in sin, that grace may abound?

2. God forbid. How shall we that are dead to sin, live any longer therein?

3. Know ye not, that so many of us as were baptized into Jesus Christ were baptized into his death?

4. Therefore we are buried with him by baptism into death: that like as Christ was raised up from the dead by the glory of the Father, even so we also should walk in newness of life.

5. For if we have been planted together in the likeness of his death, we shall be also in the likeness of his resurrection:

6. Knowing this, that our old man is crucified with him, that the body of sin might be destroyed, that henceforth we should not serve sin.

7. For he that is dead is freed from sin.

8. Now if we be dead with Christ, we believe that we shall also live with him:

9. Knowing that Christ being raised from the dead dieth no more; death hath no more dominion over him.

10. For in that he died, he died unto sin once: but in that he liveth, he liveth unto God.

11. Likewise reckon ye also yourselves to be dead indeed unto sin, but alive unto God through Jesus Christ our Lord.

12. Let not sin therefore reign in your mortal body, that ye should obey it in the lusts thereof.

13. Neither yield ye your members as instruments of unrighteousness unto sin: but yield yourselves unto God, as those that are alive from the dead, and your members as instruments of righteousness unto God.

14. For sin shall not have dominion over you: for ye are not under the law, but under grace.

15. What then? shall we sin, because we are not under the law, but under grace? God forbid.

16. Know ye not, that to whom ye yield yourselves servants to obey, his servants ye are to whom ye obey; whether of sin unto death, or of obedience unto righteousness?

17. But God be thanked, that ye were the servants of sin, but ye have obeyed from the heart that form of doctrine which was delivered you.

18. Being then made free from sin, ye became the servants of righteousness.

19. I speak after the manner of men because of the infirmity of your flesh: for as ye have yielded your members servants to uncleanness and to iniquity unto iniquity; even so now yield your members servants to righteousness unto holiness.

20. For when ye were the servants of sin, ye were free from righteousness.

21. What fruit had ye then in those things whereof ye are now ashamed? for the end of those things is death.

22. But now being made free from sin, and become servants to God, ye have your fruit unto holiness, and the end everlasting life.

23. For the wages of sin is death; but the gift of God is eternal life through Jesus Christ our Lord.

Chapter 6:1

Deliverance from Sin's Power

In chapter 5 the results of the discovery of peace with God (v. 1), and of "justification of life" (v. 18), and of reigning in life through Christ (v. 17), are things of experience, of rejoicing. But the question of a holy walk under God's abounding grace (v. 20) is now brought up in chapter 6. In this chapter we are clearly taught that it is possible for us to be delivered from the power of indwelling sin. This deliverance comes only through the victory provided in the death and resurrection of the Lord Jesus Christ.

The sixth chapter brings up and answers a question which naturally grows out of chapter 5, verses 20 and 21: ". . . Where sin abounded, grace did much more abound: that as sin hath reigned unto death, even so might grace reign through righteousness unto eternal life by Jesus Christ our Lord."

Verse 1: *"What shall we say then? Shall we continue in sin, that grace may abound?"*

The question is: If abounding grace is produced by abounding sin, then must we not conclude that we are to persist in sin in order that it result in more and more grace? In other words, if man is assured that God's grace saves and keeps, then does it not stand to reason that man, knowing this, will naturally become careless in his daily living?

The answer to such a question is simply this: The believer has been born again, and through the new birth the believer has received a new nature, "created in righteousness and true holiness" (Eph. 4:24). Because of this new nature, the believer has new desires—and not only new desires, but a new power that indwells the heart to help the believer fulfill the new desires planted within the bosom.

The grace that saves us *teaches* us. Please read Titus 2:11-15 very carefully; weigh every word—and you will notice that the grace of God that saves us also sets up a classroom in our heart and teaches us. The grace of God teaches us to deny ungodliness and worldly lusts, and to live a sober godly life in this present world, looking for the glorious appearing of the Lord Jesus Christ. You can rest assured that a believer who is looking for the second coming of Christ will be very careful what he practices in his daily living. So the marvelous grace of God not only saves us—but the grace of God sustains us, teaches us, preserves us. Thank God for His marvelous grace!

The answer to the question raised in verse 1 Paul gives in the next verse:

Verse 2: *"God forbid. How shall we that are dead to sin, live any longer therein?"*

Shall we who name the name of Jesus, who profess to be followers of the Lamb of God, continue sinning, that grace may abound? The answer is, *"GOD FORBID."* We who are *born into* the family of *God* have *died out of* the family of the *devil*. We as Christians have shared Christ's death, and in sharing Christ's death, we died to sin. We were by nature the children of the devil, but upon receiving the Lord Jesus Christ we were translated out of the kingdom of darkness "into the kingdom of His dear Son"—or the kingdom of light (Col. 1:13). We who are believers have been raised from the deadness of sin, and planted by the power of the Holy Ghost into the body of Christ. *God forbid* that we continue in sin. *"How shall we that are dead to sin, live any longer therein?"*

Verse 3: *"Know ye not, that so many of us as were baptized into Jesus Christ were baptized into His death?"*

Just what does Paul mean here? Is he speaking of water baptism? Is he saying that all who have been baptized in water have been baptized into the death of Jesus Christ? I think not.

To get the answer, let us look at I Corinthians 12:12, 13: "For as the body is one, and hath many members, and all the members of that one body, being many, are one body: so also is Christ. FOR BY ONE SPIRIT ARE WE ALL BAPTIZED INTO ONE BODY, whether we be Jews or Gentiles, whether we be bond or free; and have been all made to drink into one Spirit." From these verses

195

we learn that all believers, the moment they believe—yea, the split second they believe—are baptized by the Holy Ghost into the body of Christ. The same subject is discussed in Galatians 3:26-28:

"For ye are all the children of God by faith in Christ Jesus. For as many of you as have been baptized into Christ have put on Christ. There is neither Jew nor Greek, there is neither bond nor free, there is neither male nor female: for ye are all one in Christ Jesus."

Believers are all sons of God through faith in Christ Jesus. Paul declares that as many as were "baptized into Christ have put on Christ." Inspired of the Holy Ghost, he goes further, to teach that there can be "neither Jew nor Greek," there can be "neither bond nor free" . . . "for ye are all ONE IN CHRIST JESUS."

Here in Romans 6:3 we are taught not only that we have been *"baptized into Jesus Christ"*—but through this baptism into Christ we have been baptized also *"into His death."* The death referred to here is the death of Christ on the cross of Calvary. Our baptism into the death of the Lord Jesus took place the moment we believed. That second, we were joined to Him by the Holy Spirit. We were made *"members of His body, of His flesh, and of His bones"* (Eph. 5:30). And from the time we believed on Christ as our personal Saviour, we have been reckoned partakers in all He ever did for us in His life, His death, or His resurrection.

Christ died for us "according to the Scriptures" (I Cor. 15:3); and when He died, we died in His death. That is the way God reckons it. Jesus was buried; He rose again. When we are baptized into His body by the Holy Spirit, we share in His death, burial, and resurrection. The Scriptures state it this way: "We thus judge (reckon), that IF ONE (MAN) DIED FOR ALL, THEN WERE ALL DEAD" (II Cor. 5:14).

The second we believe on the Lord Jesus Christ and accept His finished work for our salvation, we share in all that He did for us through His life, His suffering, His death, burial, and resurrection. Even now, believers "SIT TOGETHER IN HEAVENLY PLACES IN CHRIST JESUS" (Eph. 2:6). Paul tells us that "our conversation (our citizenship) is in heaven; from whence also we look for the Saviour" (Phil. 3:20). The Head of the Church is Christ; the Foundation of the Church is Christ; the Church is the body of Christ; believers are members of the body; therefore, *positionally* we sit together with Christ in heavenly places *now*.

Tremendous truth? Yes—and it can be appreciated only by the spiritually minded who are willing to accept God's Word as it is, without human interpretation. Verse 3 certainly does not refer to water baptism. Verse 3 speaks of the baptism of the Spirit. When we believe, we are united (or joined) to the body of Christ through the baptism of the Holy Spirit (I Cor. 12:12, 13).

Verse 4: *"Therefore we are buried with Him by baptism into death: that like as Christ was raised up from the dead by the glory of the Father, even so we also should walk in newness of life."*

In this verse the symbol of water baptism is taken up. Because we have been joined to Christ by the baptism of the Holy Spirit, thus being baptized "into His death," we submit ourselves to the rite of water baptism, in which are symbolized the death, burial, and resurrection of the Lord Jesus Christ in our place. We are to *repent* and be baptized (Acts 2:38); we are to *believe* and be baptized (Mark 16:16). In answer to the eunuch's question, "Here is water; what doth hinder me to be baptized?" Philip replied, *"IF THOU BELIEVEST with all thine heart, thou mayest (be baptized)"* (Acts 8:36, 37).

To teach that water baptism is essential to salvation, or to teach that water baptism saves or washes away sins, is to make void the grace of God and the shed blood of Jesus Christ. Water baptism has nothing to do with saving us. It plays no part in our salvation, our redemption. It is an outward expression to an unbelieving world, that we have embraced with the heart the death, burial, and resurrection of our Lord and Saviour Jesus Christ. We are baptized in water to testify (through water baptism) that we are born again, dead to the world, raised to *"walk in newness of life"* — even *"as Christ was raised up from the dead by the glory of the Father."*

Verse 5: *"For if we have been planted together in the likeness of His death, we shall be also in the likeness of His resurrection."*

This verse tells why there should be a new walk in pointing out the *power* of that walk. The reason is that if we are one with Christ in His death, so shall we be one with Him in His resurrection. In other words, if we become actually united to Him *"in the likeness of His death"* — which in our baptism we profess — so shall we also be united *"in the likeness of His resurrection"* (our emersion from the watery grave) to "walk in newness of life." When we are born again, old things pass away and all things become new. We prove our faith by walking in "newness of life." When some people tell me they are saved, I wonder what they were saved FROM!

When we believe on the Lord Jesus Christ from the heart unto salvation, we experience all that He experienced. By that I mean we die to the world, and we are given new life (or "newness of life") in Him. True believers are IN Christ, and Christ is IN the believer. What Paul is clearly teaching here is that no one can share in Christ's resurrection except he first die. The resurrection to a new life is the result of dying to the world with Christ.

We are buried in order to be raised (John 12:24). Here Paul clearly reveals the union between the believer and Christ—for the thought is, if we have gone into the baptism in union, why should we not come out in union? As someone has said, "The oneness in *immersion* is proof of the oneness in *emersion.*"

Verse 6: *"Knowing this, that our old man is crucified with Him, that the body of sin might be destroyed, that henceforth we should not serve sin."*

"Our old man" is our old selves before we were saved, contrasted with the *"new man,"* which is what we are and have in Christ. Paul uses this same expression in Ephesians 4:22 and Colossians 3:9. The words *"our old man is crucified"* are addressed to faith, and faith only. In Galatians 2:20 the same assertion is repeated: *"I am crucified with Christ: nevertheless I live; yet not I, but Christ liveth in me:* and the life which I now live in the flesh *I live by the faith of the Son of God,* who loved me, and gave Himself for me."

Paul is saying, "I died when Jesus died on the cross." When Jesus hung on the cross, the passers-by saw only *one Man* dying on that cross; but God the Father saw *more* than one Man. God saw more than a physical body. God saw the *spiritual* body, the mystical body of Christ—the Church of the living God. By grace Paul was in Christ as He hung on the cross, and what happened to Jesus on the cross happened to Paul, since he was in Christ. What happened to Paul happened to every born again believer from then until this day, and to every believer from this day until the Church is completed and caught up to meet Jesus in the air.

We must not confuse "the old man" with "the flesh." The flesh is not changed. Wuest gives a very good explanation of the Greek words in this verse, which is most enlightening. He says:

"There are two words in Greek which mean 'old': *archaios*, which means 'old in point of time,' and *palaios*, which means 'old in point of use.' The second is used here. Trench defines the word as follows: 'old in the sense that it is more or less worn out.' It describes something that is worn out, useless, fit to be put on the scrap pile, to be discarded. Thus, the old man here refers to that person the believer was before he was saved, totally depraved, unregenerate, lacking the life of God.

"The word 'body' is *soma*, the human body. The word 'sin' is in the genitive case, here, the genitive of possession. The reference is therefore to the believer's physical body before salvation, possessed by or dominated and controlled by the sinful nature. The person the believer was before he was saved was crucified with Christ in order that his physical body which before salvation was dominated by the evil nature, might be destroyed,

Paul says. The word 'destroyed' is *katargeo,* 'to render idle, inactive, inoperative, to cause to cease.' Thus, the entire idea is, 'knowing this, that our old man, that person we were before we were saved, was crucified with Him, in order that our physical body which at that time was dominated by the sinful nature, might be rendered inoperative in that respect, namely, that of being controlled by the sinful nature, in order that no longer are we rendering a slave's habitual obedience to the sinful nature.' . . . Here the fact is stated, that this disengagement of the believer from the evil nature has been brought about by God with the result that the believer no longer renders a slave's obedience to the evil nature habitually as he did before God saved him."

When we believe on the Lord Jesus Christ, we become a new man. We are regenerated, and a regenerated person is to be distinguished from a person who has never been saved. As a new man we become partaker of divine nature and divine life (II Pet. 1:4; Col. 3:3, 4). The Bible does not teach that the old man is made over or improved— or, as we would say, "overhauled." (Read II Corinthians 5:17; Galatians 6:15; Ephesians 2:10; and Colossians 3:10.) When we believe, the new man is Christ formed in the believer (Gal. 2:20; 4:19; Col. 1:27; I John 4:12).

When God saves us, He saves us *from sin, TO righteousness;* and we will read later in this same chapter, "to whom ye yield yourselves servants to obey, his servants ye are . . . ." So if we continually practice sin, we are the servant of sin; but if we are born again we are a new creation in Christ Jesus and we walk in newness of life.

Verse 7: *"For he that is dead is freed from sin."*

The word *"dead"* in this verse is mystical—death is a release; death liberates from all claims. That is, although the believer lives in the same physical body, the flesh has no claim on the spirit. Having been crucified with Christ releases the believer from any claim the flesh had on him. "All claims against him are cancelled, such is the force of the statement" *(Lightfoot).*

That answers the question: "Why is it that so many church members are up today and down tomorrow, shouting God's praises today and in the gutter tomorrow?" The answer is simply this: They reform . . . they decide to do better, live better, *be* better. They have a conscience in their bosom that convicts them of the need to live right; but instead of permitting God to make them right by giving them a new heart, they try within their own power and ability to remodel their heart and their life—and it is impossible. The reason some people cannot live right is that they have never been *made* right. I believe it is possible for a born again person to backslide; but I believe just as fervently that ninety per cent of the people who

203

claim to be backsliders have never been saved in the first place. They "joined," they "united," they "made a decision" to live better. But one can do all of that and still not be born again. The new birth is becoming a new creation by exercising faith and receiving into one's heart Christ Jesus, who died that we might live.

In verse 7, the believer is pictured as the criminal who has paid the penalty for his crime: He was guilty, he deserved death; he was sentenced to death; he died—and now there is nothing against him! He is *"freed from sin"!* When we grasp this tremendous truth we can say:

> *"I do believe, I now believe*
> *That Jesus died for me;*
> *And through His blood, His precious blood,*
> *I am from sin set free!"*

Verses 8-10: *"Now if we be dead with Christ, we believe that we shall also live with Him: knowing that Christ being raised from the dead dieth no more; death hath no more dominion over Him. For in that He died, He died unto sin once: but in that He liveth, He liveth unto God."*

The fact of verse 8—*"that we shall also live with Him"*—rests upon the assurance of verses 9 and 10: *Christ,* who died for sinners, has been *"raised from the dead,"* and *"dieth no more; death hath no more dominion over Him"!* And since this is true concerning Christ, it is also true concerning those who have died in Him—and every true believer died in Him. As already pointed out, all true believers are united to the body of Christ by the baptism of the Holy Spirit. When we share the death of Christ by believing in His finished work, we share His life through the union with Him by the power of the Holy Spirit. The death of Jesus Christ on Calvary completely and entirely fulfilled the Law and answered every demand of righteousness. Jesus died on the cross, and with His own shed blood He paid the penalty of sin "ONCE FOR ALL" (Heb. 7:27; 10:10).

As to the life unto which we are raised, it is not a life unto *sin*, for sin has no claim upon it. It is to be lived *"unto God."* In II Corinthians 5:14, 15 we read: "For the love of Christ constraineth us; because we thus judge, that if One died for all, then were all dead: and that He died for all, *that they which live should not henceforth live unto themselves, but unto Him which died for them, and rose again."*

Verses 11-13: *"Likewise reckon ye also yourselves to be dead indeed unto sin, but alive unto God through Jesus Christ our Lord. Let not sin therefore reign in your mortal body, that ye should obey it in the lusts thereof. Neither yield ye your members as instruments of unrighteousness unto sin: but yield yourselves unto God, as those that are alive from the dead, and your members as instruments of righteousness unto God."*

The truth presented in verses 11 through 13 will work a miracle in the heart of any believer who will accept these verses and put them into practice.

"Likewise reckon... yourselves to be dead indeed unto sin...." Here the Holy Spirit is exhorting us to adopt for ourselves the reckoning of God. God "reckons" us to have died to sin the moment we receive His Son and the shed blood of His cross for the atonement and for salvation from sin. Therefore (or even so) let *us* reckon it thus.

"...but alive unto God...." God reckons us to have been brought again from the dead, even the death that sin produces, unto the life which is ours in Christ Jesus.

By God's grace and power, we who are saved have been born again, and we actually possess a new life—a new life in God; because it is God's own life, we have been made partakers of "divine nature." Therefore we are God's beloved children, having heard the precious words of life given to us by Jesus, the Word in flesh; believing that God sent Him into the world that we through Him might have eternal life and that we shall not be brought into judgment, but that we have passed (not *WILL pass* at some future date) out of death into life eternal. Please read John 5:24—and if you have not already memorized it, do so. Let the truth of that verse be your daily portion.

The truth declared in verses 12 and 13 is simply this: "Do not let sin therefore reign as the king in your mortal body, causing you to be in subjection to its lustful cravings. Do not yield your members to the enemy to be used in unrighteous acts, which serve as weapons against you and your spiritual victory. On the contrary, surrender your members . . . yes, even your entire body . . . to God as living, risen from the deadness of sin. Surrender your members to God—every member of your body—to be used as weapons against sin in order that you may enjoy your spiritual birthright—victory over sin . . . complete victory through the power of God" *(Weymouth)*.

Notice particularly in verse 12 that our present body is *"mortal"*; that is, subject to physical death. (We are waiting for the redemption of the body at Christ's coming—Rom. 8:23.)

"Let not sin therefore reign in your mortal body . . . ." Sin is present in our members, and ready to reign as king if permitted. That is, our bodies have not yet been redeemed from the possibility of sin's being king, if we permit it. The believer is directed to *reject* this reigning of sin, which would involve our obeying the desires of the flesh.

Note the important word *"therefore."* This looks back to the first part of chapter 6, in which our death with Christ unto sin has been established. Because of our union with Christ, the

207

"members" of the body must not be yielded at any time *"unto sin... as instruments of unrighteousness."*

Paul now goes from the negative to the positive: *"...but yield yourselves unto God...."* The Christian who counts upon the fact that divine nature has been implanted will obey Paul's exhortation to "yield yourselves unto God." To *yield* means to *present for service.* Paul is saying, "Put yourselves at once, and once for all, at the disposal of God. Present yourselves not only as forgiven sinners, but *as those that are alive from the dead."* The Christian should live every day of his life with the consciousness of this fact in mind—that he is dead to sin and alive unto God.

It is the spiritual birthright of every born again child of God to enjoy complete and total victory over the world, the flesh, and the devil; and if we as believers do not have and enjoy total victory over the world, the flesh, and the devil, it is not God's fault; it is our fault. God has provided the power; and if we refuse to use that power, received in the finished work of Jesus Christ and the shed blood of His cross, it is our fault. It is not God's fault. In the words of Paul, "We are more than conquerors through Him that loved us" (Rom. 8:37).

Verse 14: *"For sin shall not have dominion over you: for ye are not under the law, but under grace."*

When the Christian obeys the instructions laid down in verses 12 and 13 relative to his adjustment to the evil nature and the divine nature, Paul emphatically states, *"Sin shall not have dominion over you."* And he gives the reason: *"for ye are not under the law, but under grace."*

The truth of this tremendous verse confuses the legalists, because they believe exactly the opposite. They would say, "Sin SHALL have dominion over you—unless you see yourself to be under law and not under grace." The legalist reasons that Christians are kept from sinning through the terror of the Law. The legalist would make the Law to be a ministration not of condemnation and death, but a ministration of justice and life. (Compare II Corinthians 3:1-18.)

Romans 6:14 can be understood and accepted only by the believer who accepts the fact that Christ IS "the end of the law for righteousness" (Rom. 10:4). The wages of sin is death—both physical death and eternal death in hell. "The sting of death is sin; and the strength of sin is the law. But thanks be to God, which giveth us the victory through our Lord Jesus Christ" (I Cor. 15:56, 57). Victory over death, hell, and the grave is brought about by the complete and utter abolition of the Law ... which is "done away in Christ" (II Cor. 3:14; Eph. 2:15). The Gospel in its power and beauty can never be fully seen until this point is settled.

Writing to the Galatian believers, Paul said: "For as many as are of the works of the law are under the curse: for it is written, Cursed is every one that continueth not in all the things which are written in the book of the law to do them. But that no man is justified by the law in the sight of God, it is evident: for, The just shall live by faith. And the law is not of faith: but, The man that doeth them shall live in them. *Christ hath redeemed us from the curse of the law, being made a curse for us:* for it is written, Cursed is every one that hangeth on a tree: . . .

"Wherefore then serveth the law? It was added because of transgressions, till the Seed should come to whom the promise was made . . . . But before faith came, we were kept under the law, shut up unto the faith which should afterwards be revealed. Wherefore the law was our schoolmaster to bring us unto Christ, that we might be justified by faith. But after that faith is come, we are no longer under a schoolmaster" (Gal. 3:10-25).

The argument in verses 1 through 14 here in Romans 6 is that the believer is not led into a sinful life, by consideration of the fact that he is saved by grace and that he is not under law. On the contrary, having been saved by God's grace, he receives by regeneration a new nature in the inner man, which plants in the heart new desires and furnishes new power never before experienced. Therefore, "we are *more than conquerors* through

Him that loved us." The believer, having died to sin, is alive unto God; and God is working in Him, both to will His good pleasure and to *do* His good pleasure (Phil. 2:13). Paul testifies here what David said in Psalm 23—namely, *"He leadeth me in the paths of righteousness for His name's sake."*

God wants His child to be victorious and successful in the spiritual life, a million times more than *we* could ever want to be victorious or successful Christians. The Good Shepherd leads the sheep in the paths of righteousness (or *right living*) for His name's sake. The Holy Ghost leads the believer around the pitfalls of the devil and the cesspools of sin—not that we might brag or boast, but "for His name's sake," because we bear the name *Christian.* When we believe on the Lord Jesus Christ we become a Christian, and He does not want us to disgrace His name. Therefore God puts within us a new nature and gives to us a new power to carry out the new desires that come with our new nature.

Verse 15: *"What then? Shall we sin, because we are not under the law, but under grace? God forbid."*

Paul again asks and then answers his own question. He knew this question was sure to arise, because human societies and human governments know no way to restrain men from sin except by law and its penalty. Concerning rulers Paul said,

". . . he is the minister of God, a revenger to execute wrath upon him that doeth evil" (Rom. 13:4).

The assertion *"we are not under the law, but under grace"* was made to turn the justified man's eyes from Moses to Christ, from law to grace. That this can lead to license to sin Paul vehemently denies: *"God forbid!"* — and the remainder of the chapter is occupied with a fuller answer to the question raised.

Verse 16: *"Know ye not, that to whom ye yield yourselves servants to obey, his servants ye are to whom ye obey; whether of sin unto death, or of obedience unto righteousness?"*

"Know ye not . . . ?" Paul only reminds his readers what the result of sin must be. They already knew that to whom we yield our members to obey, to that one we are servant—*"whether of sin unto death, or of obedience unto righteousness."* The answer is found in the nature of sin. Its immediate effect is slavery; its ultimate outcome is death. "When lust hath conceived, it bringeth forth sin: and *sin, when it is finished, bringeth forth death"* (James 1:15).

Verse 17: *"But God be thanked, that ye were the servants of sin, but ye have obeyed from the heart that form of doctrine which was delivered you."*

"But God be thanked . . . ." Paul thanks God

that the Roman believers, who had been *"the servants of sin,"* had become obedient *"from the heart to that form of doctrine . . ."*—that of salvation by Christ on the cross. Whereas before salvation they were slaves to the evil nature, they were in salvation delivered to the teachings of grace, so that they became slaves of righteousness. That is, in salvation God constituted the believer inwardly so that he would react to the doctrines of grace by nature (divine nature) in such a way as to receive and obey them.

". . . that form of doctrine which was delivered you." "The Greek text reads, 'the form of doctrine into which you were delivered.'" *(Wuest).* It is true that the doctrine of grace was delivered to us and we by the grace of God believed. But that is not what Paul says; his statement is stronger. It is not the form of doctrine which was delivered to the Romans, but a doctrine (the Gospel) *into which* they were delivered—or *cast,* as in a *mold.* In other words, as one commentator states it, "The teaching to which they had heartily yielded themselves had stamped its own impress upon them."

Verse 18: *"Being then made free from sin, ye became the servants of righteousness."*

This verse continues the thought of the last—the happy condition into which the believer is brought by heart obedience to the Gospel. The first part of the verse is also a repeated statement of verse 7 of this chapter; that is, that the believer is *"made free from sin."* In becoming free from sin the Christian has become *the bondservant "of righteousness."* In other words, by the wonderful change wrought in him by salvation, he has come to the place where *righteousness* is his master, instead of *sin.* Jesus tells us in the Sermon on the Mount that we cannot serve two masters (Matt. 6:24).

To make the words *"free from sin"* denote what is called "eradication of the sin principle" or "eradication of the old nature"—a sinlessness of the flesh—is a terrible perversion. Paul constantly preached and testified to the contrary. Our *bodies* will not be redeemed (no matter how much we may be blessed or filled with the Holy Spirit) until the redemption of the body at Christ's second coming. Until that time sin will still be in the flesh, although those who obey with the heart that word of the cross unto which they have been delivered, will find themselves in a state of blessed relief from sin's bondage.

We do not abstain from sin because of the fear of the Law; but we abstain from sin because of the power of the indwelling Holy Ghost in our heart—"Not after the law of a carnal commandment, but after the power of an endless life" (Heb. 7:16).

God does not want us to sin; but if a believer DOES sin, we have an Advocate with the Father—

Jesus Christ, who did no sin—and He pleads our case; He is our propitiation (I John 2:1, 2).

Verse 19: *"I speak after the manner of men because of the infirmity of your flesh: for as ye have yielded your members servants to uncleanness and to iniquity unto iniquity; even so now yield your members servants to righteousness unto holiness."*

Paul here explains why he was using the illustration drawn from human relations—that of a slave—throughout this passage. He declares *the "infirmity"* (or frailties) *of our flesh* to be such that we must necessarily be in bondservice—either to sin, or unto God. Rome was full of slaves, and freedom was most difficult to secure. So Paul speaks in human terms—*"after the manner of men"*—a great truth: that we must be servants of God or of sin. Man hates this fact, for he boasts of his independence; but it is all a delusion.

Our Lord Himself (and Scripture generally) sets forth that only those who know the truth and walk therein are truly free. The Jews in John 8:32-36 rebelled when our Lord told them, "Ye shall know the truth, and the truth shall make you free. . . . If the Son therefore shall make you free, ye shall be free indeed." There is no real freedom out of Christ, in whose service is *perfect freedom.*

Verse 20: *"For when ye were the servants of sin, ye were free from righteousness."*

In other words, there is no middle ground: We are either sons of God or sons of the devil. We are either the possessors of divine nature, or we are controlled by the old nature which brings death. If we have received the new nature given by Almighty God when we believe on His Son Jesus Christ, then we have One within us who is greater than he who is without (I John 4:4); therefore we are conquerors, victorious over the world, the flesh, and the devil. Our members are not captured by lust, but we are delivered through the Power within (the Holy Ghost) who leads us into paths of right living for His (Jesus') name's sake.

Verses 21 and 22: *"What fruit had ye then in those things whereof ye are now ashamed? for the end of those things is death. But now being made free from sin, and become servants to God, ye have your fruit unto holiness, and the end everlasting life."*

In verse 21 Paul is saying, "Look back to the old sinful life, to the things you did then. What reward did it bring? Only a fruitage of which you are *ashamed,* the *end* of which is *death.*"

"But now . . . ." Paul continues by saying, in effect, "But the opposite of this is your case now. You well know that in your old life you were free men in respect of God's righteousness, and bondsmen in respect of sin. But now you are cut loose from sin and united to righteousness, because you

216

have been redeemed by the shed blood and baptized into the body of Christ by the Holy Ghost. Therefore, you are no longer bondsmen in respect to sin, but you are bondsmen to righteousness and holiness. Just as you in the old days allowed your members to be dominated and controlled by sin, so now you should (since you are Christians) commit your members unreservedly to the Holy Spirit, as means of serving and promoting personal holiness in daily living."

The Apostle is saying, "You have experienced what real living is; and now that you are free men insofar as sin is concerned, you are bondsmen in relationship to the God who saved you. You now have, as the fruit of your daily living, holiness; and the end of your holy living is *everlasting life.*"

It is just as natural for a sinner to practice sin as it is for water to run downhill or for the sun to rise in the morning; but it is equally *un*natural for born again children of God to practice sin. They do not . . . because they are new creations; they have become servants of God, bondslaves to righteousness, possessing divine nature, indwelt by the Holy Spirit. Therefore they live righteous and holy lives through the divine nature and the divine power that abides in their bosom.

"Free from the law, O happy condition,
 Jesus hath bled, and there is remission;
 Cursed by the law and bruised by the fall,
  GRACE HATH REDEEMED US ONCE FOR ALL!

217

"Now are we free—there's no condemnation,
  Jesus provides a perfect salvation;
'Come unto me,' O hear His sweet call,
  Come, and He saves us ONCE FOR ALL!

"'Children of God,' O glorious calling,
  Surely His grace will keep us from falling;
Passing from death to life at His call,
  BLESSED SALVATION, ONCE FOR ALL!"

Verse 23: *"For the wages of sin is death; but the gift of God is eternal life through Jesus Christ our Lord."*

We could spend hours here—and I could write a book on this verse, because this is the verse the minister used the night I was born again. There is another verse in this same Epistle that gave me the blessed assurance of salvation, but this is the verse that brought me to Christ. That night I heard God's minister deliver a sermon on *The Wages of Sin.* He proved to me from God's Word that sinners go to hell when they die. (I am of the conviction that we need more "hell-fire and damnation" preaching and less of this anemic social gospel that declares "the fatherhood of God, the brotherhood of man"—a doctrine that is certainly foreign to the Word of God.)

The young man who stood in the pulpit and preached the night I was saved, convinced me that I was on the road to hell—and I faced the fact that hell would be my eternal destiny unless

I called on God for salvation. I will always have
a warm spot in my heart for this verse of Scripture . . . for even though the first part of the verse
is very sad, the climax of the verse is glorious!

"The wages of sin" is singular. It makes no
difference from which angle we look at sin, nor
how carefully we may analyze sin, we always get
the same answer: "The wages of sin *is death."*
No man (or angel) ever sinned and got away with
it! If you are reading these lines and you are not
washed in the blood, if you are a sinner, and if
you continue in sin and get away with it, you will
be the first being who ever sinned against God
and did not reap the penalty. The only way to
escape the damnation of sin is to receive the Gift
of God—Jesus Christ.

Yes, sin pays wages. The devil's pay envelope
contains eternal death . . . eternal separation from
God . . . eternal separation from everything beautiful
and lovely . . . eternal separation from the glories of
heaven . . . eternal separation from all godly mothers
. . . eternal separation from all godly loved ones.
The devil's pay envelope contains everlasting torment . . . everlasting misery . . . everlasting woe . . .
everlasting pain. Sin pays wages in fire and brim-
stone!

". . . but the gift of God is eternal life . . . ."
I am so thankful that salvation from hell is God's
gift. In spite of the fact that we have all sinned
and come short of the glory of God, God so loved

219

all, that He gave His only begotten Son; and Jesus so loved all, that He came and laid His life down that we might have life. The only way any poor sinner can stay out of hell and go to heaven is to receive the Lord Jesus Christ by faith (John 1:12, 13; 3:16; Eph. 2:8). Salvation is God's gift, minus works.

"... *through Jesus Christ our Lord.*" Greek scholars tell us that the word "through" is *"in"* in the original. So the pure Greek would read, "The gift of God is eternal life *IN Jesus Christ our Lord.*" Salvation and Jesus cannot be separated. *"Christ in you"* is the only hope of glory. "And this is the record, that God hath given to us eternal life, and this life is IN HIS SON. He that hath the Son hath life; and he that hath not the Son of God hath not life" (I John 5:11, 12).

It is utterly impossible for me or any other minister to overemphasize the fact that salvation and Jesus are inseparable. Jesus Christ *is* our salvation. He is *the Way,* and all other ways are counterfeits of the devil. He is *the Truth,* and all else that is branded truth is the devil's lie. He is *the Door—THE Door,* the ONLY Door, the singular Door; all other doors open into the pits of the damned.

Jesus Christ is the Author and He is the Finisher of our faith. We are saved by God's grace... grace is Jesus... grace becomes ours by faith. Faith comes by hearing, and hearing by the Word of

God. "In the beginning was the Word, and the Word was with God, and the Word was God" (John 1:1). Jesus said, "I and my Father are one" (John 10:30). Therefore salvation, grace, faith, Jesus are all one and the same—you cannot separate them. Saving faith can become ours only by hearing the Word of God (John 5:24; Rom. 10:17). When we hear the Word, we are hearing Jesus because the Word testifies of Him. It is absolutely impossible to be saved apart from Jesus Christ.

In the Gospel, Jesus is the center, the very soul, of the message of redemption. The Gospel finds man dead in trespasses and sin, because all men have sinned and come short of the glory of God, and "the wages of sin is death." But the Gospel brings to us the message that raises dead sinners to life in Christ Jesus. From the very moment we are regenerated, we become a partaker of the Christ-life within.

Hear these glorious words from the inspired pen of the Apostle Paul:

"If ye then be risen with Christ, seek those things which are above, where Christ sitteth on the right hand of God. Set your affection on things above, not on things on the earth. For ye are dead, and *your life is hid with Christ in God. When Christ, WHO IS OUR LIFE,* shall appear, then shall ye also appear with Him in glory" (Col. 3:1-4).

To speak of salvation apart from Jesus Christ

is to advertise total ignorance in the teaching of the Gospel of the Lord God Almighty. Jesus Christ is the hub of the wheel of salvation, and every spoke points to the hub—*Jesus Christ*, the virgin-born, only begotten, sinless Son of God!

"Buried with Christ, and raised with Him too;
    What is there left for me to do?
Simply to cease from struggling and strife,
    Simply to walk in newness of life.

"Risen with Christ, my glorious Head,
    Holiness now, the pathway I tread;
Beautiful thought, while walking therein:
    He that is dead is freed from sin.

"Living with Christ, who dieth no more,
    Following Christ, who goeth before;
I am from bondage utterly freed,
    Reckoning self as dead indeed.

"Living for Christ, my members I yield,
    Servants to God, forevermore sealed:
Not under law, I am now under grace,
    Sin is dethroned, and Christ takes its place.

"Growing in Christ: no more shall be named
    Things of which now I am truly ashamed.
Fruit unto holiness will I bear;
    Life evermore, the end I shall share."

Chapter VII

1. Know ye not, brethren, (for I speak to them that know the law,) how that the law hath dominion over a man as long as he liveth?

2. For the woman which hath an husband is bound by the law to her husband so long as he liveth; but if the husband be dead, she is loosed from the law of her husband.

3. So then if, while her husband liveth, she be married to another man, she shall be called an adulteress: but if her husband be dead, she is free from that law; so that she is no adulteress, though she be married to another man.

4. Wherefore, my brethren, ye also are become dead to the law by the body of Christ; that ye should be married to another, even to him who is raised from the dead, that we should bring forth fruit unto God.

5. For when we were in the flesh, the motions of sins, which were by the law, did work in our members to bring forth fruit unto death.

6. But now we are delivered from the law, that being dead wherein we were held; that we should serve in newness of spirit, and not in the oldness of the letter.

7. What shall we say then? Is the law sin? God forbid. Nay, I had not known sin, but by the law: for I had not known lust, except the law had said, Thou shalt not covet.

8. But sin, taking occasion by the commandment, wrought in me all manner of concupiscence. For without the law sin was dead.

9. For I was alive without the law once: but when the commandment came, sin revived, and I died.

10. And the commandment, which was ordained to life, I found to be unto death.

11. For sin, taking occasion by the commandment, deceived me, and by it slew me.

12. Wherefore the law is holy, and the commandment holy, and just, and good.

13. Was then that which is good made death unto me? God forbid. But sin, that it might appear sin, working death in me by that which is good; that sin by the commandment might become exceeding sinful.

14. For we know that the law is spiritual: but I am carnal, sold under sin.

15. For that which I do I allow not: for what I would, that do I not; but what I hate, that do I.

16. If then I do that which I would not, I consent unto the law that it is good.

17. Now then it is no more I that do it, but sin that dwelleth in me.

18. For I know that in me (that is, in my flesh,) dwelleth no good thing: for to will is present with me; but how to perform that which is good I find not.

19. For the good that I would I do not: but the evil which I would not, that I do.

20. Now if I do that I would not, it is no more I that do it, but sin that dwelleth in me.

21. I find then a law, that, when I would do good, evil is present with me.

22. For I delight in the law of God after the inward man:

23. But I see another law in my members, warring

against the law of my mind, and bringing me into captivity to the law of sin which is in my members.

24. O wretched man that I am! who shall deliver me from the body of this death?

25. I thank God through Jesus Christ our Lord. So then with the mind I myself serve the law of God; but with the flesh the law of sin.

The Law Cannot Produce a Holy Life

In the first six chapters of Romans, we find three clear statements concerning the Law:

1. ". . . by the deeds of the law there shall no flesh be justified in His sight . . ." (3:20).

2. ". . . the law entered, that the offence might abound. . ." (5:20).

3. ". . . ye are not under the law . . ." (6:14).

The theme of chapter 7 is that the Law cannot produce a holy life; it cannot produce holy living. We have learned in previous chapters that the Law could not produce *justification,* and it is just as true that the Law cannot produce *sanctification.*

Chapter 7 falls into three divisions:

1. Born again believers enjoy freedom from the Law (verses 1-6).

2. Though the Law makes sin to abound, the Law of God is not sinful, but holy (verses 7-13).

3. The Law cannot deliver from the flesh (verses 14-25).

Verse 1: *"Know ye not, brethren, (for I speak to them that know the law,) how that the law hath dominion over a man as long as he liveth?"*

Paul was addressing intelligent people who knew the law as a principle. They lived in Rome where the very meaning of law—and the force through law—was well known. The Apostle is speaking of the law as a principle (civil law) rather than the Law of Sinai, although he has in view throughout the illustration the freedom of the believer from the Law given to Moses on Mount Sinai. Paul says that it is common knowledge that the (civil) law has power over man so long as he lives. When he dies, he has passed out of the realm where law can have jurisdiction over him.

Just so, the Law of God can have dominion over a person as long as he remains in the domain where the Law can have jurisdiction over him— and that is in an unsaved state. But when a believer has been identified with Christ in His death, burial, and resurrection (ch. 6), he has passed out of the realm where the Law has power over him.

Verses 2 and 3: *"For the woman which hath an husband is bound by the law to her husband so long as he liveth; but if the husband be dead, she is loosed from the law of her husband. So then if, while her husband liveth, she be married to another man, she shall be called an adulteress: but if her husband be dead, she is free from that law; so that she is no adulteress, though she be married to another man."*

In these verses Paul uses the marriage relation as a basis to illustrate how the Christian is freed from the Law. Here the case is brought before us of a married woman *"bound by the law"*—permanently bound; there is no release. The illustration is simple enough: The marriage relation continues in force between the two parties as long as they both shall live.

Verse 3 is self-explanatory and perfectly clear. If a married woman marries another man than her husband while her husband is alive, she is guilty of adultery; *"but if her husband be dead, she is free from that law; so that she is no adulteress, though she be married to another man."* On the death of the husband, the wife is released, or "loosed"; literally, "she has been brought to naught as respects the law of her husband." Before her husband died, she was truly a wife; but after the husband is dead, she is a wife no longer. She remains a woman; but she has become dead to the law which bound her to a man (her husband)—and her death to the law which bound her to a husband brings about her freedom insofar as the marriage relation is concerned.

Verse 4: *"Wherefore, my brethren, ye also are become dead to the law by the body of Christ; that ye should be married to another, even to Him who is raised from the dead, that we should bring forth fruit unto God."*

The third verse emphasizes the rigor of the marriage law in its demand that the husband and wife remain one (Gen. 2:24; Matt. 19:4-6). Verse 4 now brings in the conclusion: Believers are made dead to the Law as the wife is dead to marital law. It is God's law that a woman should be considered dead in her husband's death; wherefore, under a similar law believers may be reckoned dead in Christ's death. The point reached is this: As the woman died to the marriage law in the death of her husband, so *"brethren, ye also,"* in like manner, died to the whole Mosaic Law by the means of *"the body of Christ"* on the cross.

But how did the Mosaic Law affect Gentiles, who were not under it? In a very unique sense they were under it. It was against them (Col. 2:14). When Moses shut up the Jew under the Law, he shut out the Gentiles. God's way was to remove the barrier of the Law by breaking down this "middle wall of partition." Christ reconciled both Jew and Gentile unto God "in one body by the cross," so that both have access by the Spirit unto the Father (Eph. 2:13-18).

Paul told the Romans, *"Ye . . . are become dead to the law . . . that ye should be married to Another, even to Him who is raised from the dead . . . ."* We are now *joined* to the risen Christ; we *live* unto Him: "For the love of Christ constraineth us; because we thus judge, that if One died for all, then were all dead: and that He died for all, *that they which live should not henceforth live unto themselves, but unto Him which died for them, and rose again.* Wherefore henceforth know we no man after the flesh: yea, though we have known Christ after the flesh, *yet now henceforth know we Him no more"* (II Cor. 5:14-16). Through the truth of these tremendous verses we learn:

1. In the reckoning of Almighty God, when the Lord Jesus Christ died on Calvary's cross, the believer died with Him.

2. When Jesus arose from the dead and walked from the tomb, every born again believer rose from the dead with Him; that henceforth we born again believers should live—not to ourselves, but unto the Lord Jesus, in whom we died when He died and rose again with Him when He rose from the dead.

3. In the third place, the Christ we now know is not a Babe in a manger; He is not the Man of Galilee working miracles; He is not the Christ nailed to a cross or lying in a tomb. *The Christ we now know is the Christ seated at the right hand of God the Father.* He is not the Christ according to the flesh; He is the same Christ (in a sense)— but He is not now in the body in which He conquered the world, the flesh, and the devil, and in which He fulfilled the Law. He is now seated at the right hand of God the Father in His resurrection body—a glorious body, one such as we will have when we meet Him in the first resurrection.

Yes, there is a sense in which He is the same Jesus Christ as He was before the cross; but in a Gospel sense, He is far, far different. Our faith is not in the Christ of Galilee—but in the Christ of eternal glory; not in the Man Jesus who walked on the shores of Galilee doing good, working miracles, nineteen hundred years ago—but in the Lord Jesus Christ who sits at the right hand of the Majesty on high, making intercession for us, pleading our case before a holy God (Heb. 7:25).

This eternal Bible fact needs to be emphasized today as never before. We hear people cry out, "Go back to the Christ of the Gospels!" But I would like to say to you that the words of the Epistles are the words of Jesus just as truly as are the words of the Gospels. The words of the Epistles are the teachings of Christ, risen from the dead, glorified at the Father's right hand, pleading our case to the eternal God.

The marriage illustration given here in Romans chapter 7 goes a little deeper: We are "married" to the risen Christ *that we should bring forth fruit unto God.*" In our natural condition—that is, "children of wrath, even as others" (Eph. 2:3)—and joined (or married) to sin and lust, our fruit coming through that marriage is, of course, things that would make us ashamed . . . ungodliness and lust. But now, being made free from sin by having become servants to God through believing on His Son Jesus Christ, we have our fruit unto holiness

(Rom. 6:22). The heavenly purpose of marriage on earth is that children may be born and reared. God gave Noah the command to replenish the earth, and it is in the program of God that children be born into the homes. Children are the logical issue of the marriage relationship. Likewise, just as in our former marriage to sin and ungodliness we produced uncleanness and iniquity (Rom. 6:19), it is the purpose of our new marriage (having been joined in holy relation to the risen Christ by faith in His shed blood) that we should "bring forth fruit unto God."

Verses 5 and 6: *"For when we were in the flesh, the motions of sins, which were by the law, did work in our members to bring forth fruit unto death. But now we are delivered from the law, that being dead wherein we were held; that we should serve in newness of spirit, and not in the oldness of the letter."*

"When we were in the flesh . . . ." Notice that Paul did not say "in the *body,*" but "in the *flesh.*" This is the condition of all who are not saved, as we see from verses 8 and 9 of chapter 8: "They that are *in the flesh* cannot please God. *But ye are not in the flesh, but in the Spirit, if so be that the Spirit of God dwell in you. . . ."* Paul is saying that when we were still unsaved, before we became believers, *"the motions* (or passions) *of sins, which were by the law, did work*

231

in our members to bring forth fruit unto death."

"But now"—that is, since we are born again and are new creatures in Christ—*"we are delivered from the law, that being dead wherein we were held"* (or "having died to that in which we were constantly being held down"). That in which the believer was constantly held before he was saved is the evil nature. The point is, as Paul has so clearly shown, that the power of the evil nature has been broken in the believer.

". . . that we should serve in newness of spirit, and not in the oldness of the letter." It is not merely that we have been delivered from the bondage of sin, in order that we might walk in newness of *human* spirit, but that we might serve "in newness of THE Spirit"—the Holy Spirit of God, who originates and penetrates our Christian life.

"The letter" here refers to the written Word of God as found in the Old Testament, the Law being only a collection of precepts and prohibitions, while the Gospel is the message of freedom and liberty, ruled by the Spirit and produced through the power of the Spirit. The Spirit brings liberty: *". . . where the Spirit of the Lord is, there is liberty"* (II Cor. 3:17).

The "newness" is the new spiritual state—or our union with Christ through the power of the Holy Spirit. The "oldness of the letter" means the former state—being under the Law, "the ministration of death" (II Cor. 3:7). "The letter killeth,

but the Spirit giveth life" (II Cor. 3:6). The Law
could bring forth only "fruit unto death," but the
Spirit produces holy fruit unto life. Believers now
being married to a new Husband—the risen Lord
Jesus Christ—must change our ways.

It is true that we are still servants—yea, bond-
servants; but it is a service in perfect freedom and
liberty, whereas in the "old letter" we were servants of sin and drudgery. We now serve Him
whom we have never seen, yet believing, we serve
with "joy unspeakable and full of glory" (I Pet.
1:8). We are now under the dispensation of the
Spirit—or the Dispensation of Grace—not law.
Therefore we must be spiritual in our thoughts,
words, and deeds. We must serve in the spirit;
we no longer worship in the outer court . . . we
worship within the veil.

Verses 7 and 8: *"What shall we say then? Is
the law sin? God forbid. Nay, I had not known
sin, but by the law: for I had not known lust,
except the law had said, Thou shalt not covet.
But sin, taking occasion by the commandment,
wrought in me all manner of concupiscence. For
without the law sin was dead."*

In verse 7 we come to the second division of
the subject under discussion. Again, Paul asks
and answers his own question: *"Is the law sin?
God forbid."* Although it has been shown (in
chapter 5, verse 20) that "the law entered, that the

233

offence might abound," the Law nevertheless is not sinful, but holy. This is proved by the fact that "by the law is the knowledge of sin" (Rom. 3:20). A sinful law would be incapable of revealing the sinfulness of sin. It is because the Law is perfect as a standard of righteousness and godliness, that it (the Law) so clearly manifests the presence of evil. The Law shows the exceeding sinfulness of sin (Rom. 7:13), and by this divine standard every man is convicted of sin: "For there is no difference: for all have sinned, and come short of the glory of God" (Rom. 3:22b, 23).

Paul explains this by saying, ". . . *for I had not known lust* (a passionate craving, or coveting) *except the law had said, Thou shalt not covet.*" In other words, without the Law or the commandment, sin—though present in the heart of Saul of Tarsus—was unsuspected and unrecognized even by himself. His conscience was not disturbed, he was not troubled . . . *"For without the law, sin was dead."*

Verses 9 and 10: *"For I was alive without the law once: but when the commandment came, sin revived, and I died. And the commandment, which was ordained to life, I found to be unto death."*

What Paul is saying here is simply this: "I felt that I was alive before I knew the law." ". . . *but when the commandment came . . . .*" What does

234

Paul mean by this expression? From Paul's own testimony, in the Book of Acts and other places in the Epistles, he was brought up on the commandments at his mother's knee, and he studied the commandments under the great teacher Gamaliel; but there came a day when Paul's eyes were opened and he saw what the commandments really meant. He realized that, far from being the means of grace and redemption, they were the means of death and condemnation.

Sin was there all the time, to be sure—but until the day the commandment came upon him with all of its crushing, condemning force, his conscience was asleep; sin did not disturb it. The strength of sin that brought the sting of death to the Apostle Paul, was the Law. When the Law was joined to sin in his consciousness and he saw what the Law really was and what the Law could really do, the conscience within him that had been dead, came to life, and he *"died."* (Read I Corinthians 15:56, 57; II Corinthians 3:7-9.)

The Law was never given to be a ministration of life, but of death (II Cor. 3:7). And yet Paul could write of the commandments as being *"ordained to life,"* because Moses had said, "The man which doeth those things shall live by them" (Rom. 10:5; Lev. 18:5). Saul of Tarsus—like every other sinner—found himself without power to do these things; and so the Law, which was unto life, he *"found to be unto death."*

235

Paul (Saul of Tarsus) was "a Pharisee of the Pharisees" and a devout Judaist. He lived after "the straightest sect" of the Pharisees, and he is saying in these verses: "I felt that I was alive when I knew no law; but when the commandment came, sin came to life and I died. The very commandment whose end I thought was life, I found to be, to me, death. I realized for the first time the real sentence brought upon me by the law."

Concerning Romans 7:7-25, Dr. Scofield tells us in his footnote in the Scofield Reference Bible:

"Paul's religious experience was in three strongly marked phases: (1) He was a godly Jew under the law. That the passage does not refer to that period is clear from his own explicit statements elsewhere. At that time he held himself to be 'blameless' concerning the law (Phil. 3:6). He had 'lived in all good conscience' (Acts 23:1). (2) With his conversion came new light upon the law itself. He now perceived it to be 'spiritual' (Rom. 7:14). He now saw that, so far from having kept it, he was condemned by it. He had supposed himself to be 'alive,' but now the commandment really 'came' (v. 9) and he 'died.' Just when the apostle passed through the experience of Romans 7:7-25 we are not told. Perhaps during the days of physical blindness at Damascus (Acts 9:9); perhaps in Arabia (Gal. 1:17). It is the experience of a renewed man, under the law, and still ignorant of the delivering power of the Holy Spirit (Rom. 8:2). (3) With the great revelations afterward embodied in Galatians and Romans, the apostle's experience entered its third phase. He now knew himself to be 'dead to the law by the body of Christ,' and, in the power of the indwelling Spirit, 'free from the law of sin and death' (Rom. 8:2); while 'the righteousness of the law' was wrought in him (not *by* him) while he walked after the Spirit (Rom. 8:4). Romans 7 is the record of past conflicts and defeats experienced as a renewed man under law."

Verses 11 and 12: *"For sin, taking occasion by the commandment, deceived me, and by it slew me. Wherefore the law is holy, and the commandment holy, and just, and good."*

"Taking occasion" means "to make a start from a place, a base of operations" *(Wuest).* The Law is not sin, but sin found *occasion* in the Law. This verse supports verse 10 in showing the process by which the Law brought about death. Paul is saying that sin, taking the commandment as a starting point, an occasion, *"deceived me, and by it slew me."*

Verse 12 is the conclusion of verse 11. The *holiness* and *goodness* of the Law is proved by the fact that the Law slays every sinner with whom it comes in contact. The Law must do this—else the Law would be neither *"holy"* nor *"just"* nor *"good."*

God has not changed His mind about His law

nor about sin. The Law of Sinai has been described by some as "the concept of the mind of God as to what man ought to be," and it has its penalty: *"The soul that sinneth, it shall die"* (Ezek. 18:20).

"So then, if a soul under the law sins and dies not, that is indisputable proof that the law is evil, unholy, and unjust. A holy law must of necessity impose and enforce its penalty. This explains the connection between verses 11 and 12: 'For sin seized the advantage, and by means of the commandment it completely deceived me, and also put me to death. So that the law is holy, and the commandment is holy and righteous and good'" *(Wuest).*

"Christ is the end of the law for righteousness to every one that believeth" (Rom. 10:4), and Jesus said, "Think not that I am come to destroy the law . . . I am not come to destroy, but to fulfil" (Matt. 5:17). "What the law could not do, in that it was weak through the flesh" (Rom. 8:3), God sent Jesus in flesh to do—and Jesus did in flesh what the Law could never have done; therefore God can be holy and just, and yet justify the ungodly. That is exactly what God does when we put our faith in the finished work of the Lord Jesus Christ. When we receive Jesus, who said, "It is finished" (John 19:30), He is our salvation. He is our redemption; and God has accepted us as His sons—His heirs—and we are joint-heirs with

Jesus Christ. But this is not on the merit of works or law, but on the grounds of His finished work.

Verses 13 and 14: *"Was then that which is good made death unto me? God forbid. But sin, that it might appear sin, working death in me by that which is good; that sin by the commandment might become exceeding sinful. For we know that the law is spiritual: but I am carnal, sold under sin."*

Again Paul asks a question, and then gives the answer. He is asking, "Did *that which is good* become death to me?" Then he thunders out, *"God forbid!"* In the final analysis, it was not the Law that actually put Saul of Tarsus to death, but *sin—by means of the Law.* And in this there was a divine intention, namely, *that sin "might appear sin,"* might come out in its true colors, by *"working death"* for man through *"that which is good."* Paul wants us to fully understand that "the letter killeth"; it is the *Spirit* that makes alive. What an awful thing sin is, that by the holy and just law of God it can bring death to God's creatures.

In verse 14, Paul says, *"I am carnal . . . ."* Paul has three words to describe man: *"natural"* (I Cor. 2:14)—the unsaved man; *"carnal"* (I Cor. 3:1-4)—the saved man who has not found deliverance from the power of sin in the fullness of the Spirit; and *"spiritual"* (I Cor. 3:1)—the believer who is living his life in the fullness of the Holy Spirit.

Paul has been speaking of himself up to this point, as the days before he was born again; but the struggle he now proceeds to describe is not that of an unregenerate man trying to save himself, but rather of a regenerate man trying to live right. It is the conflict between the old nature and the new living together in the believer. The new nature cannot sin—("Whosoever is born of God doth not commit sin; for His seed remaineth in him: and he cannot sin, because he is born of God"—I John 3:9)—while the old nature can do nothing but sin.

By the closing verses of chapter 7 we are to learn that as the Law was unable to justify a sinner and make him a child of God, so it is equally unable to sanctify the believer as to his walk. It matters not how hard one may attempt to keep the Law, if that person is successful in keeping part of the Law, and yet he offends in one point, he is guilty of all (James 2:10). Therefore, no believer has reached perfection—and the Law accepts only perfection; it refuses to recognize imperfection. So when one puts himself under the Law he brings upon himself the curse of the Law.

Some teach that we are free from the Law insofar as the Law bringing life is concerned, but that in the rule of our daily living we are still under the Law. There is certainly no Scripture for such a doctrine. I remind you again: "Christ is the *end* of the law for righteousness to every one that believeth" (Rom. 10:4). Sin shall not have dominion over the Christian, because he is *not under law* but under grace (Rom. 6:14). The person who mixes law and grace, or who teaches that salvation is by grace but he must obey the rules of the Law, is under the Law, and sin does have dominion over him. That person will soon discover the strength of sin, the defeat of sin, and discover that the Law is holy and blameless, but he is *carnal,* *"sold under sin."*

It will be a happy day in the experience of the Christian who reads these lines, when that Christian embraces the Bible truth that salvation is all grace, pure grace, minus law. We are saved by grace, we are kept through grace, and we will stand in the presence of Almighty God free from condemnation because of the finished work of the Lord Jesus Christ and not because of any work we have done in this body.

Verses 15-17: *"For that which I do I allow not: for what I would, that do I not; but what I hate, that do I. If then I do that which I would not, I consent unto the law that it is good. Now then it is no more I that do it, but sin that dwelleth in me."*

In these verses we have two *"I"*'s. They are contending one with the other; they represent the

241

old nature and the new nature of Paul. In other words, Saul of Tarsus is in conflict with Paul the Apostle. They both live in one body.

Many believers are in spiritual ignorance concerning the two natures of a Christian. Because of this spiritual ignorance, many believers suffer defeat and heartache which they would never know if they understood the difference between the inner man and the flesh. As long as we live in this life, we will have a warfare between the Spirit of God and the flesh. Paul faces this solemn fact in chapter 7 of our present study.

"For that which I do I allow not . . . ." Now Paul explains his situation. *"Allow"* is "to know by experience, to understand." He says, "For that which I do, I do not understand." The very thing he desires to do—that is, to do good—this he does not do; and that which he *hates*, this is the thing he *does* do. It is clear that Paul is recounting his experiences as a saved man. He desires to do good, and he hates sin. No unsaved man does that. The failure of Paul to achieve his purpose is found in the fact that he is attempting in his own strength that which can be accomplished only in the supernatural power of the Holy Spirit.

In verse 16 Paul says, *". . . I consent unto the law that it is good."* This is shown as the Apostle points out that the Law does not desire what he does. In doing evil against his will, his will agrees with the Law, "that it is good."

242

Paul cries out in verse 17, *"It is no more I that do it, but sin that dwelleth in me."* Beloved, these words were spoken by a born again man. It was not Saul of Tarsus who spoke these words; it was Paul the Apostle. He recognized the presence of the flesh. (Please read Galatians 2:20; Colossians 1:15; 3:3; I Peter 1:23; II Peter 1:4.)

Verses 18-20: *"For I know that in me (that is, in my flesh,) dwelleth no good thing: for to will is present with me; but how to perform that which is good I find not. For the good that I would I do not: but the evil which I would not, that I do. Now if I do that I would not, it is no more I that do it, but sin that dwelleth in me."*

Paul's failure cannot be blamed on, nor accredited to, his wrong attitude toward the holy law of God. He declared it was indwelling sin (the evil nature indwelling a believer) that brought about his failure to live as he wished to live. He confesses in verse 18 that he desires to do good, he *wants* to do good, and he knows the good he should do—but he is powerless to perform it.

"To will" is literally "the being constantly desirous." That is, Paul was constantly desirous of doing God's will. This *"will"* that was constantly *"present with"* him came from his new nature—the divine nature within (II Pet. 1:4). But while the desire to do God's will is always with him, the ability or power *"to perform that which*

243

is good" is not. Certainly these are the words of a pathetic person. He cries out again in verse 20: *"Now if I do that I would not, it is no more I that do it, but sin that dwelleth in me."*

Verse 21: *"I find then a law, that, when I would do good, evil is present with me."*

The word *"law"* in this verse refers to the *law of sin* which Paul speaks of as "in his members" (v. 23). Dr. Scofield points out that there are six "laws" mentioned in Romans:

1. The Law of *Moses*—which condemns (3:19).
2. Law simply as a *principle* (3:21).
3. The law of *faith*—which brings saving grace and excludes all works and self-righteousness (3:27).
4. The law of *sin* in the members of the body, which is victorious over the law of the mind (7:21, 23, 25).
5. The law of *the mind,* which consents to the Law of Moses which is holy and righteous, but cannot keep the Law because of the law of sin in the members of the body (7:16, 23).
6. The law of *the Spirit,* which delivers the believer from the law of sin and death (8:2).

Verses 22 and 23: *"For I delight in the law of God after the inward man: but I see another law in my members, warring against the law of my mind, and bringing me into captivity to the law of sin which is in my members."*

Verses 22 and 23, introduced by *"for,"* unfold what Paul means by verse 21. To *"delight"* means to *rejoice* and is "stronger than 'I consent' in verse 16" *(Wuest)*. Paul delights *"in the law of God."* This delight is not in that which is outward in doing it, but in the *"inward man,"* the new nature that comes into the heart when a sinner is born again—in his wish, in his consent, in his hate of what the Law condemns. A proof of his delight in the Law is his persistent effort to keep the Law in spite of constant failure. Paul's delight in the Law reveals himself as a *saved man* throughout this struggle. No unsaved person is conscious of a moral struggle within himself, for he has but one nature.

"But I see another law . . . ." The word *"law"* here (as in vv. 21 and 25) means an inward principle or action operating with the fixedness and regularity of the Law. Paul is speaking of *"the law of sin,"* or the tendency to do evil in his own members. This law is also called (in Galatians 5:17, 24) "the flesh" which "lusteth against the Spirit, . . . the flesh with the affections and lusts"; that is, the sinful principle in the regenerate.

But the Apostle found *two* "laws" within him: The one, "the law of sin"; the other, *"the law of the mind,"* or the holy principle of the new nature. When he says he *"sees"* one of these principles *"warring against"* the other and *"bringing"* him *"into captivity"* to itself, he is not referring to his actual condition at the time he was writing this Epistle. Chapter 7 is not the *present experience* of Paul; rather, it is a *delivered* person describing the state of an undelivered one. He is simply describing the two conflicting principles in every born again person.

Verse 24: *"O wretched man that I am! Who shall deliver me from the body of this death?"*

The battle Paul has described is so severe he cries out, *"O wretched man that I am!"* How can this be called a normal Christian experience? It is a legal experience written to show that whatever else the Law can do, it can deliver no man, saint or sinner, from the flesh. We are "delivered from the law" by "being dead" (in Christ) to that in which we were held (v. 6).

"Who shall deliver me from the body of this death?" The Apostle speaks of the "body" here with reference to the "law of sin" which he had said was in his members; and he calls it *"the body of this death"* as feeling as he wrote, the horrors of that death (chap. 6:21 and chap. 7:5) into which it dragged him down. But the language is not that of a sinner; it is the cry of a living but agonized believer weighed down under a burden which is not himself, but which he longs to shake off from his renewed self. Nor does it imply ignorance of the way of relief at the time referred to. It was

designed only to prepare the way for that outburst of thankfulness for the divinely prepared way of deliverance which immediately follows.

Verse 25: *"I thank God through Jesus Christ our Lord. So then with the mind I myself serve the law of God; but with the flesh the law of sin."*

"I thank God through Jesus Christ our Lord." This is the ready answer of praise to the despairing question of verse 24. Jesus Christ is the "channel" of deliverance.

"So then with the mind" Paul delights in *"the law of God; but with the flesh the law of sin."* Paul is saying, "Such then is the unchanging character of these two principles within me. God's holy law is dear to my renewed mind and has the willing service of my new man, although that corrupt nature which still remains in me listens to the dictates of sin."

Many believers suffer many defeats, simply because they have not learned to walk in the Spirit and thereby refrain from fulfilling the lust of the flesh. "Christ in you" is "the hope of glory," and Christ reigning in your heart and in your daily practices of life brings victory. We are overcomers because greater is He that is within, than he that is without (I John 4:4). Whosoever is born of God overcomes the world—but the victory comes only by faith (I John 5:4). It is not by keeping the Law, or trying to practice the Law, that we are victorious over the world, the flesh, and the devil. We can never be victorious except through the power of the Holy Spirit within. The Spirit of God draws us to God. He is the attending Physician at the spiritual birth. We are born of the Spirit; He baptizes us into the body of Christ when we accept Jesus by faith. He seals us until the day of redemption—and from the moment we are born again until that glad day when we stand in the presence of our Redeemer, it is the Holy Spirit of God who leads us in the path of victory over the world, the flesh, and the devil.

In Romans chapter 7 we hear the pitiful cry of a believer who is a bondslave from the standpoint of the flesh, his members bondslaves to sin; but in chapter 8 we will hear the victorious cry of a believer who has discovered the power of the indwelling Spirit to give victory! In chapter 7 we hear the believer crying, "O wretched man that I am! Who shall deliver me . . . ?" And then in chapter 8 we hear the same believer crying out in victory, "Who shall separate us from the love of Christ? . . . WE ARE MORE THAN CONQUERORS THROUGH HIM THAT LOVED US" (ch. 8:35, 37).

Chapter VIII

1. There is therefore now no condemnation to them which are in Christ Jesus, who walk not after the flesh, but after the Spirit.

2. For the law of the Spirit of life in Christ Jesus hath made me free from the law of sin and death.

3. For what the law could not do, in that it was weak through the flesh, God sending his own Son in the likeness of sinful flesh, and for sin, condemned sin in the flesh:

4. That the righteousness of the law might be fulfilled in us, who walk not after the flesh, but after the Spirit.

5. For they that are after the flesh do mind the things of the flesh; but they that are after the Spirit the things of the Spirit.

6. For to be carnally minded is death; but to be spiritually minded is life and peace.

7. Because the carnal mind is enmity against God: for it is not subject to the law of God, neither indeed can be.

8. So then they that are in the flesh cannot please God.

9. But ye are not in the flesh, but in the Spirit, if so be that the Spirit of God dwell in you. Now if any man have not the Spirit of Christ, he is none of his.

10. And if Christ be in you, the body is dead because of sin; but the Spirit is life because of righteousness.

11. But if the Spirit of him that raised up Jesus from the dead dwell in you, he that raised up Christ from the

dead shall also quicken your mortal bodies by his Spirit that dwelleth in you.

12. Therefore, brethren, we are debtors, not to the flesh, to live after the flesh.

13. For if ye live after the flesh, ye shall die: but if ye through the Spirit do mortify the deeds of the body, ye shall live.

14. For as many as are led by the Spirit of God, they are the sons of God.

15. For ye have not received the spirit of bondage again to fear; but ye have received the Spirit of adoption, whereby we cry, Abba, Father.

16. The Spirit itself beareth witness with our spirit, that we are the children of God:

17. And if children, then heirs; heirs of God, and joint-heirs with Christ; if so be that we suffer with him, that we may be also glorified together.

18. For I reckon that the sufferings of this present time are not worthy to be compared with the glory which shall be revealed in us.

19. For the earnest expectation of the creature waiteth for the manifestation of the sons of God.

20. For the creature was made subject to vanity, not willingly, but by reason of him who hath subjected the same in hope.

21. Because the creature itself also shall be delivered from the bondage of corruption into the glorious liberty of the children of God.

22. For we know that the whole creation groaneth and travaileth in pain together until now.

23. And not only they, but ourselves also, which have the firstfruits of the Spirit, even we ourselves groan within ourselves, waiting for the adoption, to wit, the redemption of our body.

24. For we are saved by hope: but hope that is seen

is not hope: for what a man seeth, why doth he yet hope for?

25. But if we hope for that we see not, then do we with patience wait for it.

26. Likewise the Spirit also helpeth our infirmities: for we know not what we should pray for as we ought: but the Spirit itself maketh intercession for us with groanings which cannot be uttered.

27. And he that searcheth the hearts knoweth what is the mind of the Spirit, because he maketh intercession for the saints according to the will of God.

28. And we know that all things work together for good to them that love God, to them who are the called according to his purpose.

29. For whom he did foreknow, he also did predestinate to be conformed to the image of his Son, that he might be the firstborn among many brethren.

30. Moreover whom he did predestinate, them he also called: and whom he called, them he also justified: and whom he justified, them he also glorified.

31. What shall we then say to these things? If God be for us, who can be against us?

32. He that spared not his own Son, but delivered him up for us all, how shall he not with him also freely give us all things?

33. Who shall lay anything to the charge of God's elect? It is God that justifieth.

34. Who is he that condemneth? It is Christ that died, yea rather, that is risen again, who is even at the right hand of God, who also maketh intercession for us.

35. Who shall separate us from the love of Christ? Shall tribulation, or distress, or persecution, or famine, or nakedness, or peril, or sword?

36. As it is written, For thy sake we are killed all the day long; we are accounted as sheep for the slaughter.

37. Nay, in all these things we are more than conquerors through him that loved us.

38. For I am persuaded, that neither death, nor life, nor angels, nor principalities, nor powers, nor things present, nor things to come,

39. Nor height, nor depth, nor any other creature, shall be able to separate us from the love of God, which is in Christ Jesus our Lord.

Deliverance and Righteousness
Through the Indwelling Holy Spirit

One outstanding Bible scholar of the past made this statement: "If the Word of God was a ring, and the Epistle of Romans its precious stone, chapter eight would be the sparkling point of the jewel." I think all believers agree that Romans chapter 8 is one of the most precious and one of the most beloved chapters in the entire Word of God.

In chapter 8 we find the climax to the argument begun in chapter 3:21; that is, the subject of Gospel righteousness through faith in the finished work of the Lord Jesus. Chapter 3, verses 21-31, clearly teaches us that righteousness is by faith. In chapter 4 we are taught that this Gospel righteousness by faith does not contradict Old Testament Scriptures. Chapter 5 teaches us that by Gospel righteousness, obtained through the finished work of the Lord Jesus Christ, we are kept by the power of God, through faith in the finished work of our

Saviour. Chapter 6 shows that sinful living is neither produced nor encouraged by the Gospel teaching of salvation by grace through faith, but that we are *dead* to sin and "alive unto God through Jesus Christ our Lord." The born again believer can trust in Jesus to *keep* him, instead of depending upon his own ability, which could never provide victory over the old nature. Divine nature brings victory to the believer. Chapter 7 teaches that the believer's sanctification by the Law is utterly impossible. And now, in chapter 8 we will learn that through the Holy Spirit who dwells in every believer, we are able to live a godly life—but only as we allow the Holy Spirit to lead us day by day.

Verse 1: *"There is therefore now no condemnation to them which are in Christ Jesus, who walk not after the flesh, but after the Spirit."*

It is a wonderful thing for the believer to discover the indwelling Holy Spirit as the Spirit of life and power, and to know that condemnation has been removed. The first verse of this wonderful chapter reminds us that *"now"*—yes, NOW— we are free from condemnation. Authorities on the Greek language tell us that Romans 8:1 reads as follows in the original: "Therefore, now there is not even one bit of condemnation to those who are in Christ Jesus" *(Wuest's Translation of the New Testament).*

Our standing *"in Christ Jesus"* is stated in this verse: We are NOW delivered from condemnation. The proposition set forth here is that the believer is absolutely and forever free from all condemnation. This is the result of believing the Gospel of the marvelous grace of God, placing trust in the finished work of the Lord Jesus Christ. Such faith has bestowed upon the believer a righteousness—even the righteousness of God—which nothing can soil or destroy. Yes, God's OWN righteousness is *imputed* unto the believer at the beginning of his Christian experience—the very second he believes on the name of the Son of God.

Dr. Scofield says, "Imputation is the act of God whereby He accounts righteousness to the believer in Christ, who has borne the believer's sins in vindication of the law."

We have been justified by faith in Jesus Christ (Rom. 5:1), and justification is the act of God whereby God declares righteous one who believes on His only begotten Son, Jesus Christ. *In Christ* we stand free from condemnation. There is no condemnation from the Law, for Jesus fulfilled the Law. There is no condemnation because of our sin inherited through Adam's sin, for Jesus (the last Adam) bought back everything Adam lost, He did what the first Adam failed to do. There is no condemnation from any source because we are *in Christ Jesus,* born of His Spirit, washed in His blood, *hid with Christ in God.* What a position!

No condemnation! Can it be
This message sweet is meant for me?
For me, who but for God's free grace
Would occupy the sinner's place?

No condemnation! When? and how?
The word is clearly written—*"Now."*
'Tis wrought through Christ, and Christ alone;
Naught but His blood can sin atone.

No condemnation! Fully free!
Though Satan cast his darts at me,
Accuse me oft, and try me sore,
In Christ I stand condemned no more.

No condemnation! No more dread
That God's fierce wrath will touch my head.
His Word is true, His promise sure;
It shall forevermore endure.

No condemnation! Joy untold!
My heart cannot its praise withhold
From Him who freely bore for me
My condemnation, set me free!
                              —*G. K. Horne*

". . . who walk not after the flesh, but after the Spirit." This is not a condition for being saved, but a *fact* concerning one who has been born again. Paul does not base his assertion of no condemnation to the saint upon the saint's conduct, but upon his position in Christ. His position in Christ has liberated him from the compelling power of the evil nature and made him a partaker of the

divine nature, a new inner condition which produces in every Christian a desire and a motive to be obedient to the Lord's commandments.

Verse 2: *"For the law of the Spirit of life in Christ Jesus hath made me free from the law of sin and death."*

In verse 2 we are taught that by the higher and more powerful *"law of the Spirit of life"* the believer is delivered and *made free* from two other laws; namely, *"the law of sin"* and *the law of "death."* "The law of sin" is clearly defined in chapter 7, verses 21-23. Chapter 7 presents the believer seeking to live a righteous life through obedience to the Law, but within himself he finds another law warring (fighting) against the law of his mind and bringing him into slavery under the law of sin in the body, or in the "members."

In chapter 8 we find the believer discovers deliverance through the Holy Spirit abiding within, dwelling daily—yea, moment by moment—in the heart. I John 4:4 tells us that we are overcomers because "greater is He that is in you, than he that is in the world." John is telling us that the Holy Ghost within is more powerful, and greater, than the spirit of the devil without.

The law of the Spirit of life also delivers from the law of death, which is described in Romans 7:7-11. Even though the Law of Moses was in itself spiritual, holy, righteous, pure, and good, it became unto Saul of Tarsus a law of death; and it was indeed unto Israel a yoke which they were not able to bear (Acts 15:10). Here in Romans 8 the believer is seen as yielding himself to the indwelling Holy Spirit of God, who by divine power delivers the believer from the law of death.

Verse 3: *"For what the law could not do, in that it was weak through the flesh, God sending His own Son in the likeness of sinful flesh, and for sin, condemned sin in the flesh."*

"For what the law could not do . . . ." The Law of Moses was unable to produce in man the obedience that the holy law demanded. In other words, the Law demanded what it could not produce. Romans 3:20 tells us, "By the deeds of the law there shall no flesh be justified in His sight." The Law could never produce justification; yet the Law demanded perfect obedience, perfect purity, perfect righteousness.

The Law *"was weak through the flesh"*—i. e., having to address itself through a corrupt nature. The Law itself was not weak—but it was powerless *on account of the flesh.* The Law—holy, just, and good—could command, but the flesh was not subject to it and could not be. How could sinful flesh obey holy, sinless law?

So—what the Law could not do, *Almighty God did. He sent "His own Son in the likeness of sinful flesh"*—a very remarkable expression. Jesus was made in the reality of our flesh, but only in the *likeness* of its sinful condition. He took our nature as it is in us, compassed with infirmities, with nothing to distinguish Him as man from sinful men, save that He was *without sin* (Heb. 4:15).

"*. . . and for sin*"—literally, "and about sin" or "on the business of sin"—"*condemned sin in the flesh*"—that is, caused it to lose its power over men. The expression is a general one and speaks not only of Christ's mission to atone for sin but also in virtue of that atonement to destroy its dominion and power over believers.

By the cross of Jesus sin is condemned, for God sent Jesus as a sin-offering. All men had gone astray; all had sinned and come short of the glory of God (Isaiah 53:6; Rom. 3:23). All were under condemnation. Sin in the flesh—all centering in the Lamb of God on the cross—was put to death in order that the righteousness of God (demanded by the law of God) might be fulfilled in the believer.

Verse 4: "*That the righteousness of the law might be fulfilled in us, who walk not after the flesh, but after the Spirit.*"

"*That the righteousness of the law*"—the righteous demands or the precepts of the Law, meaning here the obedience which the Law calls for— "*might be fulfilled in us . . . .*" Wuest says this means to "find its full accomplishment, not merely be performed by us, for the Apostle has a deeper meaning—namely, that the aim of God in giving the Law might be accomplished in us, *in our sanctification,* which is the ultimate end of our redemption (Eph. 2:10; Col. 1:22)." The work of being fulfilled is not ours, but the work of God by His grace.

"... *who walk not after the flesh, but after the Spirit.*" Here, as in verse 1, the believer is defined as one who walks—not according to the flesh—but according to the Spirit. Here again "who walk not" is a *result* of being born again, not a *condition* to being born again.

To walk according to the flesh, as set forth in this verse, is to reject the gift of pure Gospel righteousness in Christ, and Christ alone. To walk according to the flesh is to seek to establish one's own righteousness by keeping the Law—or by doing the works of the Law. This is the natural thing and is what the flesh is ever prone to try. On the other hand, to walk according to the Spirit of God is to receive the Lord Jesus Christ by faith, trusting in Him as Saviour and Lord.

Verses 5 through 8 draw a contrast between the believer and the unbeliever, the born again and the sinner. These verses mention those who are "after the flesh" and those who are "after the Spirit." Rotherham's translation of this passage reads as follows: "For they who according to flesh have their being, the things of the flesh do prefer, but they according to the Spirit the things of the Spirit; for what is preferred by the flesh is death, whereas what is preferred by the Spirit is life and peace; inasmuch as what is preferred by the flesh is hostile toward God, it does not submit itself, neither in fact can it; they moreover who in flesh have their being, cannot please God."

Verse 5: *"For they that are after the flesh do mind the things of the flesh; but they that are after the Spirit the things of the Spirit."*

"The flesh" here is the evil nature. *"They that are after the flesh"* are unsaved people who are dominated by the indwelling sinful nature. They *"do mind . . ."*—literally, "direct their mind to something; to seek or strive for." The word speaks of a deliberate setting of one's mind upon a certain thing. Therefore, those who follow the flesh have their interest in *"the things of the flesh";* but those who follow the Holy Spirit have their interest in the things of God, *"the things of the Spirit."* Those who are indwelt by the Holy Spirit desire the things of the Spirit, because He leads us, as we will see later in this chapter. Those who follow the lust of the flesh, the lust of the eye, and the lust of the world, are not guided by the Spirit of God. From this verse we see that the desires of the heart show our position spiritually, whether we are saved or lost. And

the possession of the heart determines the practices of life.

Verses 6 and 7: *"For to be carnally minded is death; but to be spiritually minded is life and peace. Because the carnal mind is enmity against God: for it is not subject to the law of God, neither indeed can be."*

"For to be carnally minded"—literally, "to have the mind of the flesh"—*"is death . . . ."* It not only *ends* in death, but even now is carrying death in its bosom, so that such are "dead while they live" (I Tim. 5:6).

". . . but to be spiritually minded" (or "minding of the Spirit")—i. e., the pursuit of spiritual things, thus a mind that is controlled or dominated by the Holy Spirit—*"is life and peace."* If we have uppermost in our minds the interest of the flesh, then of course that means death; but if the uppermost desire of our heart and life is the interest of the things of the Spirit, that means life and peace. We possess the life that God is, and peace. The Greek word for peace means "to bind together that which has been separated." Thus the believing sinner is bound together with God and His life, after having been separated by sin.

"Because the carnal mind is enmity (hostility, hatred) *against God . . . ."* Such a regard to the flesh is in fact hostility to God, because it is opposed to His law and His plan for the salvation

of the soul. The minding the things of the flesh also leads to the hatred of God Himself because He is opposed to it and has expressed His abhorrence of it.

". . . for it is not subject to the law of God, neither indeed can be." The brief statement, *"neither indeed can be,"* is very emphatic. The carnal mind does not subject itself to the law of God, for *it cannot.* The carnal mind is in such a state there neither is nor can be the least subjection to the law of God.

Verse 8: *"So then they that are in the flesh cannot please God."*

Verse 8 is a definite statement easily understood. It is a solemn declaration of the attitude of Almighty God toward those out of Christ: *". . . they . . . cannot please God."* All unbelievers are without faith, and "WITHOUT FAITH IT IS IMPOSSIBLE TO PLEASE HIM" (Heb. 11:6).

Almighty God deals with men through His Son, the Lord Jesus Christ, and ONLY through the Lord Jesus Christ. "Whosoever will may come," but all who come to God must come God's way. Jesus said, *"I am the Way, the Truth, and the Life: NO MAN COMETH UNTO THE FATHER, BUT BY ME"* (John 14:6). Anyone coming to God in Jesus Christ is welcome; but those who try to approach God—or "climb up"—some other way, are thieves and robbers (John 10:1), and they will fail to enter the Father's house—"for there is none other name under heaven given among men, whereby we must be saved" (Acts 4:12).

Hear this solemn declaration: "He that despised Moses' law died without mercy under two or three witnesses: *Of how much sorer punishment, suppose ye, shall he be thought worthy, who hath trodden under foot the Son of God, and hath counted the blood of the covenant, wherewith he was sanctified, an unholy thing, and hath done despite unto the Spirit of grace?* For we know Him that hath said, Vengeance belongeth unto me, I will recompense, saith the Lord. And again, The Lord shall judge His people. *It is a fearful thing to fall into the hands of the living God*" (Heb. 10:28-31).

Paul wants us to clearly understand that all flesh (the natural man) is under the condemnation and the terrible wrath of Almighty God. There is no salvation, no way to approach God, except through the Lord Jesus Christ and His shed blood.

In the true sense of the word, all unbelievers are treading under foot the Son of God. By their actions they are testifying that the blood of the covenant is not clean . . . they are not willing to accept the cleansing power of the blood of Jesus, shed on the cross for the remission of sin. They have heard about the Son, they have heard about His sufferings, they have heard about His death; but they are not willing to accept the Son of God as God's love-gift to them. They are not willing to put their trust in the shed blood of God's Son; they repudiate the blood of the everlasting covenant when they reject the finished work of Jesus Christ as the only necessity for salvation from condemnation and the eternal wrath of God.

Verse 9:   *"But ye are not in the flesh, but in the Spirit, if so be that the Spirit of God dwell in you.   Now if any man have not the Spirit of Christ, he is none of His."*

Let me point out that in verses 9 through 11 there are four phrases used which all mean "the indwelling Spirit in the believer." You will notice in verse 9, *"the Spirit of God,"* and again in verse 9, *"the Spirit of Christ."* Then in verse 10, *"if Christ be in you,"* and in verse 11, *"His Spirit that dwelleth in you."* All these statements teach the doctrine of the indwelling Holy Spirit.

In his first epistle to the Corinthians, Paul clearly states the Bible fact that *the body of the believer "is the temple of the Holy Ghost."* He says, "... which is *IN you,* which ye have of God," and he goes on to declare that we are not our own, but we are "bought with a price" and therefore should glorify God in our body (I Cor. 6:19, 20).

The Holy Spirit does not take up His abode in the believer at some time *after* regeneration; but the moment the unbeliever believes on the Lord Jesus Christ and is born again by the power of the Holy Spirit, he is that split second indwelt by the Holy Spirit. From that moment forward, the Holy Spirit abides in the believer, and he is sealed "unto the day of redemption" (Eph. 4:30).

Here in verse 9 we are assured that if the Spirit of God is dwelling in us, we *"are not in the flesh,"* according to God's reckoning. On the other hand, this verse clearly teaches that any person who does not possess the Holy Spirit is not a child of God: *". . . if any man have not the Spirit of Christ, he is none of His."*

For one to speak of being a Christian and not possessing the Holy Spirit is to advertise pure Bible ignorance. Jesus said to Nicodemus, *"Except a man be born of water and of the Spirit, he cannot enter into the kingdom of God"* (John 3:5). On another occasion Jesus said, "No man can come to me, except my Father which hath sent me draw him" (John 6:44). And then Jesus taught that it is *the Holy Spirit* who convicts, convinces, and draws men to God (John 16:7-11).

The Holy Spirit of God *leads* the children of God (Rom. 8:14). The Holy Spirit *assures* the children of God (Rom. 8:16). The Holy Spirit *seals* the believer (Eph. 4:30). The Holy Spirit *fills* the believer (Eph. 5:18), and the Holy Spirit *indwells* the believer (Rom. 8:9). The believer's body is the house in which the Holy Ghost lives (I Cor. 6:19, 20). I repeat: According to Romans 8:9, "If any man have not the Spirit of Christ," he certainly does not belong to God. It is utterly impossible to be saved apart from the ministry of the Holy Spirit.

Verse 10: *"And if Christ be in you, the body is dead because of sin; but the Spirit is life because of righteousness."*

When Christ dwells in a man, *"the body is dead because of sin."* The saints are subject to physical death and die, because of Adam's sin. But the spirit, the saint's own personal spirit, is alive, in that the Holy Spirit energizes it with divine life. It has the life of Christ, because of His righteousness imparted through faith. The *"righteousness"* here mentioned is comprehensive, in that it includes justification and sanctification.

Paul is teaching pure grace. Pure grace is "Christ in you." Christ is God's grace brought down to man (John 1:14). When Christ comes to dwell in us in the Person of the Holy Spirit, then we are dead—dead to the flesh, dead to the Law—because "Christ is the *end* of the law for righteousness to every one that believeth" (Rom. 10:4). But we are *alive unto God* because the Spirit of God abides in us. We have been made partakers of divine nature (II Pet. 1:4).

To the Galatian believers, Paul said: *"I am crucified with Christ* (to be crucified is to die): *nevertheless I live; yet not I, but Christ liveth in me: and the life which I now live in the flesh*

I live by the faith of the Son of God, who loved me, and gave Himself for me" (Gal. 2:20).

Paul was dead—yet he was speaking. He was dead—yet he was alive. Only the spiritually minded can understand this. Paul told the Colossians, *"Ye are dead,* and your *life* is hid with Christ in God"* (Col. 3:3). All believers are dead to the flesh but alive unto God. Ephesians 2:6 tells us we "sit together in heavenly places in Christ Jesus." Yes, NOW we are the sons of God. NOW we sit together in heavenly places in Christ Jesus. NOW we are dead to the flesh, but we are alive unto God. And the miracle occurs only through *"Christ in you"* (Col. 1:27).

Verse 11: *"But if the Spirit of Him that raised up Jesus from the dead dwell in you, He that raised up Christ from the dead shall also quicken your mortal bodies by His Spirit that dwelleth in you."*

". . . raised up Jesus . . . raised up Christ . . . ." Notice the change of the name from *Jesus* (the Man who died on the cross), whom God raised from the dead, to *Christ,* the covenant Head. He was raised not only as Jesus the Man, but as *Jesus Christ,* who stands for all that are in Him.

"He that raised up Christ from the dead shall also quicken your mortal bodies . . . ." *"Shall quicken"* means "to cause to live, to make alive, to give life." Although the spirit of man who has

The Epistle to the Romans

accepted Christ will never be subject to death, the body, on the other hand, *is* subject to death. Christians, like sinners, grow sick and die, and this will go on until "the adoption, to wit, the redemption of our body" (v. 23). Here in verse 11 the future resurrection of the believer's body is in view. Our Lord was raised from the dead. This is physical resurrection. The bodies of the dead saints will be "quickened," or raised from the dead, at the time of the Rapture through the instrumentality of the Holy Spirit—*"His Spirit that dwelleth in you."*

Verses 12 and 13: *"Therefore, brethren, we are debtors, not to the flesh, to live after the flesh. For if ye live after the flesh, ye shall die: but if ye through the Spirit do mortify the deeds of the body, ye shall live."*

We are no longer *"debtors . . . to the flesh."* Once we were "sold under sin" (7:14); but now that we have been set free from that hard master and become servants to righteousness, we owe nothing to the flesh.

"For if ye live after the flesh, ye shall die . . . ." The Apostle is not satisfied with assuring the Roman believers that they are under no obligation to the flesh, to hearken to its suggestions, without reminding them where it will end if they do. A person who lives habitually under the dominion of sin is an unsaved person.

268

Wuest translates these verses as follows: "So then, brethren, we are those under obligation, not to the flesh, to live habitually under the dominion of the flesh. For, assuming that you are living habitually under the dominion of the flesh, you are on the way to dying. But, assuming that by the Spirit you are habitually putting to death the deeds of the body, you will live."

Paul is saying, "Brethren, we are not debtors to the flesh, to live after the flesh (or, to crave the things of the flesh); but we have within us the Holy Spirit, who leads us into spiritual thinking, spiritual living, and spiritual practices of life."

If we live after the flesh, we die; if we love the world, the love of God is not in us. The lust of the flesh, the lust of the eyes, and the pride of life are not of the Father, but are of the world. The world will pass away, and the lust of the world will pass away; but we who do the will of God will abide forever (I John 2:15-17). (The only way any person can do the will of God is to be possessed by God and indwelt by the Holy Spirit.)

Paul comes now to a new line of thought, opening into the final subject in this chapter: the glory awaiting the justified believer.

PART IV

BLESSINGS OF THE GOSPEL:
BELIEVERS' SONSHIP AND ETERNAL GLORY

In Part IV of Romans we see believers as God's sons and heirs, cheered by the prospect of the eternal glory prepared for us. Paul also assures us of the Holy Spirit's intercession for us, and he proclaims the security we possess in Christ Jesus. This section of this marvelous chapter has always been a great blessing to me.

Verses 14 and 15: *"For as many as are led by the Spirit of God, they are the sons of God. For ye have not received the spirit of bondage again to fear; but ye have received the Spirit of adoption, whereby we cry, Abba, Father."*

In verse 14 we learn that *"as many as are led by the Spirit of God, they are the sons of God."* This verse teaches me that if I am a son of God, the Holy Spirit leads me—and if I am not led by the Holy Spirit, I am not God's son. Insofar as I am concerned, that puts some people in a very bad position, spiritually speaking. You will never convince me that God's Holy Spirit leads Christians to go the places some people go, do the things they do, keep the company they keep. I am persuaded to believe that a person led by the Holy Spirit will walk in paths of righteousness. (Read Psalm 23.) All sons of God are led by the Holy

Spirit. The Holy Spirit is no respecter of persons (or sons); therefore He leads all sons in paths of righteousness for the name's sake of Jesus. (The Holy Spirit is in the world to glorify Christ—not to glorify Himself. Read John 16:12-15.)

"For ye have not received the spirit of bondage again to fear . . . ." We who are believers are not in bondage, nor are we under law. We are under grace. We are not *afraid* . . . fear has been removed (I John 4:17, 18). We are God's sons on the merit of the finished work of His only begotten Son, and salvation removes fear. Born again children of God do not fear death or the judgment; nor do they fear meeting God.

". . . but ye have received the Spirit of adoption . . . ." "Adoption" means literally, "placing as a son." Thus the Holy Spirit is "the Spirit of adoption" who places children of God (born ones) as adult sons in a legal standing before God and in relation to Him. Thus we are able to *"cry, Abba, Father."* The expression here is "Abba, the Pater," *Abba* being the Hebrew and Chaldean word for *Father,* and *Pater* the Greek form of the same word. As Paul uses it here our Lord used it in Mark 14:36, and the words are found again in Galatians 4:6, in much the same connection as here.

Verses 16 and 17: *"The Spirit itself beareth witness with our spirit, that we are the children of God: and if children, then heirs; heirs of God,*

271

*and joint-heirs with Christ; if so be that we suffer
with Him, that we may be also glorified together.''*

Verse 16 is precious. The Holy Spirit within us
*''beareth witness with our spirit, that we are the
children of God.''* ''Beareth witness'' is to ''bear
joint witness with some other person, to bear joint
testimony with some other person.'' The testimony
of our own spirit is borne in that cry of *conscious
sonship*—''Abba, Father.''

What is this witness of the Spirit? I assure you
that it is not a mere ''feeling.'' How foolish it
would be for a child to fall into the delusion that
he must have certain ''feelings'' to prove he is a
child of his parents. It is just as foolish for a
child of God to expect the ''witness'' of the Spirit
to be a ''feeling.'' Our own spirit tells us we are
God's children, but the voice with which it speaks
is prompted and inspired by the Holy Spirit Himself. Thus ''in the mouth of two witnesses'' the
thing is established.

The Apostle had before called us *sons* of God
(v. 14); here the word changes to *''children''* (begotten ones) with all the rights and prospects of
children, which we will see in verse 17. If you
cannot bow your head and ask in prayer, ''Dear
God, am I your child? Am I saved?'' and get an
answer through the witness of the Spirit, then I
would be afraid to die, with your brand of religion!
If you do not know you are saved just as surely as
you know you are breathing, I doubt your salvation.

Do not tell me that God abides in you, and yet you do not know it! To me, that is an impossibility. The Holy Spirit testifies to us through our spirit (the inner man) that we are God's children. Do you have the witness of the Spirit? If you do not, fall on your knees this very moment and give God your heart.

"And if children, then heirs . . . ." Paul, inspired of God, declares, "If we are children, then we are heirs . . . *heirs of God* . . . and we are *joint-heirs with Christ . . . ."* We ARE sons of God, born into God's family through the miracle of God's grace and the operation of the Holy Spirit. We are heirs of God. And since we are God's sons by the new birth, we are joint heirs with Jesus. Think of it—God's heirs and Christ's co-heirs; not joint heirs in the sense of dividing the inheritance but in the sense of entering into the whole inheritance together with Him.

". . . if so be that we suffer with Him . . . ." The *"if"* here is not conditional; it is rather that we are joint heirs with Christ *"since* we suffer with Him." This suffering is not penal and not in the contest with our own flesh, but comes to His followers because, like Him, they live in opposition to the world that hates them (I John 3:13). Paul told the Philippians: "For unto you it is given in the behalf of Christ, not only to believe on Him, *but also to suffer for His sake"* (Phil. 1:29). And to Timothy he said, *"Yea, and ALL*

that will live godly in Christ Jesus shall suffer persecution" (II Tim. 3:12).

". . . that we may be also glorified together." We share in His sufferings now, but is it not wonderful to know that one day we shall share in His glory?

Verse 18: *"For I reckon that the sufferings of this present time are not worthy to be compared with the glory which shall be revealed in us."*

I suppose no person, apart from the Lord Jesus Christ, ever suffered as Paul suffered. Paul was beaten, he was stoned, he was dragged outside the city for dead; and yet this man who knew suffering possibly as no other but Jesus cried out, "I reckon that the sufferings of this life are not worthy to be compared with the glory we shall share in the life to come!" To *"reckon"* is "to compute, calculate." The word implies reasoning. Paul, after a process of reasoning, arrived at the conclusion that the suffering he had endured, when set over against the coming glory, sank into insignificance.

The Greek word here translated *"in us"* would be better translated *"toward us."* The glory of God is already revealed *in* us in great measure; but when Jesus comes, the glory of God will be revealed *toward* us. Please read I Peter 1:11, and you will find Peter testifying to the sufferings of *Christ* and the glory that should follow. *Our* sufferings and glory are closely identified with *His*

274

sufferings and glory. If we suffer with Him we will be glorified with Him; but if we deny Him He will deny us (II Tim. 2:12).

Verse 19: *"For the earnest expectation of the creature waiteth for the manifestation of the sons of God."*

When Jesus shall appear, we are to be manifested with Him in glory. (Read Colossians 3:4.) Our manifestation as the sons of God in the glory of our Father is dealt with here in this verse.

Jesus will be revealed in the clouds of heaven, with power and great glory—"and every eye shall see Him, . . . and all kindreds of the earth shall wail because of Him" (Rev. 1:7). He will come in the clouds and in great glory; and we (the bride of Christ, the true Church) will come with Him. I am not here referring to *the Rapture,* but to *the Revelation.* Jesus first comes FOR His Church in the Rapture; then He will come in great glory in the Revelation, WITH His Church, and "every eye shall see Him." Jude speaks of His coming "with ten thousands of His saints" (Jude 14).

So great is this glory that the material world (the creation of earth, the animal kingdom, etc.) itself is pictured as standing on tiptoe with expectancy, longing for and looking to the glory that is about to be revealed when the children of God shall be manifested in the likeness of their Lord. (Read I John 3:1-3.)

God's sons—yes, even the most spiritual of God's people—look with longing to the glorious future when Jesus comes. Our present condition is painful, certainly not an ideal condition as we live in the flesh today. We long for the glory that is to come because the future will bring redemption to the body; we will have a glorious body just like the body Jesus had when He came out of the tomb. In the same way, creation looks to, hopes and longs for, the same future. NOW all creation is under the curse, but in the future all creation will be glorified and delivered from the curse.

Verses 20 and 21: *"For the creature was made subject to vanity, not willingly, but by reason of Him who hath subjected the same in hope. Because the creature itself also shall be delivered from the bondage of corruption into the glorious liberty of the children of God."*

These verses assure us that all creation will be delivered from the terrible suffering and death brought upon the whole creation by sin. Verse 20 gives a reason for the "earnest expectation" (v. 19), drawn from the present condition of creation— namely, the cursed condition. Verse 21 gives a reason for the *"hope"* mentioned in verse 20. Creation originally was not cursed; it was good. It was not *"subject to vanity"*; it was perfect. Perfection cannot create imperfection, and in the beginning when God created the heaven and the earth, there was no vanity, there was no curse. Creation is not *in* its original state, nor is creation as it WILL be.

In Genesis 1:2 we read that the earth was "without form, and void; and darkness was upon the face of the deep." God never created the earth without form, and void! God brought order out of chaos; but again judgment struck and the curse was pronounced upon all creation when man fell (Gen. 3:17-19). But creation will be restored again when Jesus shall come again to bring peace on earth, good will toward men, and *will deliver the whole creation "from the bondage of corruption into the glorious liberty of the children of God."* The whole creation is promised liberty and glory when Jesus delivers this entire universe from the curse that grips it now. What a day that will be!

Verses 22 and 23: *"For we know that the whole creation groaneth and travaileth in pain together until now. And not only they, but ourselves also, which have the first-fruits of the Spirit, even we ourselves groan within ourselves, waiting for the adoption, to wit, the redemption of our body."*

Certainly no one would deny the universal sufferings of the whole world—not only man, but the whole of creation. The Spirit of God tells us here that *"the whole creation groaneth and travaileth in pain,"* looking forward to the day when the sons of God will be revealed with Christ in glory.

The reason is given in verse 23, which says, in effect: "Not only creation, but those of us who *have the first-fruits* of salvation, the indwelling of the Spirit of God, *WE groan . . .*"—and if we who have God's best groan and travail in pain, then it is no wonder the other members of God's creation groan and travail under the curse! We are *"waiting for . . . the redemption of our body"*—looking for that glorious morning when we will be raised in His likeness (Phil. 3:21).

Before we can enjoy "the glorious liberty" in its fullness, the liberty Jesus purchased through His shed blood, "this corruptible must put on incorruption, and this mortal must put on immortality. So when this corruptible shall have put on incorruption, and this mortal shall have put on immortality, THEN shall be brought to pass the saying that is written, Death is swallowed up in victory" (I Cor. 15:53, 54). Not until death has been swallowed up in victory, not until death (the last enemy) shall be destroyed (I Cor. 15:26), can this glorious liberty be realized.

Verses 24 and 25: *"For we are saved by hope: but hope that is seen is not hope: for what a man seeth, why doth he yet hope for? But if we hope for that we see not, then do we with patience wait for it."*

"For we are saved by hope"—or, "in that hope were we saved." The moment a person is saved,

the Holy Spirit of God immediately directs the believer's attention to the "blessed hope" set before him. Read Hebrews 12:1, 2. According to those verses, Jesus did not *enjoy* the cross . . . He ENDURED it. He saw the glory beyond the cross; and we, as believers, share that glory even now.

Things are not to go on forever as they are at the present time. God's marvelous grace that brings salvation will deliver us from the corruption of sin and death, even in the body. These bodies will be changed if we are living when the Rapture takes place. If we die and the flesh returns to dust, these bodies will be raised incorruptible and we will be like the Lord Jesus Christ. According to Titus 2:11-14, the grace of God that brings salvation teaches us to *look for "that blessed hope"* and the glorious appearing of our great God and our Saviour Jesus Christ, who loved us and gave Himself for us, that He might redeem us and make unto Himself a peculiar people, zealous of good works. Yes, in hope were we saved.

The attitude of hope, so distinctive of the Christian, implies that there is more in store for him than anything that is his already. Hope suggests something unseen, unrealized; for what a man sees, what he already has, he does not hope for. *"But if we hope* (the Christian's condition) *for that we see not, then* (as said in verse 23) *do we with patience wait for it."*

Verses 26 and 27: *"Likewise the Spirit also helpeth our infirmities: for we know not what we should pray for as we ought: but the Spirit itself maketh intercession for us with groanings which cannot be uttered. And He that searcheth the hearts knoweth what is the mind of the Spirit, because He maketh intercession for the saints according to the will of God."*

"The Spirit also helpeth our infirmities"—our "want of strength; weakness." The weakness spoken of here is not physical but is defined by the context, which speaks of *prayer.* The Spirit helps in every way—but in the matter of prayer He does in the heart what Christ does before God (v. 34); He *intercedes in our behalf.* The earnest manner of His intercessions is shown in the words *"with groanings which cannot be uttered,"* yearnings whose depth is beyond the power of words to convey.

God the Father *"searcheth the hearts"* of the saints, and He (God) *"knoweth what is the mind of the Spirit."* God knows the meaning of the Spirit's groan and interprets the inarticulate desires of the heart, *"because He* (the Spirit) *maketh intercession for the saints according to the will of God."*

These verses should give much comfort—even to the weakest saint. What a promise they contain! The Spirit helps us when we pray. When we are

280

burdened and broken with grief and heartache, the Holy Spirit groans within us—and God understands the groanings of the Spirit, even the groanings which cannot be uttered, because the Spirit utters requests according to the will of God. I am sure most Christians who read these lines recall one time or another when you were so burdened you could not utter words in prayer. All you could say was, "O Lord . . . have mercy!" or words similar to those. But the Holy Ghost knows the burden, the desire, the longing of the heart of the believer; therefore He helps us in such an hour.

You will notice there are *three "groanings"* mentioned in chapter 8. First, we hear the groanings of the whole creation (v. 22). Second, the children of God, even the most spiritual, groan (v. 23). Then, the Spirit groans as He makes intercession for the saints (v. 26). One day all these groanings will cease, and we will experience the glorious deliverance that is coming in the "salvation ready to be revealed in the last time" (I Pet. 1:5).

The next verse in this chapter is one of the most beloved in all the Bible, from the first verse of Genesis to the last verse of Revelation:

Verse 28: *"And we know that all things work together for good to them that love God, to them who are the called according to His purpose."*

This verse opens with assurance: *"We know"*!

But WHAT do we know? We know *"that all things"*—not a few things, not the good things, not the glorious things, but ALL things—*"work together for good to them that love God . . . ."* The sunshine, the rain, the gladness, the sadness, the heartache, the heartbreak—whatsoever, whensoever—they ALL work together for our good and for God's glory if we love Him!

". . . to them who are the called according to His purpose." "His purpose" is the heart of this verse. If salvation were offered to us conditionally —that is, if it were left to our faithfulness, our obedience, our prayerfulness, or our ability—then the case would be hopeless and out of the question. History proves that man, under probation, breaks down. The Law was such a system. Under the Law, life was offered as a condition of obedience *to* the Law: "The man which doeth those things shall live by them" (Rom. 10:5). But the Law proved to be a burden which man alone could not bear (Acts 15:10). The Law was a ministration of condemnation and a ministration of death (II Cor. 3:7-9).

In the marvelous Gospel of the grace of God, all conditions are swept aside. The invitation of the Gospel is to "whosoever will" . . . "whosoever shall call" . . . "let him that is thirsty come"; the invitation is simply, *"Come."* Almighty God does the rest. Jesus said, "Come unto me, all ye that labour and are heavy laden, and I will give you rest" (Matt. 11:28). Notice the words in that marvelous invitation: "Come—YOU come; come unto me—come all—I WILL GIVE YOU REST!" The part of man is simply "Come," and when man comes, God Almighty handles the rest of the transaction.

I know that such a doctrine is difficult for some to accept, but it will be a happy day in your life when you accept it. God's Word says: "Let him that thinketh he standeth take heed lest he fall" (I Cor. 10:12). "Have faith in God" (Mark 11:22). ". . . this is the victory that overcometh the world, even our faith" (I John 5:4). Your ability, your faithfulness, your obedience, and your praying without ceasing are not enough. Victory is in *Jesus,* and unless you are totally and entirely surrendered—body, soul, and spirit—to Him, and walk by faith, you cannot have victory.

Yes, the sinner is invited to "Come" . . . come in all the vileness sin has brought, all the weakness the flesh has . . . and submit to the loving arms of Jesus! He saves, strengthens, and keeps. When the vilest of sinners, the weakest of sinners, the least deserving of sinners, comes to the Lord Jesus and by faith falls into His loving arms . . . from that moment forward Jesus undertakes for him; and thereafter, Jesus sees to it that all things work together for good unto him who puts his trust in the finished work of Jesus. This is the eternal purpose which He purposed before the world was.

With such a salvation, based upon such an eternal purpose, it cannot be otherwise than that *all things* — whether we understand or not — shall work together for good "to them that love God" . . . those who are the children of God by faith in the finished work of His Son Jesus Christ.

Verses 29 and 30: *"For whom He did foreknow, He also did predestinate to be conformed to the image of His Son, that He might be the firstborn among many brethren. Moreover whom He did predestinate, them He also called: and whom He called, them He also justified: and whom He justified, them He also glorified."*

Verse 29 troubles many people, but it is very easily understood if we let the Spirit speak and forget what man has said or what man teaches. Because of such a marvelous salvation, and because all things are working together for good to them that love God, we know that since He *foreknew* us, He also *predestinated us "to be conformed to the image of His Son"* — that is, all believers are predestined to be conformed to the image of the Son of God. All truly born again, blood-washed, redeemed believers will become conformed to the image of the Son of God. We are bone of His bone, flesh of His flesh; divine nature abides in our bosom . . . therefore we will become conformed to the image of His Son.

"Moreover whom He did predestinate, them He

also called . . . .'' Jesus called us with a holy calling. He also *justified* us, and He has also *glorified* us—we now sit together in heavenly places in Christ Jesus (Eph. 2:6). Our conversation is *now* in heaven, from whence we look for the Saviour (Phil. 3:20). We are a heavenly people, and one day we will be like our wonderful Saviour. We will see Him as He is, and we will be like Him (I John 3:1-3).

You will notice that the wording in verses 29 and 30 here in Romans chapter 8 is in the past tense. In other words, we HAVE been called, we HAVE been justified—and we HAVE been glorified. Since God is sovereign, He is able to count things done even when they have not yet *been* done. You may say, "Preacher, I do not understand that." Neither do I—and if I did, it would not increase my faith in God; it would *lessen* (or decrease) my faith in God. If I could understand God, then I would be equal with God and I would have no God. I am glad that the just shall live by *faith* and not by wisdom or understanding.

Just remember that God is able to count things done even when they have not yet been done. Our glorification is according to the purpose of Almighty God, and nothing can stop the purpose of Almighty God. Having been foreknown, having been predestinated to be conformed to the image of His Son, we WILL BE conformed to the image of His Son; and we will be glorified, because God said it, and nothing in heaven, in earth, or under the earth can break the Word of God.

Verse 31:   *"What shall we then say to these things? If God be for us, who can be against us?"*

This has always been one of my favorite verses. The Holy Spirit is asking, "What indeed can any man *say to these things*—these things that have just been brought to light? *If God be for us, who can be against us?* Who can overthrow or dethrone God?" (This has been tried in the past, but since the Creator is greater than the created, no one . . . no part . . . of the creation of God can dethrone or overthrow God.)

Suppose the devil IS against us. Suppose all the forces of hell ARE allied against us. Suppose the masses of humanity be against us. It matters not. Shall we be afraid of anything if God is on our side? Could God lose a battle? Paul answers later in the chapter by saying, "We are more than conquerors through Him that loved us"! Therefore, if God be for us, who can be against us? If God is on our side we cannot lose; but if we are not on God's side, we cannot win.

Verse 32:   *"He that spared not His own Son, but delivered Him up for us all, how shall He not with Him also freely give us all things?"*

How can anything be added to this verse? God, who is rich in mercy, *spared nothing* in providing man's salvation. Heaven was emptied of God's best to provide our redemption; He *"spared not His own Son,"* the infinite price of redemption.

It would be strange if God should withdraw His power and leave us to the mercy of the devil, after He spared not His own Son, *"but delivered Him up"* to the cross *"for us all."* Would you suggest that He would leave us to the mercy of the devil after paying such a tremendous price for our salvation?

". . . how shall He not with Him also freely give us all things?" The Father, after bestowing His own Son, will not withhold the rest. All other gifts are small in comparison with the Gift of gifts but are *virtually included in it.* In Christ ALL things are ours, for we are His, and He is God's (I Cor. 3:21-23). (Read this passage carefully; it is tremendous.) All that I need is in Jesus. In Him I am more than conqueror. God gave heaven's best that I might have salvation; and thank God, Jesus my Saviour said, "I will never leave thee, I will never forsake thee." We may boldly say, "God is my helper. All my needs are supplied in Jesus; physical, spiritual, financial, mental—ALL needs are found supplied in Him!"

Verse 33: *"Who shall lay anything to the charge of God's elect? It is God that justifieth."*

Paul asks the question, then answers that question by thundering out, *"IT IS GOD THAT JUSTI-*

FIETH!" In other words, "Shall God—He who justified us—accuse us? Surely if the God who justifies us does not accuse us—since we are righteous through faith in the finished work of Jesus, cleansed by faith in His shed blood—it matters little what man may say about us, or with what judgment man judges us." (Read I Corinthians 4:3, 4.)

It is true that our archenemy Satan accuses us before God day and night—but we need not fear Satan. We need to fear GOD, because God in Christ defeated Satan and conquered everything hell hurled at Him. Therefore Satan is unable to bring anything new against us. God knows all the tricks of Satan, and it is God who justifies us in Christ Jesus when we accept Him by faith as our personal Saviour.

Verse 34: *"Who is he that condemneth? It is Christ that died, yea rather, that is risen again, who is even at the right hand of God, who also maketh intercession for us."*

Paul asks, "Can Christ, who is always making intercession on behalf of us, at the same time condemn us? He does not do both. While interceding on our behalf, He will not condemn." The Christ who *"died . . . is risen again"*; He is now *"at the right hand of God,"* and He *"maketh intercession for us."* God does not want His children to sin; but if we DO sin, "we have an Advocate

288

with the Father, Jesus Christ the righteous'' (I John 2:1)—and our Advocate does not condemn us; He makes intercession *for* us. Surely this tremendous truth should bring comfort to every believer's heart. There is nothing to fear from Him who died for us on the cruel cross, rose again for our justification, and ''ever liveth to make intercession'' for us (Heb. 7:25).

If you as a born again, blood-washed believer were to drop into the pits of the damned (which is impossible, according to John 5:24 and John 10:28, 29), Jesus would be the One to condemn you, because no one else in heaven or on earth CAN condemn you! But you must remember—it was Jesus who *died* for you, it was Jesus who purchased you at the tremendous price of His blood; and if you have accepted Him as your personal Saviour you may rest assured that the Christ who died for you, who rose again for you, will not condemn you, but will make intercession to God the Father for you. Tremendous truth!

Paul immediately goes on to ask another question:

Verse 35: *"Who shall separate us from the love of Christ? Shall tribulation, or distress, or persecution, or famine, or nakedness, or peril, or sword?"*

"The love of Christ" here does not mean our love to Christ, as if saying, "Who shall hinder us from loving Christ?" But it is *Christ's* love to *us,*

as is clear from the closing words in verse 39. It is no ground of confidence to assert, or to even feel, that we will never forsake Christ; but it is the strongest ground of assurance to be convinced that *His* love will never change.

Paul is asking, "Is there anyone, or anything, that can tear us loose or *separate us from the love of Christ*—He who loved us so much He left the Father's bosom and heaven's glory to come into the world and lay down His life for us? Can anything break us away from such love?"

"Shall tribulation"—we may be tried, we may be tested; *"or distress"*—we may find ourselves in great distress of soul, spirit, body; *"or persecution"*—we may be persecuted beyond reason; *"or famine"*—we may suffer famine until it seems we will starve for food; *"or nakedness"*—we may reach the place where we will be naked, with no clothes to cover our body; *"or peril"*—perils may come upon us; *"or sword?"*—we may die by the sword. But none of these things can separate us from the love of Christ.

Verse 36:   *"As it is written, For thy sake we are killed all the day long; we are accounted as sheep for the slaughter."*

"As it is written . . . ." Here Paul quotes from Psalm 44:22. God's children, down through the ages, have been hated and despised by the world—by the enemies of God, by the children of the devil.

But whenever such persecution has come upon the children of God, when they are *"accounted as sheep for the slaughter,"* when they are butchered by the sword, fed to the lions, or burned at the stake, there has been an increase of the devotion and faithfulness of the saints. Such persecutions have established them deeper in the love of God and in the things of Christ.

Paul suffered "bonds and afflictions," but he told the Ephesian elders: *"None of these things move me, neither count I my life dear unto myself, so that I might finish my course with joy,* and the ministry, which I have received of the Lord Jesus, to testify the Gospel of the grace of God" (Acts 20:24). And just before he sealed his testimony with his blood, he wrote these words to Timothy: *"I am now ready to be offered, and the time of my departure is at hand. I have fought a good fight, I have finished my course, I have kept the faith: Henceforth there is laid up for me a crown of righteousness, which the Lord, the righteous Judge, shall give me at that day:* and not to me only, but unto all them also that love His appearing" (II Tim. 4:6-8).

Verse 37: *"Nay, in all these things we are more than conquerors through Him that loved us."*

Paul asks questions in verse 35, makes a statement in verse 36, and then he answers in verse 37. He says, "NO! These things cannot separate us from the love of Christ." Why? "Because *we are more than conquerors through Him that loved us.*" Who can be *more* than a conqueror? He that cannot be conquered! But beloved, mark it well in your Bible, in your mind, and in your heart: We are not conquerors through *our* strength or ability; we are conquerors *through Him that loved us*—the Lord Jesus Christ. If Jesus loved us so much that He left all of heaven's glory and came to earth's sorrow to suffer as no human has suffered before or since, if He demonstrated such love for us, He will surely provide victory for all who love Him.

Verses 38 and 39: *"For I am persuaded, that neither death, nor life, nor angels, nor principalities, nor powers, nor things present, nor things to come, nor height, nor depth, nor any other creature, shall be able to separate us from the love of God, which is in Christ Jesus our Lord."*

Certainly these words were spoken under inspiration of God. God dictated these words to Paul through the Holy Ghost, and Paul penned them down. But there is no person who ever lived, apart from Jesus Christ, who was in better position to speak the words given here. Paul suffered persecution and bodily pain; he was beaten, stoned, dragged outside the city for dead, shipwrecked. Therefore he could say, "I, Paul, am thoroughly *persuaded* that *death* cannot separate us from the

love of Christ. *Life* cannot separate us from the
love of Christ. *Angels* cannot separate us from
the love of Christ. *Principalities* cannot separate
us from the love of Christ. *Powers*—however
wicked they may be—cannot separate us from the
love of Christ. *Things present*—things with us
now (lust, liquor, gambling, vice, sin, all hell)—
cannot separate us from the love of Christ. *Things
to come*—suggest them . . . any wicked invention,
all hell in all of its power—cannot separate us
from the love of Christ. *Nor height*—the high
heavens; *nor depth*—the depth of hell—*nothing*
can separate us from the love of Christ."

God knew someone might say, "The things
that separated *me* from Christ are not named
here!" So the Holy Spirit stopped all mouths by
saying, *"NOR ANY OTHER CREATURE."* You
name it . . . you suggest it . . . you manufacture it
. . . you conceive it—and God's Word answers it!
"NOR ANY OTHER CREATURE!" NO creature,
no created thing, *"shall be able to separate us
from the love of God, which is in Christ Jesus
our Lord."* Mark it, and mark it well—"the love
of God which is *in Christ Jesus* our Lord."

At the outset of this chapter, I said it is one
of the most beloved chapters in the Word of God.
It opens "in Christ Jesus" (v. 1); it closes "in
Christ Jesus" (v. 39). All of the promises therein
are ours *in Christ Jesus*. We step from chapter 7,
which describes a believer battling with the flesh,

to chapter 8, which describes the spiritual man in Christ Jesus. We are reminded that we are free from condemnation (v. 1) and that the Holy Spirit dwells within (v. 9) and leads us day by day (v. 14). We know we are saved, we know we belong to God, because the Holy Spirit testifies and brings to our heart this assurance (v. 16). Many other wonderful truths we find here. What a chapter! Memorize it. Write it in your heart. It will bless you, sustain you, strengthen you, quench your spiritual thirst, feed your spiritual hunger. The tremendous truths of Romans 8 stand out like cut diamonds in the sunlight.

Chapter IX

1. I say the truth in Christ, I lie not, my conscience also bearing me witness in the Holy Ghost,

2. That I have great heaviness and continual sorrow in my heart.

3. For I could wish that myself were accursed from Christ for my brethren, my kinsmen according to the flesh:

4. Who are Israelites; to whom pertaineth the adoption, and the glory, and the covenants, and the giving of the law, and the service of God, and the promises;

5. Whose are the fathers, and of whom as concerning the flesh Christ came, who is over all, God blessed for ever. Amen.

6. Not as though the word of God hath taken none effect. For they are not all Israel, which are of Israel:

7. Neither, because they are the seed of Abraham, are they all children: but, In Isaac shall thy seed be called.

8. That is, They which are the children of the flesh, these are not the children of God: but the children of the promise are counted for the seed.

9. For this is the word of promise, At this time will I come, and Sarah shall have a son.

10. And not only this; but when Rebecca also had conceived by one, even by our father Isaac;

11. (For the children being not yet born, neither having done any good or evil, that the purpose of God according

to election might stand, not of works, but of him that calleth;)

12. It was said unto her, The elder shall serve the younger.

13. As it is written, Jacob have I loved, but Esau have I hated.

14. What shall we say then? Is there unrighteousness with God? God forbid.

15. For he saith to Moses, I will have mercy on whom I will have mercy, and I will have compassion on whom I will have compassion.

16. So then it is not of him that willeth, nor of him that runneth, but of God that sheweth mercy.

17. For the scripture saith unto Pharaoh, Even for this same purpose have I raised thee up, that I might shew my power in thee, and that my name might be declared throughout all the earth.

18. Therefore hath he mercy on whom he will have mercy, and whom he will he hardeneth.

19. Thou wilt say then unto me, Why doth he yet find fault? For who hath resisted his will?

20. Nay but, O man, who art thou that repliest against God? Shall the thing formed say to him that formed it, Why hast thou made me thus?

21. Hath not the potter power over the clay, of the same lump to make one vessel unto honour, and another unto dishonour?

22. What if God, willing to shew his wrath, and to make his power known, endured with much longsuffering the vessels of wrath fitted to destruction:

23. And that he might make known the riches of his glory on the vessels of mercy, which he had afore prepared unto glory,

24. Even us, whom he hath called, not of the Jews only, but also of the Gentiles?

25. As he saith also in Osee, I will call them my people, which were not my people; and her beloved, which was not beloved.

26. And it shall come to pass, that in the place where it was said unto them, Ye are not my people; there shall they be called the children of the living God.

27. Esaias also crieth concerning Israel, Though the number of the children of Israel be as the sand of the sea, a remnant shall be saved:

28. For he will finish the work, and cut it short in righteousness: because a short work will the Lord make upon the earth.

29. And as Esaias said before, Except the Lord of Sabaoth had left us a seed, we had been as Sodoma, and been made like unto Gomorrha.

30. What shall we say then? That the Gentiles, which followed not after righteousness, have attained to righteousness, even the righteousness which is of faith.

31. But Israel, which followed after the law of righteousness, hath not attained to the law of righteousness.

32. Wherefore? Because they sought it not by faith, but as it were by the works of the law. For they stumbled at that stumblingstone;

33. As it is written, Behold, I lay in Sion a stumblingstone and rock of offence: and whosoever believeth on him shall not be ashamed.

PART V

THE GOSPEL DOES NOT SET ASIDE GOD'S COVENANTS WITH ISRAEL

We come now to a new section of the Epistle to the Romans, consisting of chapters 9, 10, and 11. In these chapters we will learn that God is righteous in His dealings with Israel. Men down through the ages have objected to the doctrine of justification by faith in the finished work of Jesus Christ, because it rejects the unbelieving Jews, and they reason that the doctrine of justification by faith contradicts the promises of Almighty God to His chosen people, Israel. Therefore Paul must settle this great problem, which existed even in his day.

Chapters 9, 10, and 11 are really a parenthesis; that is, they are inserted here to clear up the matter of justification by faith. You will notice chapter 12 opens with the statement, "I beseech you therefore, brethren, by the mercies of God, that ye present your bodies a living sacrifice, holy, acceptable unto God, which is your reasonable service." This verse is a continuation of the thought, or the theme, of the closing verses of chapter 8. In other words, since we are justified by faith in the finished work of the Lamb of God, since God loved us so much that He gave His Son, that by faith in the finished work of Jesus we could be freely justified from all things, nothing in heaven, on earth, or under the earth can separate us from the love of God. And since that is a Bible fact—yea, an eternal truth—we should present our bodies a living sacrifice, holy unto God.

What I am trying to point out is simply this: Chapters 9, 10, and 11 explain how God can be just and yet turn aside from Israel for a season, allowing "blindness in part" (Rom. 11:25) to come upon Israel because of her unbelief. But even though God allows this, the Gospel of justification does not hurt or hinder the covenants God made with Abraham and Israel.

It is convenient for us to forget the Jew—and easy, too—for usually Christians know almost nothing about the Jewish covenants and promises. There are many who teach that Christians are now the true Israel, and that the Church today is the recipient of the promises of God to Israel.

To the apostolic Church, the question of the relation of Judaism to the Church was a most living and burning discussion. Having brought the entire race into one common group, all condemned as sinners, and having opened the one and only way of salvation (by faith in the shed blood of Jesus Christ), naturally the following questions arose:

"What then becomes of the Davidic covenant, confirmed by Almighty God and renewed to the mother of Jesus by the angel Gabriel? Has God forgotten His covenant with David? What becomes of the repeated, specific, unconditional promise God made to restore all Israel to the land of their fathers . . . the land God specifically laid out and promised to Abraham? What has happened to the unconditional promise to restore all Israel to her land and to establish a government at the head of which shall be Messiah, who was prophesied to be the son of David and therefore the heir of David?"

Chapters 9, 10, and 11 give the Apostle's answer to these questions.

In the Jerusalem council (Acts chapter 15), James showed that God's acceptance of the Gentiles by faith without circumcision not only *did not* contradict the prophets—or deny their teaching—but, on the contrary, *agreed* with the prophets, since they had predicted the restoration as occurring *after* the return of the Lord (Acts 15:14-17).

In the same manner, Paul, in even more detail, explains that this Gospel of justification by faith in the finished work of the Lord Jesus Christ was fully foreseen by the prophets, even though they did not fully understand the grace that was to come; and that, far from having done away with the covenants to Abraham, David, and the whole house of Israel, this Gospel strengthens these promises; and when the Church is complete, Jesus WILL return to catch away His bride. Then, after the great tribulation period, Jesus WILL sit on the throne of His father David, and "all Israel shall be saved" (Rom. 11:26). Please notice: ALL ISRAEL . . . not every individual Israelite, but Israel as a nation, will be saved.

It makes no difference what preachers preach or what teachers teach, *the Church is NOT Israel.* It is spiritual robbery to take the promises made to Israel and give them to the Church. God has NOT forgotten His people, and one day God will turn again to Israel, and a nation will be born in a day. God will fulfill every promise to faithful Abraham, in every minute detail.

Paul's Great Sorrow for Unbelieving Israel

Verses 1-3: *"I say the truth in Christ, I lie not, my conscience also bearing me witness in the Holy Ghost, that I have great heaviness and continual sorrow in my heart. For I could wish that myself were accursed from Christ for my brethren, my kinsmen according to the flesh."*

Paul was a freeborn Jew. He was a Pharisee of the Pharisees. At one time he was separated from the righteousness of God in Christ Jesus, through the religion he so fervently practiced; but now, knowing the Lord Jesus Christ in the free pardon of sin, he is enjoying the grace of God that is greater than all our sins—grace that does for us what the Law never could have done.

"I say the truth . . . I lie not . . . ." This strong language was necessary, because in giving the Gospel to the Gentiles, Paul was looked upon as an enemy to his own people the Jews. He must defend himself. Let it be seen that the picture drawn here is not by an enemy but by a friend, whose heart is breaking for his brethren.

". . . I have great heaviness and continual sorrow in my heart. For I could wish that myself were accursed from Christ for my brethren . . . ."

What a testimony! In the previous chapter, Paul had been speaking of the glorious certainty possessed by the sons of God, believers in the Lord Jesus Christ. Surely this is the language of heart-breaking passion as he thought of the extreme failure, misery, and hopelessness of his own countrymen through their unbelief. Therefore he looked upon his own people and cried out, "I say the truth... the whole truth... the pure truth. My conscience bears me witness in the Holy Ghost; my heart is experiencing great heaviness. I am continually sorrowful in my heart when I think of my own countrymen, my own people—lost, blinded, doomed, headed for an endless hell. My sorrow is so deep and my heart is so broken, I could wish that myself were accursed from Christ, if it would bring my brethren, my kinsmen, my own people in the flesh, to know this wonderful salvation by faith in the finished work of the Lord Jesus Christ!"

I wonder if many mortals ever carried such a burden for their own loved ones? You recall that on one occasion *Moses*, in his anguish for Israel, cried out: "Oh, this people have sinned a great sin, and have made them gods of gold. *Yet now, if thou wilt forgive their sin—; and if not, blot me, I pray thee, out of thy book which thou hast written*" (Ex. 32:31, 32). This man Paul was no less devoted to his people than was Moses. Paul felt the sting of death and the horrors of hell when

302

he cried out for his countrymen. What he said is simply this: "I would be willing to be cut off from Christ, willing to be condemned to hell, if it would save my brethren!"

But Paul knew that even if he COULD be accursed and consigned to the pit, it would not save his brethren. Paul knew the only way they could be saved was by faith in the finished work of the Lord Jesus Christ. The only way his religious brethren could become righteous would be to accept the righteousness of God in the Lord Jesus.

Great scholars down through the ages have debated the meaning of this passage. Many great men of God have disagreed. I do not classify myself with the great authorities on the Hebrew and Greek languages, but insofar as I am concerned, I believe Paul meant exactly what he said! I believe he was so deeply moved, burdened and stirred, carrying such a heavy heart for his people (the Israelites), that he would be willing to be cut off from Christ if it would save Israel. That is exactly what I believe he meant when he uttered those words from a heart stricken with grief and broken because of the blindness of his people.

No wonder at the end of his life's journey, just before his head was chopped off by Nero's ax— just moments before he sealed his testimony with his life's blood—he could cry out, "I have fought a good fight; I have finished my course; I have kept the faith!" I do not believe any person ever lived—other than the Lord Jesus Christ—who so completely surrendered soul, spirit, and body to the will of God as did the Apostle Paul.

Verses 4 and 5: *"Who are Israelites; to whom pertaineth the adoption, and the glory, and the covenants, and the giving of the law, and the service of God, and the promises; whose are the fathers, and of whom as concerning the flesh Christ came, who is over all, God blessed for ever. Amen."*

The question was asked in Romans 3:1—"What advantage then hath the Jew?" The answer there is, "Much every way." The answer is amplified here, where Paul lists eight respects in which the nation of Israel differed from all other nations:

1. To the Israelites *"pertaineth the adoption."* They were adopted as God's people from among the nations. Their adoption, as referred to here, is not *individual* adoption, but NATIONAL—the whole twelve tribes of Israel. (The adoption referred to here is quite different from the adoption spoken of in Romans 8:15. See comments on that verse.)

2. To the Israelites *"pertaineth ... the glory."* In the Old Testament the Shekinah cloud of God's great glory led the Israelites in their wilderness wanderings.

3. To the Israelites were given *"the covenants."* The Abrahamic Covenant, the Mosaic Covenant, and the Davidic Covenant were given to the Is-raelites—and these covenants are yet theirs, despite the utter failure of the Israelites. (The *Gentiles* are *"aliens* from the commonwealth of Israel, and *strangers from the covenants of promise,* having no hope, and without God in the world"—Eph. 2:12. But now in this marvelous Day of Grace, both Jew and Gentile become sons of God by faith in the finished work of the Lord Jesus Christ.)

4. To Israel *"the law"* was given. The Gentiles "have not the law" (Rom. 2:14). Those who would mix law and grace, and those who would put us under the Law today, should make a thorough study of the Law and to whom it pertains. The Law was given to a specific people, at a specific time, in a specific place, under God-ordered con-ditions. We are not under the Law. Read Romans 6:14 and 10:4.

5. To Israel was given *"the service of God."* They alone, among all the nations of the world, had an authorized form of worship. Through their temple services, sacrifices, and priesthood they were taught the way of approach to God.

6. To Israel God gave *"the promises"*—prom-ises concerning Messiah and His reign, and the glory of the land of Israel. The promise of the Redeemer—He who would buy back what Adam lost—was peculiarly Israel's. It is true that the promise of the Redeemer was first given to the whole race in the Garden of Eden, but it was

ultimately confined to the seed of Abraham, the seed of Isaac, the seed of Jacob—and He was to come through the tribe of Judah and the house of David. We should not forget that the Lord Jesus Christ was primarily "a minister of the circumcision for the truth of God, *to confirm the promises made unto the fathers . . . ."* Jesus came first to the Jew; His mercy to the Gentiles was to come afterward (Rom. 15:8, 9). In Hebrews 7:6 Abraham is described as *"him that had the promises."*

7. *". . . whose are the fathers . . . ."* Paul no doubt means the three great fathers of the covenant, Abraham, Isaac, and Jacob (Ex. 3:6, 13; Luke 20:37). What nation in ancient history—or in any other age—ever produced such fathers as Abraham (the head of many nations), Isaac, and Jacob?

8. *". . . and of whom . . . Christ came . . . ."* Concerning Israel, there is one honor that stands above all other honors: The Christ, the Messiah, insofar as His humanity is concerned, came out of Israel. You will notice the word "whose" in this verse changes to "of whom" . . . that is, the fathers were Israel's, but the Christ—though He came through the seed of Abraham, Isaac, and Jacob—did not belong to Israel only. Christ belongs to the world!

The expression *"as concerning the flesh"*—or "so far as regards the flesh"—points to the fact that Christ was not entirely sprung from Israel, but had another nature—yes, He was God Almighty in flesh, and He came to lay His life down for the sins of the whole wide world. Insofar as His deity is concerned, Paul says He is *"over all, God blessed for ever. Amen."*

God Is Not Unfaithful or Unrighteous

Verses 6 and 7: *"Not as though the Word of God hath taken none effect. For they are not all Israel, which are of Israel: Neither, because they are the seed of Abraham, are they all children: but, In Isaac shall thy seed be called."*

Wuest translates these verses thus: "But the case is not such as this, that the Word of God is fallen powerless; for not all who are out of Israel, these are Israel, nor because they are offspring of Abraham, are all children, but in Isaac an offspring shall be named for you."

"Not as though the Word of God hath taken none effect." The emphasis is on the Word of God. Paul emphatically states that the Word of God has not failed, and cannot. The proof of no failure is that the promises were made to Israel, but they were not made to them on the ground of their natural descent from Abraham. *For not all they who are of Israel*—i. e., born of the patriarch—*are Israel;* that is, the people of God. The promise was not for ALL the nation of Israel.

The Apostle makes a distinction here between the natural Israelites and those who were men of faith. Believing *Gentiles* are not in view here, though in other places Gentile believers are also called "Abraham's children" or "Abraham's spiritual seed." Paul is dealing here only with the Israelites, and he makes a distinction between the two kinds—the natural and the spiritual Israel. (Please read Romans 4:1-3; Galatians 3:6, 7; and John 8:37-39.)

"Neither because they are the seed of Abraham are they all children"—that is, in the sense which entitles them to the inheritance—*"but, In Isaac shall thy seed be called."* God from the very first made a distinction here, and definitely announced that the seed of Abraham to which the promise belonged should come through the line of *Isaac,* not of Ishmael—though he also was called the seed of Abraham. (Read Genesis 17:19-21; 21:12, 13.)

Verses 8 and 9: *"That is, They which are the children of the flesh, these are not the children of God: but the children of the promise are counted for the seed. For this is the word of promise, At this time will I come, and Sarah shall have a son."*

The Holy Spirit is here pointing out the fact that *"they which are the children of the flesh"* (earthly descendants of Abraham) are not necessarily *"the children of God"*; but *"the children of the promise are counted for the seed"*—the spiritual seed through which Messiah would be born. If the children of the promise are the only ones "counted"—of whom Isaac is the type—it is necessary to show that Isaac was a child of promise, as verse 9 does:

"For this is the word of promise"—and Paul quotes from Genesis 18:10—*"At this time will I come, and Sarah shall have a son."* The emphatic word is *"promise."* We see that not the bodily descent, but the divine promise, constitutes the relation of belonging to Abraham's fatherhood.

Verses 10-13: *"And not only this; but when Rebecca also had conceived by one, even by our father Isaac; (for the children being not yet born, neither having done any good or evil, that the purpose of God according to election might stand, not of works, but of Him that calleth;) it was said unto her, The elder shall serve the younger. As it is written, Jacob have I loved, but Esau have I hated."*

"Not only this . . . ."—not only did Sarah receive a divine promise concerning her son, but *Rebecca* also received a divine promise concerning her two sons. Wuest comments: "The thought to be supplied is, not only have we an example of election of a son of Abraham by one woman and the rejection of his son by another, but also of the election and rejection of children by the same woman."

We must, however, keep Paul's purpose in view. He wishes to show that God's promise has not broken down, even though many of the natural descendants of Abraham have no part in its fulfillment in Christ. Paul does this by showing that there has always been a distinction among the patriarchs, between those who are connected merely by natural descent and those who are the Israel of God (or the men of faith). Paul shows that this distinction can be traced to nothing but God's sovereignty.

Paul cites here the case of Jacob and Esau, the twin sons of Isaac and Rebecca. Even before these children were born...while they were yet in their mother's womb...before they had committed any good or any sin...God said, *"The elder shall serve the younger"* (Gen. 25:23). The reason for this statement from God is simple: *"That the purpose of God...might stand."* In other words, it was in the program of Almighty God *"according to election ...not of works, but of Him that calleth."*

In the case of *Ishmael,* the son of the bondwoman, it might be held forth by some that he was set aside because he was born of a slave woman; but this argument cannot stand, as touching the case of Esau and Jacob. These boys were twins — and Esau was the first-born. God had decreed that this first-born should be subject to his younger brother, and as we have already seen, the only reason given for it is that it was according to the purpose of Almighty God.

This decree of Almighty God, however, went much further than concerning the persons of Esau and Jacob: "And the Lord said unto her, *Two nations* are in thy womb, and *two manner of people* shall be separated from thy bowels; and the one people shall be stronger than the other people; and the elder shall serve the younger" (Gen. 25:23).

"As it is written, Jacob have I loved, but Esau have I hated." There is no need for us to try to change that word "hated"; it is there, and it is God's Word. There is no need to try to soften it or make it say what it does not say.

This Scripture, which looks logically only at the original two, looks directly at their descendants. In Malachi 1:1-5 we read:

"The burden of the Word of the Lord to Israel by Malachi. I have loved you, saith the Lord. Yet ye say, Wherein hast thou loved us? Was not Esau Jacob's brother? saith the Lord: yet I loved Jacob, and I hated Esau, and laid his mountains and his heritage waste for the dragons of the wilderness. Whereas Edom saith, We are impoverished, but we will return and build the desolate places; thus saith the Lord of hosts, They shall build, but I will throw down; and they shall call them, The border of wickedness, and, The people against whom the Lord hath indignation for ever. And your eyes shall see, and ye shall say, The Lord will be magnified from the border of Israel."

This passage from Malachi is quoted to corroborate the original choice. And once the choice was made, God's love followed Jacob's seed and His hate followed Esau, showing the reality of His rejection.

After studying the Bible for many years, I have come to the place where, more than ever before, I let the Word of God speak and say what it says—and leave it alone. There is no need to try to explain away what Jehovah God has said.

Verse 14: *"What shall we say then? Is there unrighteousness with God? God forbid."*

Paul again asks and answers his own question. He asks, in effect, "If God loved Jacob and hated Esau, is God unrighteous?" And then he thunders back, *"God forbid"*! This is the language of faith. In Romans 1:17 Paul said, "The just shall live by faith"—and faith cannot for one split second tolerate the insinuation that there is or could be in any minute detail, unrighteousness with Almighty God. What God does is right; God cannot do wrong. He is righteous, and all of His acts are righteous acts. The Psalmist said: ". . . the Lord is upright: He is my rock, and *there is no unrighteousness in Him"* (Psalm 92:15).

Verse 15: *"For He saith to Moses, I will have mercy on whom I will have mercy, and I will have compassion on whom I will have compassion."*

In this verse, Paul finds the argument for his denial of injustice in God by quoting from Exodus

33:19.   The words were spoken to Moses in connection with his prayer for a general forgiveness for the people, which was refused (Ex. 32:31-35), and his request to behold God's glory, which was granted (Ex. 33:12-19).   Paul points out that even the great Hebrew captain Moses (whom it might be supposed could attain grace on the grounds of his office and merit) could not attain grace from God on ANY ground except that of God's unmerited favor.   To Moses God asserts that His gift (to behold God's glory) is of His own free grace, without any recognition of Moses' right to claim it on the ground of merit or service.

"I will have mercy...."   *Mercy* is "an outward manifestation of the inward feeling of *compassion.*" The meaning of this verse is simply this: "Whenever I have mercy on any, it shall be pure mercy. No human can do anything to deserve mercy, or contribute anything to deserve mercy.   I have mercy on whomsoever I will, simply because I am God."   *God gives mercy*—not because we seek it, but because it is God's divine will, God's sovereign will, to do it.   God is God, and He can bestow mercy and grace upon whom He will.

Verse 16:   *"So then it is not of him that willeth, nor of him that runneth, but of God that sheweth mercy."*

This verse excludes all human element.   Mercy is given—not according as men deserve it, or as they seek after it—but according to God's divine purpose and will. The conclusion follows, God's mercy is not the response to *human desire* nor to *human effort* (or works). It is not of him that *"willeth"* or wishes it, as Moses did; and it is not of him who *"runneth"* (works for it)—but it is according to God's own purpose.

I know we are in deep spiritual truth here; and the only way to understand the deep things of God is to compare spiritual things with spiritual (I Cor. 2:10-14), accepting by faith what God says.

Verse 17: *"For the Scripture saith unto Pharaoh, Even for this same purpose have I raised thee up, that I might shew my power in thee, and that my name might be declared throughout all the earth."*

Paul quotes here from Exodus 9:16. According to *Wuest's New Testament Dictionary*, "In the Hebrew the word *'raised'* means *'caused thee to stand.'* The meaning here is general, 'allowed thee to appear; brought thee forward on the stage of events.'" Pharaoh was an open adversary of God, yet God raised him up as king to fill a divine purpose—and that purpose and nothing else is the explanation of his very existence.

The purpose Pharaoh was designed to serve—and did serve—was certainly not his own, but was God's: *". . . that I might shew my power in thee, and that my name might be declared throughout all the earth."* God's power was shown in the miracles by which Pharaoh and Egypt were visited, and is proclaimed today throughout the world when the account in Exodus is read.

Verse 18: *"Therefore hath He mercy on whom He will have mercy, and whom He will He hardeneth."*

". . . whom He will He hardeneth." We are not to understand that God arbitrarily and directly forced upon Pharaoh an obstinate and stubborn heart to resist Himself. Evil cannot be laid at the door of God. God does not solicit a sinner to do evil (James 1:13). When man does wrong, that wrong comes from his own totally depraved nature (James 1:14). Therefore when Pharaoh acted in stubborn rebellion against God, all of that rebellion came as a result of his own depravity, not from God. When God is said to harden Pharaoh's heart, it is that He, in demanding the release of Israel, confronted Pharaoh with an issue he did not wish to meet. God raised him up to king, confronted him with a decision to release Israel, and Pharaoh rebelled; thus, from a direct command of God, the issue was forced upon Pharaoh, who hardened his heart. In Exodus 9:34, 35 we read:

"And when Pharaoh saw that the rain and the hail and the thunders were ceased, *he sinned yet more, and hardened his heart,* he and his servants. And *the heart of Pharaoh was hardened,* neither would he let the children of Israel go . . . ."

In the same sense as that of God hardening Pharaoh's heart, God is hardening the hearts of men today. Let me explain:

The same sun that melts the ice also bakes the clay and makes it hard—the one being reduced to water, the other being made into brick! The same Gospel that softens the hard heart of the sinner, when rejected hardens the heart. The light of the Gospel rejected becomes darkness. Every time a person hears the Word of God and recognizes his or her lost condition, but refuses to accept the Lord Jesus Christ, that person's heart is automatically hardened. He hardens his heart *by* rejecting, and God's Word hardens his heart *when* rejected. So in the true analysis of the word, God is still hardening the hearts of men.

Verse 19: *"Thou wilt say then unto me, Why doth He yet find fault? For who hath resisted His will?"*

Up to this point, the objector (that is, the objector to grace and righteous judgment from Almighty God) has taken the attitude that God's justice is open for questioning; but here the objector goes a step further. He charges God with injustice. That is, God hardened Pharaoh's heart; He willed to harden him—therefore Pharaoh did just as God willed. The implication is that Pharaoh did not resist God's will. The question then is, *"Why doth He yet find fault?"*

316

This objection has been made by sinners in all ages. It is the standing objection against grace. The objection is founded on the difficulty of reconciling the sovereignty of God with the free agency of man. It assumes what cannot be proven—that the divine purpose of God destroys the free will of man.

"For who hath resisted His will?" This does not mean that no one has offered resistance or opposition to God, but that no one has done it successfully. God has accomplished His purpose in spite of their opposition.

"Hath resisted," according to Wuest, "is the perfect tense and here speaks of a process of standing against God's will which has come to a finished end, and the resulting state, that of a confirmed and permanent stand against God." The idea is a man may resist God's will, but cannot maintain his resistance.

Paul leaves the question unanswered, for there is no answer which a finite mind can either reason out or understand, since it involves the sovereignty of God and the fact that man is a free moral agent.

Verse 20: *"Nay but, O man, who art thou that repliest against God? Shall the thing formed say to him that formed it, Why hast thou made me thus?"*

Paul is asking, "Who are YOU, O man, to

317

accuse God? You were created by God; you are the product of God's power. Would you dare bring into question the God who created you? Do you think you could succeed in establishing a case against the God who made you? Do you think you, a created being of Almighty God, could prove God unrighteous, unholy? Do you think your case against the gracious, tender, compassionate, long-suffering God would stand up in the courts of heaven?"

If it were possible for man to prove God unrighteous, then man could destroy the entire program of God. But do not worry, do not fret; man cannot justly bring an accusation against God!

"... *Why hast thou made me thus?*" The Apostle is using here language similar to that of Isaiah: "Shall the work say of him that made it, He made me not? Or shall the thing framed say of him that framed it, He hath no understanding?" (Isaiah 29:16). Again in Isaiah 45:9 we read: "Shall the clay say to him that fashioneth it, What makest thou? Or thy work, He hath no hands?"

Verse 21: *"Hath not the potter power over the clay, of the same lump to make one vessel unto honour, and another unto dishonour?"*

The argument Paul sets forth in this verse is simply this: Does not the potter have the right to mold the clay according to his will? Jeremiah adds light to this passage: "Then I went down to the potter's house, and, behold, he wrought a work on the wheels. And the vessel that he made of clay was marred in the hand of the potter: so he made it again another vessel, as seemed good to the potter to make it. Then the Word of the Lord came to me, saying, *O house of Israel, cannot I do with you as this potter?* saith the Lord. *Behold, as the clay is in the potter's hand, so are ye in mine hand,* O house of Israel" (Jer. 18:3-6). (Compare II Timothy 2:20, 21.)

Here in chapter 9 of Romans, Paul is driving home the eternal fact of the sovereignty of God. He is not contrasting or comparing the sovereignty of God with the free will of man. We will see clearly, later in this Epistle, the free will of man; but here, Paul is driving home the sovereignty of God. Some teachers use Scriptures such as the verses we are now studying, to prove their beliefs. These people are known as "hyper-Calvinists," "ultra-Predestinarians." But in Scripture such as the present verses, we must be especially careful not to fall short of what is written. We must not allow any compromise of the plain truth, the words uttered by God's Spirit. We must not compromise the Word of God to prove a point of doctrine, or a belief set forth by some denomination. We must study and rightly divide the Word of truth. We must compare Scripture with Scripture. We dare not take isolated passages to prove a point. We must take the Word of God in its entirety, and see and recognize the whole truth—not just the part that we wish to teach or preach.

Verses 22-24: *"What if God, willing to shew His wrath, and to make His power known, endured with much longsuffering the vessels of wrath fitted to destruction: and that He might make known the riches of His glory on the vessels of mercy, which He had afore prepared unto glory, even us, whom He hath called, not of the Jews only, but also of the Gentiles?"*

"What if God, willing to shew His wrath . . . ." "Willing" refers not to the determinate purpose of God but to His spontaneous will, growing out of His holy character.

". . . endured with much longsuffering the vessels of wrath fitted to destruction"—not *prepared* to serve for a manifestation of divine wrath, but appertaining to wrath. It must be understood to mean vessels who by their own acts have fallen under God's wrath.

"Fitted" is from a Greek word which means "to make fit, to equip, prepare." Here it signifies "that those referred to fitted themselves for destruction (as illustrated in the case of Pharaoh, the self-hardening of whose heart is accurately presented in the first part of the series of incidents in the Exodus narrative, which records Pharaoh's doings)" *(Vine's New Testament Dictionary).*

Wuest gives the following comment on this word:

"Vincent says: 'Literally, *adjusted . . .* not *fitted by God for destruction,* but *. . . ready, ripe* for destruction, the participle denoting a present state previously formed, but giving no hint of *how* it has been formed. An agency of some kind must be assumed. That the objects of final wrath had themselves a hand in the matter may be seen from I Thessalonians 2:15, 16. That the hand of God is also operative may be inferred from the whole drift of the chapter. "The apostle has probably chosen this form because *the being ready* certainly arises from a continual reciprocal action between human sin and the divine judgment of blindness and hardness. Every development of sin is a network of human offences and divine judgments" (Lange)'" *(The Greek New Testament by Wuest).*

In verse 23 Paul speaks of *"the vessels of mercy, which He had afore prepared unto glory."* The word "prepared" is not, according to the Bible dictionary, equivalent to "foreordained." That God prepares His people for glory means that He commences and continues the work of redemption.

". . . even us, whom He hath called, not of the Jews only, but also of the Gentiles?" The promise of salvation was not conditional to nationality. God provided salvation to all nations through the death, burial, and resurrection of His dear Son. By the death of Christ, God is able to be just and yet justify the sinner, Gentiles included. But Paul keeps the two classes (Jew and Gentile)

separate here, for he still has in mind God's dealings with the Jew, to whom the thought returns exclusively in verse 31.

These verses simply say that God has a perfect right to destroy all sinners, if He so desires. God could be righteous, and annihilate every ungodly person on the face of the earth. However, God can also be righteous and show mercy upon whom He will. He can be righteous and restrain His wrath where and when He wills . . . that is, God has a right to do what God desires to do to fulfill His will, His plan, and His purpose for His own created beings.

We may not understand these verses, but we had better believe them—and let me warn you, O man: Do not accuse God, do not reply against God, do not question God . . . because one day you will bow upon your knees before God (Rom. 14:11). Just remember that God is sovereign, God is righteous, God is holy, God is truth. God cannot do wrong!

Verses 25 and 26: *"As He saith also in Osee, I will call them my people, which were not my people; and her beloved, which was not beloved. And it shall come to pass, that in the place where it was said unto them, Ye are not my people; there shall they be called the children of the living God."*

In these verses Paul quotes from Hosea 2:23 and Hosea 1:10. By referring to the prophecy itself

it will be seen that in both cases the direct application was to Israel, while the citation in Romans
has reference to the Gentiles. Paul is setting forth
the fact that certainly in principle Hosea's prophecy
is being fulfilled in this marvelous Day of Grace—
that God would save a people (namely the Gentiles) who were not a people; strangers to the
covenants, aliens from the commonwealth of Israel,
without hope. And yet through God's sovereign
grace He calls a people *His* people who were NOT
His people.

Verses 27-29: *"Esaias also crieth concerning Israel, Though the number of the children of Israel
be as the sand of the sea, a remnant shall be
saved: for He will finish the work, and cut it
short in righteousness: because a short work will
the Lord make upon the earth. And as Esaias
said before, Except the Lord of Sabaoth had left
us a seed, we had been as Sodoma, and been made
like unto Gomorrha."*

Here Paul quotes from Isaiah 10:22, 23 and Isaiah
1:9.   This he does, to prove that it is only by
God's sovereign grace, God's free grace, that even
the remnant out of Israel is saved—not because
they deserved it, but because God ordered and
willed it, by His sovereign grace.

Verse 30: *"What shall we say then? That the
Gentiles, which followed not after righteousness,*

have attained to righteousness, even the righteousness which is of faith."

Paul is pointing out here that Gentiles who *"attained to righteousness"* did not attain righteousness through their own *willingness* or through their own *running* (v. 16), but by the sovereign grace of God they attained unto *"the righteousness which is of faith."* Paul's reference to the Gentiles appropriating a righteousness which comes by faith should not be surprising, for a righteousness of this sort can be found even by those who are not in quest of it; its nature is that it is brought and offered to men, and faith is simply the act of appropriating it.

Verses 31 and 32: *"But Israel, which followed after the law of righteousness, hath not attained to the law of righteousness. Wherefore? Because they sought it not by faith, but as it were by the works of the law. For they stumbled at that stumblingstone."*

Paul is discussing here the problem raised by the relation of the Jews to the Gospel. The Gentiles (in verse 30) are in view in contrast to Israel (in verse 32). The Gentiles were not seeking righteousness, but the Jews were—but in the wrong way: *"by the works of the law."* Here was a nation pursuing after *"the law of righteousness"* and failing in pursuit; that is, they never reached the place of righteousness or holiness that the Law demands. They said, "All that the Lord hath spoken we will do" (Ex. 19:8). But they did just the opposite; they broke every commandment God gave them.

(In chapter 10, verses 5 and 6, we will study fully the difference between "the righteousness which is of the law" and "the righteousness which is of faith.")

Here in verse 32 Paul asks, *"Wherefore?"* That is, WHY did Israel fail? Why did they never reach the state (or stage) of righteousness which the Law demands? Paul answers: *"Because they sought it not by faith, but . . . by the works of the law."*

Paul is here pointing out that the Jews, who pressed forward to the goal, did not reach the goal. They *have not attained;* but the Gentiles, who never ran (or who never pressed forward to the goal), *have* attained—*by faith.* If we lose sight of this fact, we may become doctrinally prejudiced and miss the main point the Spirit is pointing out to us here; namely, that God follows His supreme will. He is God—and beside Him there is no other.

At this point, Paul passes from the sovereignty of God to the responsibility of man. We cannot harmonize the two in human understanding, and except the Scriptures harmonize the two, we will be left hanging in thin air; that is, we MUST hold to *both.* The Word of God and reason teach us the absolute sovereignty of God—and Scripture and

325

the human conscience assert with equal force the responsibility and free will of man. The practical error arises when either one of these is denied or when one is explained in a way to exclude the other.

It must also be remembered that while man cannot save himself, moral inability does not relieve from responsibility. Man's inability to save himself lies in his sinful nature (Rom. 8:7), and· God cannot be held responsible for man's sin. "God cannot be tempted with evil, neither tempteth He any man" (James 1:13). The sinner's inability to do righteousness, his inability to do God's will, is a result of sin abiding within through the nature inherited from Adam, through whom sin moved upon all men.

We live in a world of sin, a world filled with confusion; and there is enmity between God and the natural man. God cannot acquit the wicked, but God provided a substitute: Jesus, the Lamb, paid sin's debt; and "whosoever will" may come. Whosoever comes will be accepted, because Jesus promised that He would not turn away any who come. The invitation is, "Come unto me, and I will give you rest. Come unto me, and I will in no wise cast you out. Let everyone that is thirsty come, without price and without money, and let him drink freely of the water of life."

Paul teaches, as the Holy Ghost inspired him to write, the complete and undeniable sovereignty of God—and he preaches just as fervently the free will of man. In the following chapters, he will show that Israel's failure was not God's fault, but Israel's own fault.

"For they stumbled at that stumblingstone." The "stumblingstone" is Christ (the Christ of the cross). Israel stumbled at the stumblingstone (I Cor. 1:23) because they were not pursuing righteousness by faith, but by works of the Law.

Verse 33: *"As it is written, Behold, I lay in Sion a stumblingstone and rock of offence: and whosoever believeth on Him shall not be ashamed."*

This quotation is from Isaiah 28:16. Peter uses the same Scripture in I Peter 2:6. (Also read Psalm 118:22 and Isaiah 8:14.) This verse explains the meaning of the closing words of verse 32. Israel's failure to submit themselves unto the righteousness of God consisted in their failure in their rejection of the Lord Jesus Christ, who is the righteousness of God and "the end of the law for righteousness to every one that believeth."

Faith in the Messiah was also a *"rock of offence."* Wuest gives this explanation: "The offence of the cross, at which they stumbled, is not simply the fact that it *is* a cross, whereas they expected a messianic throne; the cross offended them because, as interpreted by Paul, it summoned them to begin their religious life from the very beginning, at the foot of the Crucified, and with a sense upon

327

their hearts of an infinite debt to Him which no 'works' could ever repay."

"*. . . and whosoever believeth on Him shall not be ashamed.*" The word *"whosoever"* in this verse is proof that the Jews failed because of their lack of faith.

Here in chapter 9, we see the test of faith—real faith, true faith, saving faith. Faith trusts God! Faith believes that God is not only omnipotent, but that He is ever-present and all-wise—altogether righteous and entirely holy, without fault even in the most minute detail. Faith believes everything in spite of everything else. Faith believes that it is impossible for the Judge of all the earth to do wrong . . . He *must*, because He is God, do *right*.

Faith reads the Word of God and believes it. Faith believes that God hardens whom He will and softens the heart of whom He will. These things are beyond human reason and human understanding—but human reason and understanding have no authority over true faith. Faith believes God because God is God! Faith believes God without seeing, feeling, tasting; faith just believes God. In spite of the fact that finite man fails, faith marches on with the eye singled on God, not on finite man. Even though faith walks in the dark, faith follows on. And when we walk by faith in the dark, we know God is there, even though we cannot see Him.

When human reason fails in the laboratory, in the test tube, on the slide, under the microscope, and cries out, "A virgin birth is a scientific impossibility, a resurrection from the dead is scientifically impossible," faith still believes in the virgin birth, the bodily resurrection, and the personal return of Jesus to this earth again. The just shall live by faith, walk by faith—and not by sight. If we walk by sight, there is no further need for faith; for what a man can see, handle, feel, or taste, he does not need faith to accept.

Suppose we who believe in God bow our heads this moment and thank God for the privilege of trusting Him and walking quietly with Him, resting our hand in His hand. Though we may not know every detail of the way, we know that He who leads "knoweth the way we take."

"Thomas, did you say you do not know where I am going, and therefore you do not know the way? Thomas, *I* am the Way, the Truth, and the Life. No man cometh unto the Father but by me. Since no man cometh unto the Father but by me, then it is true that all men who come to the Father *must come by me.* Thomas, the just shall live by faith—and faith does not ask to be shown. I am the Way, and without the Way there is no going. I am the Truth, and without the Truth there is no knowing. I am the Life, and without life, Thomas, you are dead. Therefore, if you come where I am, you must come by me—and not only you, Thomas, but all men, *every* man, must come by me. The just shall live by faith, walk by faith, and by faith they shall pass through the door into the Celestial City—and Thomas, I AM THE DOOR!'' (Read John 14:1-6; 10:9.)

"Thomas, do you remember when you said, 'Unless I see the prints of the nails in His hands and thrust my hand into His side, I will not believe'? Do you remember when you did see, you did believe—and I told you that you were blessed because you had seen and believed, but those who believe without seeing are more blessed? Therefore, Thomas, by faith place your hand in my nail-scarred hand and, seeing not, follow me.'' (Read John 20:24-29.)

It is precious, it is marvelous, it is wonderful to walk by faith and not by sight! Thank God we follow Him who is invisible—yet we know He is there! We place our hand in a hand we cannot see—yet we know that hand is there, and in faith we march on day by day, not knowing the tomorrows, but knowing the Christ who knows all the tomorrows!

Have you placed your hand in that nail-scarred hand? If you have not, do it this very moment!

Chapter X

1. Brethren, my heart's desire and prayer to God for Israel is, that they might be saved.

2. For I bear them record that they have a zeal of God, but not according to knowledge.

3. For they being ignorant of God's righteousness, and going about to establish their own righteousness, have not submitted themselves unto the righteousness of God.

4. For Christ is the end of the law for righteousness to every one that believeth.

5. For Moses describeth the righteousness which is of the law, That the man which doeth those things shall live by them.

6. But the righteousness which is of faith speaketh on this wise, Say not in thine heart, Who shall ascend into heaven? (that is, to bring Christ down from above:)

7. Or, Who shall descend into the deep? (that is, to bring up Christ again from the dead.)

8. But what saith it? The word is nigh thee, even in thy mouth, and in thy heart: that is, the word of faith, which we preach;

9. That if thou shalt confess with thy mouth the Lord Jesus, and shalt believe in thine heart that God hath raised him from the dead, thou shalt be saved.

10. For with the heart man believeth unto righteousness; and with the mouth confession is made unto salvation.

11. For the scripture saith, Whosoever believeth on him shall not be ashamed.

12. For there is no difference between the Jew and the Greek: for the same Lord over all is rich unto all that call upon him.

13. For whosoever shall call upon the name of the Lord shall be saved.

14. How then shall they call on him in whom they have not believed? and how shall they believe in him of whom they have not heard? and how shall they hear without a preacher?

15. And how shall they preach, except they be sent? as it is written, How beautiful are the feet of them that preach the gospel of peace, and bring glad tidings of good things!

16. But they have not all obeyed the gospel. For Esaias saith, Lord, who hath believed our report?

17. So then faith cometh by hearing, and hearing by the word of God.

18. But I say, Have they not heard? Yes verily, their sound went into all the earth, and their words unto the ends of the world.

19. But I say, Did not Israel know? First Moses saith, I will provoke you to jealousy by them that are no people, and by a foolish nation I will anger you.

20. But Esaias is very bold, and saith, I was found of them that sought me not; I was made manifest unto them that asked not after me.

21. But to Israel he saith, All day long have I stretched forth my hands unto a disobedient and gainsaying people.

Israel's Ignorance
a Cause of Their Unbelief

In chapter 10 we will study the apparent failure

of the promises of Jehovah God to Israel. We will see that the promises have not failed, but that Israel has been set aside for a season because of their unbelief.

Verse 1: *"Brethren, my heart's desire and prayer to God for Israel is, that they might be saved."*

Here Paul declares again (as in ch. 9:1-3) his great concern for his people, Israel—expressing his *"heart's desire"* for the salvation of his brethren. The Apostle longs and prays *"that they might be saved"*; for though Abraham's seed after the flesh, they are "lost sheep" and need to be sought and found by the Good Shepherd just as truly as those "other sheep" of the Gentiles (John 10:16). But the sad thing is that although they are lost, they do not recognize their true condition.

Verses 2 and 3: *"For I bear them record that they have a zeal of God, but not according to knowledge. For they being ignorant of God's righteousness, and going about to establish their own righteousness, have not submitted themselves unto the righteousness of God."*

"I bear them record . . . ." Paul testifies that his people are zealous for God—*"but not according to knowledge."* He said they were *"ignorant of God's righteousness,"* and they sought to *"establish their own righteousness"* before God through

the labors of their own hands. Wuest says, "The righteousness the Jews desired was a righteousness that was in character their own, one tinged with their own endeavors, the product of their own efforts, one that would glorify themselves, not one characterized by what God is in His glorious Person, not one handed to them as a gift for which they would feel obligated to thank Him."

"*. . . have not submitted themselves unto the righteousness of God.*" Appropriation of God's righteousness involves not only discarding all dependence upon self and self-effort for salvation, but the heart's submission to Jesus Christ as Saviour and Lord (Rom. 10:9). This the Jews were not willing to do. They did not know the meaning of righteousness from God's viewpoint. They were zealous for God, but because of their insufficient knowledge they refused to accept the marvelous grace of God, and they refused to accept the Gospel fact stated in the next verse.

Verse 4: *"For Christ is the end of the law for righteousness to every one that believeth."*

May I pause here to say that the Jews of whom Paul wrote were not the last ones to refuse to accept this fact. We have a lot of Baptists, Methodists, and others, who preach "Grace, grace—God's grace; grace that is greater than all our sins"—and then in the next breath they put men under commandments, laws, rituals, programs, and traditions, refusing to preach and practice pure grace, salvation by grace through faith, plus nothing. I have said in my meetings—and I say it here—there is no need to make a person sign a pledge stating, "I will not dance; I will not drink alcohol; I will not go to movies; I will not play poker." If a person is right with God—if he is born again, loving God with all of his heart, soul, and strength—he will not do those things. And if he is not born again, signing a pledge will not keep him from doing such things.

Israel cried out to God, "We will keep all of your commandments, we will obey all of your laws, we will practice all of your statutes!" But very soon after this promise they were molding the golden calf. Human nature has not changed, nor will it ever change. *"Christ in you"* is the "hope of glory"—and "Christ in you" is victory over the world, the flesh, and the devil. "Christ in you" is the guarantee of entering the Pearly Gates. So there is no need of trying to mix law and grace. Law will not mix with grace, grace will not mix with law. If it is law, it is law; if it is grace, it is grace. They do not mix.

Verse 4 of this tenth chapter of Romans explains the meaning of the closing words in verse 3. The Jews failed to submit themselves unto the righteousness of God when they rejected the Lord Jesus Christ, who IS the righteousness of God and who is *"the end of the law for righteousness to every*

335

one that believeth." The promise was made to Israel in the Old Testament: "Behold, the days come, saith the Lord, that I will raise unto David a righteous Branch, and a King shall reign and prosper, and shall execute judgment and justice in the earth. In His days Judah shall be saved, and Israel shall dwell safely: *and this is His name whereby He shall be called, THE LORD OUR RIGHTEOUSNESS"* (Jer. 23:5, 6). But they refused to believe when "the Lord their righteousness" appeared. However, one day Israel will receive Him, in that day of the fulfillment of the new covenant. (Read Jeremiah 31:31-34; Hebrews 8:8-12; and Romans 11:25-27.)

Contrast Between the Way of the Law and the Way of Faith

Verse 5: *"For Moses describeth the righteousness which is of the law, That the man which doeth those things shall live by them."*

These words are quoted from Leviticus 18:5, which reads: "Ye shall therefore keep my statutes, and my judgments: which if a man do, he shall live in them: I am the Lord."

Dr. Scofield tells us that the Mosaic Covenant was given to Israel "in three divisions, each essential to the others, and together forming the Mosaic Covenant, viz.: the Commandments, expressing the righteous will of God (Ex. 20:1-26);

336

the 'judgments,' governing the social life of Israel
(Ex. 21:1—24:11); and the 'ordinances,' governing
the religious life of Israel (Ex. 24:12—31:18). These
three elements form 'the law,' as that phrase is
generically used in the New Testament. The Commandments and the ordinances formed one religious
system. The Commandments were a 'ministry of
condemnation' and of 'death' (II Cor. 3:7-9); the
ordinances gave, in the high priest, a representative
of the people with Jehovah; and in the sacrifices
a 'cover' for their sins in anticipation of the Cross
(Heb. 5:1-3; 9:6-9; Rom. 3:25, 26). The Christian
is not under the conditional Mosaic Covenant of
works, the law, but under the unconditional New
Covenant of grace (Rom. 3:21-27; 6:14, 15; Gal. 2:16;
3:10-14, 16-18, 24-26; 4:21-31; Heb. 10:11-17)."

When Moses writes that the Jew who keeps the
statutes and judgments of God shall live in them,
he does not mean that person will be given eternal
life by reason of his obedience, or his works.
Eternal life is a *gift*, both in the Old and New
Testaments, and is never *earned*.

Both Moses and Paul clearly understood and
taught that obedience to the Law would never give
a person a standing of righteousness before a holy
God. In Romans chapter 4 Paul writes that *Abraham* was saved by *faith*, not by obedience to the
Law. In the Old Testament *only faith in the
coming Sacrifice for sin* which God would offer
(the Sacrifice—the Lord Jesus Christ—symbolized

by the Levitical sacrifices) could give a person such a righteous standing.

What man ever kept the Law? No man except the Lord Jesus Christ ever kept the Law. He came not to destroy the Law (Matt. 5:17) but to *fulfill* the Law—and He did. He fulfilled every jot and every tittle of the Law in every minute detail. If no mere man could keep the Law, in what sense was this statement made by Moses and repeated by Paul? It was made in the sense that a man's obedience to the ordinance of the sacrifice offered in the tabernacle is the same as his act of faith in the coming Saviour, which would result in a righteous standing before God. One writer thinks Paul has the Pharisees and legalists in mind, and the fact that the Jewish religion had been perverted from God's system—in which salvation was given in answer to faith in a blood sacrifice—to a mere ethical cult, where Israel sought salvation by law obedience.

Verses 6-8: *"But the righteousness which is of faith speaketh on this wise, Say not in thine heart, Who shall ascend into heaven? (that is, to bring Christ down from above:) Or, Who shall descend into the deep? (that is, to bring up Christ again from the dead.) But what saith it? The word is nigh thee, even in thy mouth, and in thy heart: that is, the word of faith, which we preach."*

The words quoted here are taken from Deuteronomy 30:12-14, where Moses, near the end of his life, presses upon the people the fact that God has given testimony which man is responsible to believe. The testimony there, of course, was the revelation from Sinai. But here Paul takes Moses' words and in a wonderful way applies them to faith in Christ. (Read those verses in Deuteronomy very carefully.)

Paul says: "It is not needful that anyone should *ascend into heaven, to bring Christ down from above;* nor is it necessary for anyone to *descend into the deep, to bring Him up again from the dead."* Christ has already come down, He has died, God has raised Him from the dead—and upon this depends the entire Gospel testimony. Therefore the Apostle goes on to say, "The Gospel, the Word of God, the message of God, *is nigh thee, even in thy mouth, and in thy heart:* the message, *the word of faith, which we preach."*

Faith does not ask where God is; faith *accepts* God, knowing that God IS. I am so glad we are saved by God's marvelous grace, and God's marvelous grace becomes ours when we exercise faith in the finished work of the Lord Jesus Christ. The very faith that brings saving grace becomes ours through hearing the Word of God (Rom. 10:17).

We will never know this side of the Pearly Gates how important the Word of God is. No wonder liberals, modernists, and haters of God are doing everything in their ungodly power to discredit the

Word of God and tear down the fundamentals of the faith. When we accept the Word, we do not ask where God is, or if Christ came down from above, nor if He came back from the dead. We KNOW He did, because the Word of God tells us He did!

The next verse is a SPARKLING DIAMOND to this preacher, for it was through this verse that BLESSED ASSURANCE BECAME MINE!

Verse 9: *"That if thou shalt confess with thy mouth the Lord Jesus, and shalt believe in thine heart that God hath raised Him from the dead, thou shalt be saved."*

I stated earlier in this study that I was brought under conviction and saved the night the minister preached on Romans 6:23: "The wages of sin is death; but the gift of God is eternal life through Jesus Christ our Lord." This may seem strange to you, but although I was saved that night, I did not know HOW I was saved. I knew that I WAS saved, but frankly I did not know how it happened. I knew God did it, but I did not understand HOW God did it. I did not have perfect assurance until just a few nights later, when I went into the prayer room and I sat and listened to God's minister expound the plan of salvation. He unfolded the truth of Romans 10:9, 10—and this truth gave me the assurance of salvation which I have never doubted since that night!

Paul assures us in his letter to Titus that "God cannot lie" (Titus 1:2). Therefore, I boldly declare that anyone meeting the conditions of Romans 10:9 can be saved. What conditions are presented here?

1. *"That if thou"*—that means Oliver Greene, or you, or you, or *you!* In other words, "Whosoever readeth, this tremendous truth pertaineth to you—*that if thou shalt confess with thy mouth the Lord Jesus . . . .*" That does not mean to say simply, "I believe there is a Jesus." The *devils* believe—and they tremble (James 2:19). I do not think there are many people who do not believe there is a true God existing somewhere. Even the heathen have their gods and their religion. They know there must be a Supreme Being somewhere. But this verse does not mean to believe with the *head*, for God deals with the *heart*.

To "confess with the mouth the Lord Jesus" is to confess that God sent Jesus into the world, born of a virgin. Joseph, the husband of Mary, was His foster father—but God Almighty was the Father of Jesus. The Holy Ghost overshadowed Mary, and she conceived and brought forth Jesus. You must believe in the virgin birth—or burn in hell—regardless of what the liberal and the modernist may say about it!

Not only must you believe that Jesus was virgin born, but you must believe that He lived a sinless life, that He was arrested, condemned, and crucified.

341

You must believe that He died on the cross, shed His blood—not as a religious martyr, but He shed His blood for the remission of sin. You must believe further that He was buried, and that on the third day He rose again, bodily—not as a spirit, but as a man. I repeat: You must believe that He was born of a virgin, crucified on a cross, buried in a tomb, raised the third day. This is what it means to believe that Jesus Christ is the Son of God, confessing Him as Lord.

If Jesus was God's Son—very God in flesh— then Jesus came to do exactly what God said He *would* do; and to believe that He is God's Son is to embrace everything the New Testament teaches concerning Him.

Do you believe that Jesus Christ was born of the Virgin Mary? Do you believe He came into the world as a Babe in a manger? Do you believe He was brought up in the carpenter shop, and that Joseph, His foster father, worked with Him day by day in the little carpenter's shop in Nazareth? Do you believe that when He was about thirty years of age He came on the scene of His public ministry, John the Baptist baptized Him, and the Holy Spirit descended upon Him and remained upon Him? Do you believe that He came to lay His life down, a ransom for many? Do you believe He died on the cross for the sins of the whole wide world? Do you believe they buried Him and God raised Him from the dead the third day?

Do you believe that? If you do, you are standing at the door of salvation!

2. "*. . . and shalt believe in thine heart that God hath raised Him from the dead . . . .*" He was raised "for our justification" (Rom. 4:25). The faith that leaves this out, although it may accept everything else in the record of our Lord, is not Christian, and is not *saving* faith.

One of the nation's leading religionists once dogmatically said that the resurrection of Jesus is a myth and that He did not come out of the tomb bodily. This man's statement was carried by the leading periodicals of America—and around the world, for that matter. Also, in one leading theological school in America, a man stood on the platform and spoke to hundreds of ministerial students, and said to those young men, "It is no longer necessary to believe in the bodily resurrection of Jesus . . . it is only a myth."

If the Bible is not true, what else do we have to go by? If the Bible is not God's Word, then we are all hopeless, because this is the only Book on earth that gives any hope to a hell-deserving sinner. In I Corinthians 15:12-19 we read:

"Now if Christ be preached that He rose from the dead, how say some among you that there is no resurrection of the dead? But if there be no resurrection of the dead, then is Christ not risen: and *if Christ be not risen, then is our preaching vain, and your faith is also vain.* Yea, and we are found false witnesses of God; because we have testified of God that He raised up Christ: whom He raised not up, if so be that the dead rise not. For if the dead rise not, then is not Christ raised: and *if Christ be not raised, your faith is vain; ye are yet in your sins. Then they also which are fallen asleep in Christ are perished.* If in this life only we have hope in Christ, we are of all men most miserable."

These precious verses point out clearly that if Jesus did not rise from the dead, then our preaching is vain, it is a lie . . . and your faith is vain (that is, empty); yea, we preachers who preach the resurrection are liars, false witnesses, and if Christ did not rise from the dead your faith is empty and you are still in your sins. According to these verses, if Jesus Christ did not rise from the dead, we are all going to hell!

I dogmatically declare, without apology, without fear, favor, or hesitation, that any man who teaches or preaches that Jesus did not rise bodily from the dead is a minister of the devil and he is preaching a lie. The greatest bombshell ever to explode in the face of an unbelieving world was the resurrection of the Lord Jesus Christ. That is ONE thing the Jews did not—they *could* not—explain away.

Do you believe in your heart that Jesus came out of the tomb bodily, *alive,* and appeared to men as I Corinthians 15 clearly testifies He did? If you believe that, then—

344

3. *". . . thou shalt be saved!"* In other words, you do two things: Confess with your mouth . . . believe in your heart—then, "THOU SHALT BE SAVED!" Listen to these precious words:

"Moreover, brethren, I declare unto you the Gospel which I preached unto you, which also ye have received, and wherein ye stand; *by which also ye are saved,* if ye keep in memory what I preached unto you, unless ye have believed in vain. For I delivered unto you first of all that which I also received, how that Christ died for our sins according to the Scriptures; and that He was buried, and that He rose again the third day according to the Scriptures: and that He was seen of Cephas, then of the twelve: after that, He was seen of above five hundred brethren at once; of whom the greater part remain unto this present, but some are fallen asleep" (I Cor. 15:1-6).

Paul was saying to the believers at Corinth: "I preached unto you the Gospel, you heard the Gospel, you were saved through the Gospel. And this is the Gospel I preached: Christ died for our sins according to the Scriptures. He was buried according to the Scriptures. He rose again the third day according to the Scriptures, and He was seen of Cephas, then of the twelve, and of more than five hundred brethren at one time."

The very heart of salvation is the bodily resurrection of Jesus Christ. There have been many great religious leaders, many great men who have founded great religions (please notice I said "religions"). You cannot deny the fact that Confucius left his mark upon the world. Mohammed left his mark upon the world—and some of the later religious leaders, such as Judge Rutherford, Mary Baker Eddy and others, left their mark upon the world; but not one of those people has come back from the grave.

Jesus rose bodily from the tomb. He walked out of the tomb and appeared in that body to men—and then He ascended to heaven in that same body (Acts 1:1-11). Now *THERE IS A MAN in heaven:* "There is one God, and one Mediator between God and men, *the MAN, CHRIST JESUS*" (I Tim. 2:5). "For Christ is not entered into the holy places made with hands, which are the figures of the true; *but into heaven itself, now to appear in the presence of God for us*" (Heb. 9:24).

If you believe with all of your heart that Jesus is the Christ, if you believe He died on the cross for your sin and that He rose again from the dead, then confess that with your mouth—and *you are saved!*

Verse 10: *"For with the heart man believeth unto righteousness; and with the mouth confession is made unto salvation."*

This verse emphasizes that it is *"with the heart,"* not with the head, that man *"believeth unto righteousness."* It is not with the hands that men *work* unto righteousness. It is not with their ability that men *do good deeds* unto righteousness. It is not through the brain that men *reason* and plan a life of righteousness. No, the only way to become righteous is to *believe* with the *heart* that Jesus is the Christ of God.

Paul continues by saying, *". . . and with the mouth confession is made unto salvation."* We confess Jesus Christ as Saviour . . . we confess salvation. During the transition period there were secret disciples; but today there is no such thing as a secret disciple—a born again person who refuses to confess Jesus Christ. I do not mean that all Christians preach, or pray in public, or even testify in the church service; but *all true believers* "confess with the mouth" that Jesus is Saviour of their soul! Jesus clearly taught, "If you are ashamed of me, I will be ashamed of you." He said, "If you will confess me before men, I will confess you before my Father; but if you deny me before men, I will deny you before my Father." (Read Matthew 10:32, 33.)

So—we believe with the heart unto Gospel righteousness, righteousness that God accepts. And we confess with the mouth that we are God's child, that we have been saved.

In the paragraph closing with verse 10, we have one of the most important statements in all the Word of God, from Genesis through Revelation. Here the Holy Spirit brings into the sharpest

347

contrast possible, the two righteousnesses: "the righteousness which is *of the law*" (v. 5); and "the righteousness which is *of faith*" (v. 6), minus sight or works. One is man's impure righteousness; the other is God's pure righteousness. One is human; the other is divine. One is by man's works...it comes to the man who "doeth"; the other is by unmerited favor...grace. It comes not by works, but through faith...that is, "to everyone that believeth." One is the result of man's (or human) efforts; the other is not the result of effort, but is the gift of God in Christ Jesus, to all who will receive Him.

Israel failed at this point. They refused to accept Jesus Christ as their righteousness. They (Israel), being ignorant of God's righteousness, tried to establish their own righteousness. They refused to accept the fact that Christ is the end of the Law for righteousness. He came and offered Himself to them, but they refused to submit themselves unto Him. They cried, "Crucify Him! Let His blood be upon us and upon our children! Give us Barabbas! We want a robber!"

Let me say here, that the number one purpose in The Gospel Hour radio ministry, the books and other literature, is to reach men with the pure Gospel that brings salvation. Therefore I make no apology for taking time and space to elaborate upon the truth versus error. In this day of confusion, it is refreshing to look into "the perfect law of liberty" that is able to make us wise unto salvation, and "let God be true, but every man a liar." Read the Word and follow the principles laid down in the Word. Examine again the foundations upon which we are building. May God help us to see the truth! May God help us to turn our backs upon error!

There is no passage in all the Word of God that sets forth the fundamental propositions through which salvation comes, any clearer than the passage we are studying. In this passage we read the Gospel of God. In this passage we read the complete unfolding of the way of life eternal. What are the fundamental propositions concerning salvation which we find set forth here?

1. *Man, by nature, is definitely and assuredly unrighteous.* There is nothing clearer or more strongly emphasized in the Word of God than this fact. Man recoils at the fact of his unrighteous nature. It is humiliating to the flesh to face the corruptness of the natural man. Theologians may differ on the question of original sin and total depravity—but regardless of the theologians, God has made it very clear that "the heart is deceitful above all things, and *desperately wicked*" (Jer. 17:9), and Jesus assures us that the unregenerate heart is a cesspool of iniquity. (Please read carefully Mark 7:21-23.) Man, apart from God, is definitely unrighteous.

Of course, we do not have to turn to the Word

of God to learn that man is by nature totally depraved and unrighteous. The terrible history of the human race proves that, and Romans chapter 1 points out the wickedness of mankind. Because of the terrible, terrible wickedness and vile affections, "God gave them up." It is easy for man to point out his good qualities—but God thunders out: "There is none righteous, no, not one!" (Rom. 3:10). Again God thunders out: ". . . there is no difference: *for all have sinned, and come short of the glory of God!"* (Rom. 3:22, 23).

The Word of God clearly puts all in the same category: Jew, Gentile, educated, uneducated, rich, poor, bond or free. All unbelievers are "dead in trespasses and sins" and "past feeling." (Read Ephesians 2:1-12; 4:17-19.) The natural man "is corrupt according to the deceitful lusts" (Eph. 4:22). The mind of the natural man is "enmity against God," it cannot be subject to the law of God—therefore it "cannot please God" (Rom. 8: 7, 8). The natural man cannot receive the things of God—"they are foolishness unto him: neither can he know them, because they are spiritually discerned" (I Cor. 2:14). All unbelievers are "by nature the children of wrath" (Eph. 2:3). It is as natural for the unregenerated man to follow the lust of the flesh, as it is for water to run downhill. Man by nature is unrighteous.

2. *The natural man is ignorant of God's pure righteousness.* Since man is corrupt, the natural

man has a corrupt mind. Because of his corrupt mind, his view (his definition) of righteousness is distorted. The natural man has his own ideas concerning right and wrong, but his ideas are false because they are manufactured in an unregenerate heart. The truth of the matter is, the unregenerate cannot know the righteousness of God, because to know the righteousness of God, we must know God's Christ.

The standard of righteousness is God's righteousness—and if it is right according to God, it is RIGHT; if it is not right according to God, it is WRONG. God is absolutely righteous. "God is light, and in Him is no darkness at all" (I John 1:5). In Him there is "no variableness, neither shadow of turning" (James 1:17). "God is not a man, that He should lie" (Num. 23:19). God *cannot* lie (Heb. 6:18; Titus 1:2), because God is righteous. God cannot repudiate His promise, He cannot forget His Word—for He is righteous. God's standard is not man's standard. The natural man's ideas of right and wrong are earthly—or may we say they are corrupt, vile ideas—because they are conceived in a mind that is evil and corrupt.

Unregenerated men change "the glory of the uncorruptible God into an image made like to corruptible man" (Rom. 1:21-23). That is, the unregenerate man is continually attempting to bring God down to the level of man. But such will never happen.

What is the average man's idea concerning the requirements of a holy God? If you want the answer firsthand, just step out on any busy street and begin a conversation with a man. Ask him— and ninety-nine times out of a hundred he will say, "If a man does the very best he can, if he tries to do right in all of his ways, that is all that is expected of him. If a man pays his honest debts, treats his family right, does the very best he knows how, what else can he do?" The answer is the same answer Jesus gave to Nicodemus: "You must be born from above . . . ye must be born again." The answer is the same as the answer Jesus gave to the rich young ruler: "Come, follow me, and you will have treasure in heaven." God's requirement is *not* doing the best we can, or living the best we know how—but believing on the Lord Jesus Christ and surrendering our heart and life to Him.

God's demands are clearly set forth in His Word: "Walk before me, and be thou perfect" (Gen. 17:1). Again, "Be ye holy, for I am holy" (I Pet. 1:16; Lev. 11:44). Again, "Follow...holiness, without which no man shall see the Lord" (Heb. 12:14). Again, nothing shall enter the heavenly city "that defileth, neither whatsoever worketh abomination, or maketh a lie: but they which are written in the Lamb's book of life" (Rev. 21:27).

If any man be in Christ Jesus, he is a new creation. Old things pass away, all things become

new, and he receives the divine nature of God
(II Cor. 5:17; II Pet. 1:4). God's new creation is
"in righteousness and true holiness" (Eph. 4:24).
The only way a person can be perfect, righteous,
holy, and new, is to be in Christ. It makes no
difference how sincere a person may be in his
religious practices, he must be born again if he
hopes to see God. God accepts no less than pure
righteousness, and pure righteousness comes only
through the Lord Jesus Christ.

3. *The natural man, because of his ignorance
concerning God's demands, goes about to establish
his own righteousness according to his own thinking.* When our parents (Adam and Eve) disobeyed
God, they thought they could correct their mistake.
They attempted to do so by making for themselves
aprons of fig leaves. Everything was fine until
God Almighty stepped into the garden. They
heard His voice, they ran and hid—but their hiding
place was no good. Their excuses were to no avail;
they suffered the consequences of their disobedience. Their covering was condemned by God, and
He provided a blood-covering (Gen. chap. 3).

Cain, the son of Adam and Eve, tried to make
himself presentable to God. He brought the fruit
of the ground. I am sure he brought the very best
fruit he had, but God rejected it. God said, "Cain,
if you will do well, I will still receive you. If you
will bring a lamb, I will accept your offering; but
if you do not well, if you refuse to bring a blood-

353

offering, then sin shall rule over you." Cain refused, he murdered his brother, he lied about it, and God cursed him. He cried out, "My punishment is greater than I can bear!" (Gen. chap. 4).

The account of Adam and Eve, and that of Cain, bear out the fact that the natural man, because he is ignorant of God's righteousness, seeks to establish his own righteousness; but all of the righteousnesses of man are no better than filthy rags in the sight of God (Isaiah 64:6).

The carnal mind has always been proud, and it rebels against the truth of its total depravity. It recoils at the thought of a blood-offering. The conscience of an unregenerated person is the most elastic thing on earth. Besides being corrupt, it is elastic to the desires of the corrupt heart. Eventually, instead of accusing, the conscience *excuses* almost any act of evil; and to such a person finally nothing is sinful. The conscience becomes not only defiled, but polluted, and it becomes seared as with a hot iron (I Tim. 4:2).

4. *The only way for the unregenerated man to establish his own righteousness is by his own works, and the Bible condemns that:* "NOT by works of righteousness which we have done, but according to His mercy He saved us, by the washing of regeneration, and renewing of the Holy Ghost" (Titus 3:5). Paul was very careful to make known the eternal fact that *man cannot become righteous by works*. The plan of salvation is not

based on what man can do, nor upon man's ability to live righteously.

If man could have saved himself by his own good works, there would have been no need of salvation through the Lord Jesus Christ. If our own good works were the basis for eternal life, the work of Christ would be unnecessary and vain. If man by his own good works or ability could save himself, then the greatest tragedy of all eternity would be the cross of the Lord Jesus Christ. But the cross was NOT a tragedy; it was a divine imperative. Jesus said, "And I, if I be lifted up from the earth, will draw all men unto me" (John 12:32). To Nicodemus He said, "And as Moses lifted up the serpent in the wilderness, *even so must the Son of man be lifted up*" (John 3:14).

Salvation was born in the heart of God, displayed in the body of Christ on the cross, and becomes ours by our receiving the finished work of the Lord Jesus Christ. God does the saving; man cannot save himself, nor can he *help* God save him. We are saved entirely apart from our own efforts. We simply exercise faith in the finished work of Jesus Christ—and *for Christ's sake, according to God's mercy, HE SAVES US.*

5. *It is utterly impossible for any man to establish his own righteousness.* We have learned from the Word of God that man is by nature unrighteous and ungodly. How, then, can unrighteous man do righteous works or righteous acts? "Who can

355

bring a clean thing out of an unclean? Not one!" (Job 14:4). Again, "Can the Ethiopian change his skin, or the leopard his spots? Then may ye also do good, that are accustomed to do evil" (Jer. 13:23). Man may practice those things which he considers righteous, but in God's sight "we are all as an unclean thing, and all our righteousnesses are as filthy rags" (Isaiah 64:6). The man of wisdom enlightens us in these words: "There is a way which seemeth right unto a man, but the end thereof are the ways of death" (Prov. 14:12; 16:25). And Samuel adds: ". . . for man looketh on the outward appearance, *but the Lord looketh on the HEART*" (I Sam. 16:7).

During the days before the Flood, no doubt men thought they were making great progress: "There were giants in the earth in those days." There were also "mighty men which were of old, men of renown"; but God looked down upon those giants and men of renown, and God "saw that the wickedness of man was great in the earth, and that every imagination of the thoughts of his heart was only evil continually" (Gen. 6:4, 5). Therefore God declared He would "destroy all flesh" (Gen. 6:17). In God's eyes, all flesh is corrupt, and the works of the natural man are not righteous works, but unrighteous. Therefore, man cannot attain righteousness through works.

The works of the natural man are listed for us in Galatians 5:19-21: "Now the works of the flesh are manifest, which are these; *Adultery, fornication, uncleanness, lasciviousness, idolatry, witchcraft, hatred, variance, emulations, wrath, strife, seditions, heresies, envyings, murders, drunkenness, revellings, and such like.*"

Could righteousness be produced by a heart described in those despicable terms? When a fountain is poisoned, can it produce pure water? What could the holy law of God do for a man like that? The answer is singular: It could only *condemn* him—and that is exactly what it does. "Therefore by the deeds of the law there shall no flesh be justified in His sight: for by the law is the knowledge of sin" (Rom. 3:20). The Law is not a ministration of righteousness, but of condemnation (II Cor. 3:9).

Keep in mind that the Law demands a flawless life, perfect obedience from the cradle to the grave; and anything less cannot and will not be accepted by Almighty God. If a man keeps the whole Law, and yet stumbles in *one point,* "he is guilty of all" (James 2:10). The Scriptures say, "As many as are of the works of the law are under the curse: for it is written, Cursed is every one that continueth not in *all* things which are written in the book of the law to do them. But that no man is justified by the law in the sight of God, it is evident: for, The just shall live by faith. And the law is not of faith: but, The man that doeth them shall live in them" (Gal. 3:10-12).

It is not enough to try to do good, to be good, to do right, or to do the best you can. That will not satisfy God Almighty. God is satisfied in His Son—and ONLY in His Son. Therefore, it is impossible for any man to establish his own righteousness . . . but hallelujah! *Christ* is made unto us righteousness (I Cor. 1:30).

6. *To obtain the gift of God's righteousness in Christ Jesus is possible for any and all men.* "The Lord is not slack concerning His promise, as some men count slackness; but is longsuffering to usward, *not willing that any should perish, but that ALL should come to repentance"* (II Pet. 3:9). The gift of God is for *all*—yes, all are included, not one is excluded, in spite of the teaching of the hyper-Calvinists.

There is no difference between sinners in God's sight—"for *all* have sinned, and come short of the glory of God" (Rom. 3:23). There is no difference in respect to those who are invited. God invites all: "But now the righteousness of God without the law is manifested, being witnessed by the law and the prophets; even the righteousness of God which is by faith of Jesus Christ *unto all and upon all them that believe: for there is no difference"* (Rom. 3:21, 22). Please notice: "UNTO ALL AND UPON ALL THEM THAT BELIEVE."

White or colored; rich or poor; educated or uneducated . . . whatever you are, WHOEVER you are, WHEREVER you are . . . no matter how sinful, no matter how ungodly, no matter how vile, no matter what you have done or what you have *not* done . . . the record is clear: *"For God so loved the WORLD, that He gave His only begotten Son, that WHOSOEVER BELIEVETH IN HIM should not perish, but have everlasting life"* (John 3:16). "And He is the propitiation for our sins: and not for our's only, but also *for the sins of the whole world"* (I John 2:2). Again: He is "the living God, who is THE SAVIOUR OF ALL MEN" (I Tim. 4:10). Thank God, Jesus died on the cross, and in His death He tasted death for every man (Heb. 2:9). No man will ever stand before God and accuse God of not providing salvation for him, or accuse God of leaving him out!

To me, one of the most tremendous verses in the entire Bible concerning the fact that all can be saved, is in the Old Testament: *"ALL we like sheep have gone astray; we have turned every one to his own way; and the Lord hath laid on Him the iniquity of us ALL!"* (Isaiah 53:6). This tremendous verse opens with a big "little" word: *"All."* It closes with the same big "little" word: *"all."* ALL are in the same boat—lost, doomed, hopeless, hell-bound; but ALL are invited to come to Jesus. And those who come, He will in no wise cast out. So—Jesus purchased salvation for ALL.

7. *God's way of bestowing righteousness upon unrighteous man is singular: It is simply by faith in the finished work of Jesus—*"by grace through

359

faith" (Eph. 2:8). The only way man can become
a recipient of God's grace, the only way a man
can come into possession of the gift of God, is *by
faith*. The Word of God declares, ". . . IT IS OF
FAITH, THAT IT MIGHT BE BY GRACE . . ."
(Rom. 4:16).

We have seen man's helplessness to attain righteousness by means of the Law—or works. The
Law could only show him the *need* of righteousness; it could not *produce* the righteousness the
natural man needs—but God, in Christ, met man's
need: "For what the law could not do, in that it
was weak through the flesh, God sending His own
Son in the likeness of sinful flesh, and for sin,
condemned sin in the flesh: that the righteousness
of the law might be fulfilled in us, who walk not
after the flesh, but after the Spirit" (Rom. 8:3, 4).

What the Law could not do, *God did, by grace*.
Grace is unmerited favor—and everything we receive from God is unmerited. The unregenerated
man deserves only hell—and apart from Jesus
Christ he will suffer death in hell forever. But in
spite of what we deserve, in spite of the fact that
the wages of sin is death—*"God, who is rich in
mercy, for His great love wherewith He loved us,
even when we were dead in sins, hath quickened
us together with Christ, (by grace ye are saved;)*
and hath raised us up together, and made us sit
together in heavenly places in Christ Jesus: that
in the ages to come He might shew the exceeding

riches of His grace in His kindness toward us through Christ Jesus. *For by grace are ye saved through faith; and that not of yourselves: IT IS THE GIFT OF GOD: not of works, lest any man should boast"* (Eph. 2:4-9).

Salvation is *God's gift.* There is not one single, solitary thing man can do to merit salvation. The only way to get a gift is to *receive* it. The only way to be saved is to *receive the Lord Jesus.* The Scriptures teach: "He came unto His own, and His own received Him not. But *as many as received Him, to them gave He power to become the sons of God, even to them that believe on His name:* which were born, not of blood, nor of the will of the flesh, nor of the will of man, but of God" (John 1:11-13). "Receive . . . believe . . . accept"—that is the only way to get God's gift of salvation.

In John 3:18 we read, "He that believeth on Him is not condemned: but He that believeth not is condemned already, BECAUSE he hath not believed in the name of the only begotten Son of God." Perhaps someone is asking, "Preacher, what does it mean to believe in God?" It simply means to *believe God.* Let the Scriptures explain:

"If we receive the witness of men, the witness of God is greater: for this is the witness of God which He hath testified of His Son. *He that believeth on the Son of God hath the witness in himself: he that believeth not God hath made Him a liar; because he believeth not the record that God gave of His Son.* And this is the record, that God hath given to us eternal life, and this life is in His Son. He that hath the Son hath life; and he that hath not the Son of God hath not life" (I John 5:9-12).

God said it, you believe it—and salvation is wrought. But if you read it in God's Word, and *refuse* to believe it, then my friend, according to the Scripture I have just given you, *you have called God a liar!* You believe the witness of *men:* If your husband tells you something, you believe it; if your wife tells you something, you believe it. Children believe their parents; parents believe their children.

But you read the Word of God—"By grace, through faith, the gift of God, not of works" . . . "Not by works of righteousness which we have done, but according to His mercy He saved us" . . . "if thou shalt confess with thy mouth the Lord Jesus, and shalt believe in thine heart that God hath raised Him from the dead, thou shalt be saved. For with the heart man believeth unto righteousness, and with the mouth confession is made unto salvation." . . . "Whosoever shall call upon the name of the Lord shall be saved." . . . "If we confess our sins, He is faithful and just to forgive us our sins, and to cleanse us from all unrighteousness."—You read those tremendous truths, those gigantic promises, and then you ask,

"How can it be? I do not understand it."

You do not need to ask how it can be: "IT IS FINISHED" (John 19:30). You do not need to understand it, for we are not saved by understanding. We are saved by faith; and faith accepts what God declares *simply because God said it,* not because we understand it.

So my friend, if you will bow your head, close your eyes, and ask God in faith to save you for Jesus' sake, God will save your soul this very moment—and you will know it, because you will have the witness in your heart! In the words of Paul I ask, "How shall we escape, if we neglect so great salvation?" (Heb. 2:3). All you need do to die in your sins and burn in hell forever, is to *neglect* "so great salvation"! All you need do to be saved and stay out of hell, is to *receive* "so great salvation"! Receive Jesus now, believe on Him with your heart, confess Him with your mouth —and "THOU SHALT BE SAVED!"

Verse 11: *"For the Scripture saith, Whosoever believeth on Him shall not be ashamed."*

The *"Scripture"* to which Paul refers is Isaiah 28:16, from which he quoted in chapter 9, verse 33. Paul is showing here that salvation by faith is no new thing; that is, justification by faith has always been God's way of salvation. Although Jesus had not been born during the Old Testament era, the Old Testament saint looked *forward* to the day

363

when Jesus WOULD be born, when He would come—the Lamb of God. The New Testament saint looks *back* to Calvary for salvation.

". . . Whosoever believeth on Him shall not be ashamed." The word *"ashamed"* here, according to *Vine's New Testament Dictionary*, means "put to shame." Although it is true a person who believes on the Lord Jesus Christ for salvation will not be ashamed of Him, I believe the primary meaning is that one who believes shall not be put to shame in the sense of disappointment. Paul is not afraid that the sinner who places his faith in Christ will be defeated or disappointed. By this the Apostle means he is not afraid that salvation by faith will not work. He believes in its power to save to the uttermost.

Verses 12 and 13: *"For there is no difference between the Jew and the Greek: for the same Lord over all is rich unto all that call upon Him. For whosoever shall call upon the name of the Lord shall be saved."*

Just as there is *"no difference"* among men, Jew or Gentile, in their *sinfulness* (Rom. 3:22, 23), there is no difference in God's mercy to all, Jew or Gentile—*"for the same Lord over all is rich unto all that call upon Him."*

"For whosoever shall call upon the name of the Lord shall be saved." Here Paul quotes from Joel 2:32, which reads: "And it shall come to pass,

that whosoever shall call on the name of the Lord shall be delivered: . . . ." *"Whosoever"* is scriptural proof of the universality of God's mercy. Is it not wonderful that "whosoever" shall call upon the name of the Lord shall be saved? This includes everyone; it excludes no one. Thank God for an all-inclusive salvation!

Verses 14 and 15: *"How then shall they call on Him in whom they have not believed? and how shall they believe in Him of whom they have not heard? and how shall they hear without a preacher? and how shall they preach, except they be sent? As it is written, How beautiful are the feet of them that preach the Gospel of peace, and bring glad tidings of good things!"*

Verses 13 through 15 give us the plan of salvation in *reverse*. Let me explain what I mean:

1. *"Whosoever shall call upon the name of the Lord shall be saved."* This is a positive, clear, understandable statement: "Whosoever shall call . . . shall be saved."

2. *"How then shall they call on Him in whom they have not believed?"* In other words, the sinner's call for salvation must be preceded by believing on the Lord Jesus Christ, who is able to save—and a person will never call in faith until he first believes that Jesus is able to do for him what he is about to ask Him to do. So then— *believing* on Jesus precedes *calling* on Jesus.

3. *"How shall they believe in Him of whom they have not heard?"* The sinner cannot believe the Gospel until he *hears* the Gospel. So—hearing precedes believing, and hearing and believing precede calling. But let us go a step further:

4. *"How shall they hear without a preacher?"* It pleases God through "the foolishness of preaching" the Gospel (I Cor. 1:21), to save them that believe. So God calls and anoints men to preach the Gospel—the death, burial, and resurrection of the Lord Jesus (I Cor. 15:1-4). God's preachers preach the death, burial, and resurrection. Any preacher who denies the virgin birth, the cross, and the resurrection, is not a minister of God, but a minister of the devil.

5. *"How shall they preach, except they be sent?"* God's program for this Day of Grace is for ministers to be *sent*—yes, to be sent to every creature, to preach the Gospel of the marvelous grace of God.

Here is God's blueprint (or God's outline) for salvation: First, God calls preachers to preach His Word. (If the universal condition of salvation is to call on the Lord, only the preaching of the Gospel—to *all* without distinction—can make such a call possible.) The preacher preaches the Word; the sinner *hears* the Word and recognizes the fact that he needs a Saviour. Therefore, listening to the preacher as he preaches the pure Gospel, realizing his need of a Saviour, the sinner then believes in his heart that Jesus is *willing,* and *able,* and *ready* to save. Believing that Jesus is able to supply the need of the heart, the sinner gladly *calls,* confessing all sin, repenting from the heart, *believing* on the Lord Jesus Christ as Saviour.

Paul has now argued backward from the nature of the Gospel, which demands that men call upon the name of the Lord, to that which this call implies — a general sending forth of ministers. That such would be sent forth is confirmed by a quotation from Isaiah 52:7. Paul says, *"As it is written, How beautiful are the feet of them that preach the Gospel of peace, and bring glad tidings of good things!"*

Beloved, if you have read the past few pages of this message on Romans, and you do not see the light of salvation, I fear you are willingly in darkness and do not desire to know the way of life. I have given to you the pure Gospel. I am God's preacher. You hear what I have tried to tell you. Believe Jesus died for you; call on Him in faith — and He will save your soul!

Israel's Unbelief Was Foretold

Verses 16 and 17: *"But they have not all obeyed the Gospel. For Esaias saith, Lord, who hath believed our report? So then faith cometh by hearing, and hearing by the Word of God."*

Again, these verses and those which follow

367

are seasoned with Old Testament Scripture. Here in verse 16, Paul quotes from Isaiah 53:1.

"But they have not all obeyed the Gospel." Paul might have said, "How few have believed." This general disbelief, however, does not disprove that the "sent" messengers were God's. It actually confirms their authority, for Isaiah foresaw their unbelief and predicted it in the sad statement, *"Who hath believed our report?"*—or, "Who hath believed thy message heard from us?"

"So then faith cometh by hearing . . . ." The "call" that brings salvation demands faith—and saving faith, of which Paul is speaking, comes *"by the Word of God"* sent through His messengers.

We are saved by grace *through faith.* "Whosoever is born of God overcometh the world; and this is the victory that overcometh the world, even our *faith."* To the disciples Jesus said, *"Have faith* in God." Paul thunders out, *"Without faith* it is impossible to please Him: for he that cometh to God must believe that He is, and that He is a rewarder of them that diligently seek Him." Again, "The just shall *live by faith,"* and last, but by no means least, "Whatsoever is not of *faith* is *sin"!*

From these verses we see clearly that God Almighty deals in *faith*—and this faith comes through the Word of God. The Bible is the only authentic record we have concerning Almighty God. You can believe every word you read in the Bible . . .

about God, about Christ, about salvation, or any other subject that has to do with your life on earth and in eternity after this life. Yes, "faith cometh by hearing, and hearing by the Word of God." Failure to feed upon the Word of God is the reason some Christians do not have any more faith than they have. The more we read and study God's Word, the more faith we will have.

Verses 18 and 19: *"But I say, Have they not heard? Yes verily, their sound went into all the earth, and their words unto the ends of the world. But I say, Did not Israel know? First Moses saith, I will provoke you to jealousy by them that are no people, and by a foolish nation I will anger you."*

It has been shown that the Gospel which is necessary to faith has been universally given. Could it be that they who have not obeyed (v. 16) *"have . . . not heard?"* The answer to this is found in the Old Testament Scriptures:

"Yes verily, their sound went into all the earth, and their words unto the ends of the world." Here Paul quotes from Psalm 19:4, which reads as follows in the Amplified Bible: "Yet their voice (in evidence) goes out through all the earth, their sayings to the end of the world. Of the heavens has God made a tent for the sun."

The entire nineteenth Psalm proves that *nature itself* reveals God to man; therefore there is absolutely no excuse. All men are warned of God.

Nature reveals enough concerning God to make it the duty of man to worship the God of heaven and earth. The revelation through nature is by no means insignificant. God declares that the invisible things of Him "are clearly seen, . . . even His eternal power and Godhead; so that they are without excuse" (Rom. 1:20). Yes, the heavens *do* declare the glory of God. The skies *do* show forth the work of His hands. Day and night utter words . . . the voice of God; and there is no place on this earth where nature does not declare that there is a Supreme Being somewhere behind this great and wonderful universe. Therefore, man *is* without excuse.

"But I say, Did not Israel know?" The truth revealed in Psalm 19 certainly leaves the people of Israel without an excuse. Israel in its bigotry claimed it had a monopoly on salvation in spite of the fact that Moses and Isaiah predicted the salvation of the Gentiles.

"First Moses saith . . . ." Here Paul quotes from Deuteronomy 32:21, which reads: "They have moved me to jealousy with that which is not God; they have provoked me to anger with their vanities: and I will move them to jealousy with those which are not a people; I will provoke them to anger with a foolish nation." Moses predicted that God would *"provoke"* Israel, rejecting His salvation, *"to jealousy"* of the Gentiles by giving salvation to the latter, thus arousing in Israel a desire for the

same. The *"no people"* are the Gentiles, who are a "no people" in reference to God's heritage. Upon this basis God will provoke the nation Israel to jealousy.

The very calling of the Gentiles, predicted and interpreted as it is in the passage quoted, should itself have been a message to the Jews; it should have opened their eyes to the position in which they stood. The Gentiles were aliens from the commonwealth of Israel, strangers to the covenants of promise, referred to as "dogs" by the people of Israel. Surely if the *Gentile* nations were held responsible before God, how much more shall the nation of *Israel* be held responsible before God! To Israel, God revealed His commandments, His laws, and His righteousness. The oracles of God were committed to them; therefore they were doubly responsible to Almighty God.

Verses 20 and 21: *"But Esaias is very bold, and saith, I was found of them that sought me not; I was made manifest unto them that asked not after me. But to Israel He saith, All day long have I stretched forth my hands unto a disobedient and gainsaying people."*

In these verses Paul quotes from Isaiah 65:1, 2, which reads as follows in the Amplified Bible:

"I was ready to be inquired of by those who asked not; I was to be found by those who sought me not. I said, Here I am, here I AM to a nation

(Israel) that has not called on my name. I have spread out my hands all the day to a rebellious people, who walk in a way that is not good, after their own thoughts."

Isaiah is indeed *"very bold"* in his prophecy concerning the salvation of the Gentiles, *"them that sought me not . . . them that asked not after me."* Those who sought Him not, *found Him!* Even the heathen discover God; therefore Israel is inexcusable, and they will be judged by the God who would have saved them had they only listened to His voice and followed His will.

"But to Israel He saith, All day long have I stretched forth my hands . . . ." The hands outstretched all the day long are the symbol of that incessant pleading love which Israel through all of its history has consistently despised. God never ceased to plead with them; but they were *"disobedient and gainsaying."* But even in this rebellious state God calls them *"people,"* as opposed to the "no people" in verse 19—a hopeful word, with which the Apostle begins the next chapter: "Hath God cast away *His people?"*

Chapter XI

1. I say then, Hath God cast away his people? God forbid. For I also am an Israelite, of the seed of Abraham, of the tribe of Benjamin.

2. God hath not cast away his people which he foreknew. Wot ye not what the scripture saith of Elias? how he maketh intercession to God against Israel, saying,

3. Lord, they have killed thy prophets, and digged down thine altars; and I am left alone, and they seek my life.

4. But what saith the answer of God unto him? I have reserved to myself seven thousand men, who have not bowed the knee to the image of Baal.

5. Even so then at this present time also there is a remnant according to the election of grace.

6. And if by grace, then is it no more of works: otherwise grace is no more grace. But if it be of works, then is it no more grace: otherwise work is no more work.

7. What then? Israel hath not obtained that which he seeketh for; but the election hath obtained it, and the rest were blinded

8. (According as it is written, God hath given them the spirit of slumber, eyes that they should not see, and ears that they should not hear;) unto this day.

9. And David saith, Let their table be made a snare, and a trap, and a stumblingblock, and a recompence unto them:

10. Let their eyes be darkened, that they may not see, and bow down their back alway.

11. I say then, Have they stumbled that they should fall? God forbid: but rather through their fall salvation is come unto the Gentiles, for to provoke them to jealousy.

12. Now if the fall of them be the riches of the world, and the diminishing of them the riches of the Gentiles; how much more their fulness?

13. For I speak to you Gentiles, inasmuch as I am the apostle of the Gentiles, I magnify mine office:

14. If by any means I may provoke to emulation them which are my flesh, and might save some of them.

15. For if the casting away of them be the reconciling of the world, what shall the receiving of them be, but life from the dead?

16. For if the firstfruit be holy, the lump is also holy: and if the root be holy, so are the branches.

17. And if some of the branches be broken off, and thou, being a wild olive tree, wert graffed in among them, and with them partakest of the root and fatness of the olive tree;

18. Boast not against the branches. But if thou boast, thou bearest not the root, but the root thee.

19. Thou wilt say then, The branches were broken off, that I might be graffed in.

20. Well; because of unbelief they were broken off, and thou standest by faith. Be not highminded, but fear:

21. For if God spared not the natural branches, take heed lest he also spare not thee.

22. Behold therefore the goodness and severity of God: on them which fell, severity; but toward thee, goodness, if thou continue in his goodness: otherwise thou also shalt be cut off.

23. And they also, if they abide not still in unbelief, shall be graffed in: for God is able to graff them in again.

24. For if thou wert cut out of the olive tree which is wild by nature, and wert graffed contrary to nature into a good olive tree: how much more shall these, which be the natural branches, be graffed into their own olive tree?

25. For I would not, brethren, that ye should be ignorant of this mystery, lest ye should be wise in your own conceits; that blindness in part is happened to Israel, until the fulness of the Gentiles be come in.

26. And so all Israel shall be saved: as it is written, There shall come out of Sion the Deliverer, and shall turn away ungodliness from Jacob:

27. For this is my covenant unto them, when I shall take away their sins.

28. As concerning the gospel, they are enemies for your sakes: but as touching the election, they are beloved for the fathers' sakes.

29. For the gifts and calling of God are without repentance.

30. For as ye in times past have not believed God, yet have now obtained mercy through their unbelief:

31. Even so have these also now not believed, that through your mercy they also may obtain mercy.

32. For God hath concluded them all in unbelief, that he might have mercy upon all.

33. O the depth of the riches both of the wisdom and knowledge of God! how unsearchable are his judgments, and his ways past finding out!

34. For who hath known the mind of the Lord? or who hath been his counsellor?

35. Or who hath first given to him, and it shall be recompensed unto him again?

36. For of him, and through him, and to him, are all things: to whom be glory for ever. Amen.

Wuest introduces this chapter in the following words:

"Briefly, the ninth chapter means God is sovereign, and the tenth chapter means Israel has sinned. Both of these are presented in relative independence as explanations of the perplexing fact which confronted the Apostle; namely, that Israel did not receive the Gospel, while the Gentiles did. In chapter 11 the two are brought into relation to each other, and we are shown how in the providence of God even the sin of Israel is made to contribute to the working out of a universal purpose of redemption, a redemption which Israel also shares, in accordance with the promise of God."

God Has Not Cast Off His People

Verse 1: *"I say then, Hath God cast away His people? God forbid. For I also am an Israelite, of the seed of Abraham, of the tribe of Benjamin."*

From a historical point of view, chapter 11 is logically necessary. In the Old Testament, God promised Israel headship (or leadership) in the world worship of God, and this place they had held from the days of Moses until the day of Paul. Now God was using Paul to transfer that leadership to another nation (Matt. 21:43) . . . a spiritual nation, composed of saved persons called from all peoples (I Peter 2:9, 10). The promise of leadership was made to Israel—not on the ground of their

376

descent, as the ninth chapter of Romans clearly shows; but after all, it was a national promise. The promise belonged to the natural descent and carried with it their "advantage."

In Paul's day there were two facts evident: First, the Church had for the present displaced Israel in the leadership of God's worship in the world. In the second place, the promises made to Israel in their oracles given to them by God, were not realized in the Church, and could not be. The *Church* knows no racial distinctions, and the very essence of *Judaism* was complete separation from other people.

The first fact Paul has already considered in Romans chapters 9 and 10. Paul proved that Israel was justly displaced by God, and their blindness had come about by their own fault.

It is with the second fact that the present chapter deals. Israel as a separate people will be restored and will realize the promises made to them by Jehovah in the Old Testament. God's far-reaching plans, in the riches of His glorious wisdom for the salvation of the world, are here disclosed. In this chapter we see that Israel's failure proves to be the world's wealth at this time, and it will prove to be *their* wealth finally, in God's own good time. God has not forgotten His people, nor will He ever forget them.

Paul asks, *"Hath God cast away His people?"* Then he thunders back, *"God forbid!"* He argues,

377

"I also am an Israelite—and if the Israelites as such were cut off, I would be included. The fact that I have been saved is proof to show that God has not cast away His people."

That Israel has not been forever set aside is the theme of this chapter:

1. The conversion of Saul of Tarsus, who became Paul the Apostle, proves there is still a remnant (verse 1).

2. The fact that verses 2 through 6 speak of the remnant, proves God has not cast off Israel forever.

3. The present condition of the Jews—national unbelief—was foreseen and prophesied, according to verses 7 through 10.

4. Israel's unbelief is the Gentile's opportunity. If Israel had not rejected their Messiah, then the door of salvation would never have been opened to the Gentile. The blindness of the Jew brought light to the Gentiles—and in the end, a nation will be born in a day and God will restore all of the glory to Israel (verses 11-25).

5. Israel is judicially broken off from the good olive tree (verses 17-22).

6. Israel will be grafted in again, in God's own good time and according to God's eternal blueprint (verses 23 and 24).

7. The promised Deliverer, the Lord Jesus, who came the first time and was rejected by Israel, will come out of Zion and the nation will be saved (verses 25-29).

Chapter 11:1-4

The believer does not inherit the distinctive Jewish promises taught in the Scripture. When we believe on the Lord Jesus Christ and are saved, we do not receive the promises God made to Abraham. True, the Christian is of the heavenly seed of Abraham (Gen. 15:5, 6; Gal. 3:29) and partakes of the spiritual blessings of the Abrahamic covenant (Gen. 15:18), but Israel as a nation always has its own place in God's program; and Israel is yet to have its greatest exaltation as the chosen earthly people of Jehovah God. Israel is an earthly people, with earthly blessings. The *Church* is a *heavenly* people, a royal priesthood, called to sit together in heavenly places in Christ Jesus.

The Church and Israel are not one and the same. The Church is the body of Christ, the bride of Christ, and He is the Head and the Saviour of the body. The Church did not inherit the promises made to Abraham. To Abraham was promised the land, a kingdom, a King. Jesus is the King who will reign over the house of Jacob forever—but Jesus is not the King of the Church; He is the HEAD of the Church and the Saviour of the body. (Read Ephesians 1:22, 23; 5:22-32; I Corinthians 12:12-14; Colossians 1:18.) It is spiritual robbery to take the blessings, the promises, God gave to Abraham and to Israel, and apply them to the Church and to this Dispensation of Grace.

Verses 2-4: *"God hath not cast away His people*

which He foreknew. Wot ye not what the Scripture saith of Elias? how he maketh intercession to God against Israel, saying, Lord, they have killed thy prophets, and digged down thine altars; and I am left alone, and they seek my life. But what saith the answer of God unto him? I have reserved to myself seven thousand men, who have not bowed the knee to the image of Baal.''

"God hath not cast away His people which He foreknew.'' God would not cast away His people because in His own eternal decree before the world began, He selected as His chosen people the nation Israel. They were His own, the receiver of His law. We must take "foreknew" to mean that Israel stood before God's eyes *from eternity* as His people, and in the immutableness of His sovereign love with which He made the nation His, lies the impossibility of its rejection. (Read Hebrews 6:13-17.)

"Wot ye not what the Scripture saith of Elias?" The Old Testament reference to Elijah is found in I Kings 19:10-18. Elijah said, *"Lord, they have killed thy prophets, . . . and they seek my life.''* Elijah thought that he was alone, that out of all Israel he was the only one left who had been true to God. But Elijah was sadly mistaken. God had preserved a remnant of *"seven thousand men"* who had not turned aside to worship Baal; they *had not "bowed the knee to the image of Baal.''*

Verses 5 and 6: *"Even so then at this present time also there is a remnant according to the election of grace. And if by grace, then is it no more of works: otherwise grace is no more grace. But if it be of works, then is it no more grace: otherwise work is no more work."*

"Even so then at this present time . . . ." Paul was better acquainted with his days than Elijah had been with the period to which he belonged. Paul knew that in every church there were some Jews who had accepted Christ, *"a remnant according to the election of grace."* They had not "bowed the knee" to the Baal of unbelief. Paul himself was a part of this "remnant according to the election of grace." Paul was a Jew—but he was a preacher of the marvelous grace of God.

"And if by grace, then is it no more of works . . . ." Verse 6 is spiritual dynamite against those who try to mix law and grace. What Paul is saying in this verse is simply this: Grace is God's unmerited favor to man, "works" is man seeking to present to God a human ground for blessing. The two principles are utterly opposed. If the remnant was selected on the grounds of grace, their legal works had no part whatsoever in the selection; else the grace would have lost its character as grace. Could it be made clearer? Could it be made plainer, that law and grace positively do not mix?

Let me point out here that in the history of
Israel, the remnant may be discerned as *spiritual*
Israel within *national* Israel. The remnant does
not apply to all Israel, but to the part of Israel
that has obeyed God throughout their history. In
Elijah's day, there were seven thousand who had
not bowed their knees to the image of Baal (I
Kings 19:18). Then later, in the day of Isaiah,
there was a "very small remnant" for whose sake
God still withheld judgment and did not destroy
the nation (Isaiah 1:9). During the captivities
described in Ezekiel, there were faithful Jews like
Daniel, Shadrach, Meshach, Abednego, Esther,
and Mordecai. Then, at the end of the seventy
years of Babylonian captivity, it was the remnant
that returned under Ezra and Nehemiah, to rebuild
the wall around Jerusalem.

When John the Baptist (the forerunner of the
Lord Jesus Christ) came on the scene, the remnant
seemed to be Simeon and Anna, and "them that
looked for redemption in Jerusalem" (Luke 2:25-38).
During the Church Age, the remnant is made up
of all believing Jews (Rom. 11:5).

After the Church is raptured out of the earth,
during the reign of the Antichrist and the course
of the Great Tribulation, a remnant out of all
Israel will return to the Lord Jesus Christ and
receive Him as their Messiah, and will become His
witnesses here on earth (Rev. 7:3-8). They will
preach the Gospel of the Kingdom to every creature

on this earth. Many of these will be killed (Rev. 6:9-11; 7:9-17). Some will be spared, and will enter the Millennium (Zech. 12:6; 13:9).

Verse 7: *"What then? Israel hath not obtained that which he seeketh for; but the election hath obtained it, and the rest were blinded."*

The Jews as a people have not obtained that which they sought (that is, salvation by their own obedience to the Law). They sought salvation by their own merit, and as salvation is by grace through faith, they as a people failed of obtaining God's favor, and were rejected.

Verse 7 tells us that the *elect remnant* of Israel . . . that is, *spiritual* Israel . . . *obtained* what the *nation* (or natural) Israel failed to find. But since the remnant were saved by *grace,* there was no injustice done to the rest.

"Were blinded," according to *Vine's New Testament Dictionary,* "signifies *to harden* (from *poros,* a thick skin, a hardening)."

Verse 8: *"(According as it is written, God hath given them the spirit of slumber, eyes that they should not see, and ears that they should not hear;) unto this day."*

Paul says all in Israel not included in the remnant chosen to salvation by sovereign grace were hardened (v. 7). He explains this hardening in that *God gave them a "spirit of slumber,"* an insensibility of heart that made them insensible to the Gospel, *sightless eyes*, and *deaf ears*. How are we to understand this, in the light of God's Word that says Jesus died for the world, and "whosoever will may come"? *Moses* records the fact that God hardened *Pharaoh's* heart, but not until Pharaoh had first hardened his own heart. The original hardening came from Pharaoh's own free will and a depraved nature. God only hardened Pharaoh's heart by forcing him to an issue which he did not want to meet. The more he rebelled, the more hardened his heart became. So in the same manner Israel was forced into a decision. Israel rejected Jesus, and the more they did so the harder their heart became. Spiritual light rejected blinds the eyes.

Here in verse 8 Paul quotes (not literally) from Isaiah 29:10 and Deuteronomy 29:4 to show that the Jews' own Scriptures taught them clearly beforehand that they could not reject Almighty God and not suffer the consequences. The teaching is very solemn. Long-drawn-out, continued abuse of God's goodness and grace automatically brought terrible, horrible punishment upon the chosen of God...Israel.

The principle is unfolded in Isaiah's dreadful commission, recorded in Isaiah chapter 6. Isaiah saw a vision of the King, Jehovah of hosts. The vision filled Isaiah with horror because of his own sinful condition and the sinful condition of his people. Whether it be Isaiah, you, or me...there is nothing that will reveal unto man his utter hopelessness, uncleanness, and total depravity, like a look at the Lord. When Isaiah saw Him, he cried out, "Woe is me! for I am undone; because I am a man of unclean lips, and I dwell in the midst of a people of unclean lips: for mine eyes have seen the King, the Lord of hosts" (Isaiah 6:5).

A seraph flew unto the Prophet Isaiah with a live coal from God's altar, and touching Isaiah's mouth with the live coal, announced the purging and the forgiveness of his sins. A voice was then heard—Jehovah spoke: "Whom shall I send, and who will go for us?" Then Isaiah cried out, "Here am I; send me!"

I want you to notice the commission Almighty God gave to Isaiah in verses 9 and 10:

"And He (Jehovah) said, *GO, and tell this people* (Israel, God's chosen people), *Hear ye indeed, but understand not; and see ye indeed, but perceive not. Make the heart of this people fat, and make their ears heavy, and shut their eyes; lest they see with their eyes, and hear with their ears, and understand with their heart, and convert, and be healed.*"

The Prophet, hearing these terrible words of judgment, must have been terrified! In agony he cried out to Jehovah, "LORD, HOW LONG?" Then Jehovah answered: "Until the cities be wasted without inhabitant, and the houses without

man, and the land be utterly desolate, and the
Lord have removed men far away, and there be a
great forsaking in the midst of the land. But yet
in it shall be a tenth, and it shall return, and shall
be eaten: as a teil tree, and as an oak, whose
substance is in them, when they cast their leaves:
so the holy seed shall be the substance thereof"
(verses 11-13). (In verse 13 Jehovah reveals to
Isaiah that the holy seed, the spiritual seed, will
never pass away, will never cease to be.)

Again and again the prophecy found in Isaiah
chapter 6 is quoted in the New Testament, and
its fulfillment definitely pointed out:

In Matthew 13:13-17, replying to a question as
to why He had begun to teach the people in parables, *our Lord* replied: "Because they seeing see
not; and hearing they hear not, neither do they
understand. *And in them is fulfilled the prophecy
of Esaias,* which saith, By hearing ye shall hear,
and shall not (in no wise) understand; and seeing
ye shall see, and shall not (in no wise) perceive:
for this people's heart is waxed gross, and their
ears are dull of hearing, and their eyes they have
closed; lest at any time they should see (perceive)
with their eyes and hear with their ears, and
should understand with their heart, and should be
converted, and I should heal them. But blessed
are your eyes, for they see: and your ears, for
they hear. For verily I say unto you, That many
prophets and righteous men have desired to see

those things which ye see, and have not seen them; and to hear those things which ye hear, and have not heard them." (Also see Mark 4:12 and Luke 8:10. I would like to suggest that you turn in your Bible and read these chapters in their entirety.)

John tells us that some of those who *heard* the Lord were unable to believe: "But though He had done so many miracles before them, yet they believed not on Him: That the saying of Esaias the prophet might be fulfilled, which he spake, Lord, who hath believed our report? and to whom hath the arm of the Lord been revealed? Therefore *they could not believe*, because that Esaias said again, He hath blinded their eyes, and hardened their heart; that they should not see with their eyes, nor understand with their heart, and be converted, and I should heal them. *These things said Esaias, when he saw His glory, and spake of Him*" (John 12:37-41).

These words of Isaiah are also referred to in Acts 28:25-28: "And when they agreed not among themselves, they departed, after that Paul had spoken one word, *Well spake the Holy Ghost by Esaias the prophet unto our fathers*, saying, Go thou unto this people, and say, Hearing ye shall hear, and shall not understand; and seeing ye shall see, and not perceive: For the heart of this people is waxed gross, and their ears are dull of hearing, and their eyes have they closed; lest they should see with their eyes, and hear with their ears, and understand with their heart, and should be converted, and I should heal them. Be it known therefore unto you, that the salvation of God is sent unto the Gentiles, and that they will hear it."

Thus we learn that upon Israel had come that which was prophesied... that is, the consequences of hearing the Word of God but refusing to *obey* the Word. (Read James 1:22-25.) This judicial hardening continues upon Israel even unto this very day. Nineteen centuries have come and gone since the Epistle to the Romans was dictated to the Apostle Paul and he penned it down! Israel as a nation is still hardened. Israel is still far, far from God.

Verses 9 and 10: *"And David saith, Let their table be made a snare, and a trap, and a stumblingblock, and a recompence unto them: Let their eyes be darkened, that they may not see, and bow down their back alway."*

Here Paul quotes from Psalm 69:22, 23. This Psalm has to do with the sufferings of the Lord Jesus Christ. If anyone doubts that Christ is the theme of Psalm 69, compare verse 9 with John 2:17 and Romans 15:3. Then read Psalm 69:21, and compare it with Matthew 27:34, 48; Mark 15:23, 36; Luke 23:36; and John 19:28-30. Read Psalm 69:22 and compare with Romans 11:9, 10. Compare Psalm 69:25 with Matthew 23:38; Luke 13:35; and Acts 1:20.

The Speaker in the sixty-ninth Psalm is undoubtedly the Lord Jesus Christ. Hear Him as He cries out: "Reproach hath broken my heart; and I am full of heaviness: and I looked for some to take pity, but there was none; and for comforters, but I found none. They gave me also gall for my meat; and in my thirst they gave me vinegar to drink" (verses 20, 21). Surely anyone who knows anything about the Gospels and the prophecies concerning the suffering Christ, would readily admit that these words could have been spoken by none other than the Lamb of God! This Scripture I have just given you was literally fulfilled on the cross.

The Jew's carnal security—that is, his carnal pride and self-confidence while trusting in the Law of Moses—proved to be his spiritual ruin. In other words, the Jew was self-confident, self-righteous, self-satisfied. He had his faith in his own ability to establish his own righteousness, and such a confidence in his own ability proved to be the downfall and the ruin of the Jewish nation. Today such a spirit will prove to be the ruin of the Gentile.

Verses 11 and 12: *"I say then, Have they stumbled that they should fall? God forbid: but rather through their fall salvation is come unto the Gentiles, for to provoke them to jealousy. Now if the fall of them be the riches of the world, and*

*the diminishing of them the riches of the Gentiles;
how much more their fulness?"*

That Israel has fallen cannot be denied; but is
this the end of Israel? Does God have no future
for Israel? Must we accuse God of being unfaithful
to Israel, to the covenant He made with Abraham?
Has Israel stumbled and fallen beyond the reach
of God's hand? Paul answers: *"God forbid!"* No,
God has not forgotten His people. Abraham asked,
"Shall not the Judge of all the earth do right?"
(Gen. 18:25). The answer is: "Yes!" Jehovah God
made a covenant with Abraham that was everlasting. Every promise God made to His people,
Israel, will be fulfilled in its entirety.

God has a purpose, a divine purpose, an eternal
purpose, in the stumbling of Israel: *"... through
their fall salvation is come unto the Gentiles."*
But that is not the only purpose God had in permitting national Israel to be blinded. Notice:
". . . through their fall salvation is come unto the
Gentiles, *FOR TO PROVOKE THEM* (the Jews)
TO JEALOUSY." Jealousy is literally *"to stimulate
alongside,* and its force here is *to excite to rivalry"*
(Strong). God in His providence used the stumbling of Israel as an occasion to bring His salvation to the Gentiles, and this latter as a means
whereby He could incite in Israel a desire for the
salvation they had rejected.

In verse 12 we read: *"Now if the fall of them*
(Israel) *be the riches of the world, . . . how much*

more their fulness?" Everything worth-while that has come to the Gentile world has come through Israel; and if blessings such as these have come through the stumbling and the falling of Israel, what wealth is in store for them in the great return, when all Israel shall be saved!

One day Israel will accept Him whom they pierced, a nation will be born in a day, and God will give to Israel every square inch of ground He promised to Abraham. The glorious Kingdom Age will run its course of one thousand glorious years right here on this earth, King Jesus will sit on the throne in Jerusalem and reign over the house of Jacob—and we, the Gentile bride, will reign with Him.

It is God's plan to bless the whole wide world through the Jew—and God will do this in His own appointed time, according to His own blueprint of the ages:

"He shall cause them that come of Jacob to take root: *Israel shall blossom and bud, and fill the face of the world with fruit"* (Isaiah 27:6).

"Arise, shine; for thy light is come, and the glory of the Lord is risen upon thee. For, behold, the darkness shall cover the earth, and gross darkness the people: but the Lord shall arise upon thee, and His glory shall be seen upon thee. And *the Gentiles shall come to thy light, and kings to the brightness of thy rising* (resurrection from the dead)" (Isaiah 60:1-3).

And so the Scriptures clearly teach that Israel must come into their blessing from Jehovah before the *Gentiles* receive the fulness of God's blessings upon them. The Psalmist said: "God be merciful unto us, and bless us; and cause His face to shine upon us; Selah. That thy way may be known upon earth, thy saving health among all nations. . . . *God shall bless us; and all the ends of the earth shall fear Him*" (Psalm 67:1, 2, 7).

Paul Warns the Gentiles

Verses 13 and 14: *"For I speak to you Gentiles, inasmuch as I am the apostle of the Gentiles, I magnify mine office: If by any means I may provoke to emulation them which are my flesh, and might save some of them."*

I love all of the Word of God—and every word in the Bible is God's Word. I believe it is all inspired. I love it from Genesis to Revelation; but I must confess that I am somewhat partial to the writings of Paul. Paul testified that God separated him from his mother's womb (Gal. 1:15, 16) to be the apostle to the Gentiles. Since I am a Gentile, and a believer, I am a member of the Gentile bride (Acts 15:13-18). Perhaps that is the reason the writings of Paul are so precious to me—especially the Book of Romans.

Paul was God's *"apostle of the Gentiles."* He was a chosen vessel, ordained by God a minister to the Gentiles (Acts 9:15). Even though he was a freeborn Roman Jew, he was not ashamed of his office as a minister to the despised Gentiles. Instead of being ashamed, he "magnified" his office. He let one and all know that he was happy to carry the message to the people to whom God sent him. He testified, ". . . *I magnify mine office: If by any means I may provoke to emulation them which are my flesh, and might save some of them.*"

Wuest puts it this way: "I do my ministry honor, if by any means, possibly, I may provoke to jealousy those who are my flesh, and save some of them."

Paul had a deep, burning desire to see his own dear people come to the knowledge of salvation. He was willing to make any personal sacrifice if it would win even just a few of his kinsmen according to the flesh.

Verse 15: *"For if the casting away of them be the reconciling of the world, what shall the receiving of them be, but life from the dead?"*

"The casting away" of Israel the nation temporarily, was a channel through which God brought the Gospel of salvation to the Gentiles, with the view of bringing Israel back into fellowship with Himself and His service in the Millennium.

"The receiving of them" refers to that wonderful moment when the Lord returns to the Mount of Olives (Zech. 14:4) and "all Israel shall be saved"

(Rom. 11:26). This will be *"life from (among) the dead,"* in that the nation will be saved by the grace of God out from a spiritually dead state and from among those who remain spiritually dead. (Read Ezekiel chapters 36 and 37.)

I repeat what I said previously: The best is just ahead—that is, the glorious kingdom God promised to Abraham; and we, the Gentile bride, will reign with Jesus, our Bridegroom. What a glorious day that one thousand years of "peace on earth" will be!

Verse 16: *"For if the firstfruit be holy, the lump is also holy: and if the root be holy, so are the branches."*

"Firstfruit" does not apply exhaustively to harvest, but is a general term referring to the first portion of everything which is offered to God. The reference here is to Numbers 15:18-21. A handful of dough was presented to God as a token of the lump from which the dough was taken. By "the firstfruit" Paul means the saved Jewish remnant, and of course that included himself and all believers in Israel at the time he uttered those words. By *"the lump"* Paul means the entire nation of Israel—all twelve tribes.

"The root" refers strictly to *Abraham.* The natural branches are the descendants of Abraham according to the flesh—that is, through Isaac and Jacob, "the heirs with him of the same promise."

Verses 17-24: *"And if some of the branches be broken off, and thou, being a wild olive tree, wert graffed in among them, and with them partakest of the root and fatness of the olive tree; boast not against the branches. But if thou boast, thou bearest not the root, but the root thee. Thou wilt say then, The branches were broken off, that I might be graffed in. Well; because of unbelief they were broken off, and thou standest by faith. Be not highminded, but fear: For if God spared not the natural branches, take heed lest He also spare not thee. Behold therefore the goodness and severity of God: on them which fell, severity; but toward thee, goodness, if thou continue in His goodness: otherwise thou also shalt be cut off. And they also, if they abide not still in unbelief, shall be graffed in: for God is able to graff them in again. For if thou wert cut out of the olive tree which is wild by nature, and wert graffed contrary to nature into a good olive tree: how much more shall these, which be the natural branches, be graffed into their own olive tree?"*

In these verses Paul is clearly teaching us that through unbelief Israel has been cut off for a season, and God has turned from them to the Gentiles. However, if the Gentiles continue not in faith, if they believe not, they too will be cast aside by Almighty God.

The *"branches . . . broken off"* refers to the

rejection of the nation Israel, the Dispersion in A. D. 70 and God's act of setting them aside temporarily, as the channel through which He could bring salvation to the Gentiles.

The *"wild olive tree" grafted in* refers to the act of God of breaking down the middle wall of partition between Jew and Gentile at the cross, and including the Gentile with the Jew in one body, the Church (Eph. 2:11-19; 3:6).

Paul's figure is that the Jewish nation is a tree from which some branches are cut off, but which remains living because of the root (and therefore all the branches connected with it are still alive). Into this living tree, the wild branch (the Gentiles) is grafted, drawing life from the root (v. 17).

". . . boast not against the branches." The warning is that the wild branches should not gloat or boast over the natural branches (which were cut off), for they draw their life from the same root. It is very plain that the Gentiles receive their blessing through the Jew, not the Jew through the Gentiles (v. 18).

Paul also testifies here that God has acted *"contrary to nature"* (v. 24); that is, the process of grafting is to insert a *good branch* into an *inferior tree.* The case is reversed here in Paul's figure. Wuest says, "Graft the good upon the wild, and as the Arabs say, it will conquer the wild; but you cannot reverse the process with success. . . . It is only in the Kingdom of Grace that a process thus contrary to nature can be successful." And it is in this circumstance—"that which was contrary to nature"—that Paul is magnifying God's mercy shown to Gentiles, a wild branch grafted into the natural and causing them to flourish and bring forth fruit unto eternal life.

"If God spared not the natural branches, take heed lest He also spare not thee." Verse 21, I think, should be interpreted that the nation Israel and the Gentiles *as a race* are in view—not an individual Gentile. In other words, Paul is not speaking of an individual Gentile who boasts against the Jew being cut off, but is saying that if God spared not His own chosen people *"because of unbelief"* (v. 20), why would He spare Gentiles?

If verse 21 is interpreted to mean *nations*, it should be clear that Paul is not speaking of individual saved Gentiles being cut off from their salvation, but the unsaved *nation* being cut off, as unsaved Israel was cut off in the Dispersion. (In the future God will bring salvation to His covenant people, Israel—and it will be perfectly logical for God to do that because Israel *is* the natural olive tree and God is able to bring them back and save them as a nation.)

There is one thing I want to point out before leaving this portion of Scripture, and that is a statement in verse 22: *"Behold therefore the goodness and severity of God."* Today we are hearing a lot about the "good" God, the "loving" God, the "fatherhood of God," the "brotherhood of man," and statements such as "The loving God would not permit a soul to go to hell," "God is too GOOD to allow men to burn in hell." Yes, God *is* a "good" God. God is a long-suffering God. God is a merciful God—but I would like to remind the liberals and the modernists that God Almighty is *"a consuming fire"!* (Heb. 12:29). I would also like to remind them that "God judgeth the righteous, and *God is angry with the wicked every day"* (Psalm 7:11). And again, "The wicked shall be turned into hell, and all the nations that forget God" (Psalm 9:17). And again: "It is *a fearful thing* to fall into the hands of the living God" (Heb. 10:31). And again: "As I live, saith the Lord, every knee shall bow to me, and every tongue shall confess to God" (Rom. 14:11). Yes, God is a good God, God is love; but God can be severe. God wants to be good to you and to me, and God *will* be good to us if we will allow Him. But if we refuse and rebel, God can be severe!

This fact is outstanding in the history of Israel. The Israelites were enslaved in Egypt, in captivity in Babylon; and Titus, the Roman emperor, butchered millions of them. Following their more recent history we find that the Nazi regime annihilated six million! Down through the pages of history, when Israel has rebelled against God, God has dealt with them in utmost severity. (Read Psalm 78.)

398

The Nation Israel Is Yet to Be Saved

Verse 25: *"For I would not, brethren, that ye should be ignorant of this mystery, lest ye should be wise in your own conceits; that blindness in part is happened to Israel, until the fulness of the Gentiles be come in."*

A *mystery* in Scripture is "a hidden purpose or counsel of God which, when revealed, is understood by the believer." Paul refers here to *"this mystery"*—*"that blindness in part is happened to Israel . . . ."* He says to his brethren in the church (believers) that *he does not want us to "be ignorant"* concerning why the blindness has happened to Israel, *"lest ye (believers) should be wise in your own conceits."* Paul goes on to enlighten us that this blindness is not forever, and that it is only "in part" because there is a saved remnant, even today, and this blindness will continue *"until the fulness of the Gentiles be come in."*

"The fulness of the Gentiles" refers to the completion of the purpose of Almighty God in this Dispensation of Grace—or, the Church Age—when He is calling out from among the Gentiles a people for His name . . . the Church, which is His body. (Read Acts 15:14; I Corinthians 12:12, 13; Ephesians 1:22, 23; 4:11-13.) When the Church is complete and caught out of this earth to meet the Lord Jesus in the air, God will turn again to Israel; and when they see Jesus whom they pierced, they will accept Him, a nation will be born in a day, and God will save His people, Israel.

"The fulness of the Gentiles" must be distinguished from "the *times* of the Gentiles," mentioned in Luke 21:24. "The *times* of the Gentiles" refers to the time from Nebuchadnezzar's deportation of David's kingdom to the defeat of the Antichrist at the end of the Tribulation—the time the Gentiles rule over the Jews. The term *"fulness* of the Gentiles"* refers to the completion of the body of Christ, made up of Jew and Gentile saved from Pentecost to the Rapture.

Verses 26 and 27: *"And so all Israel shall be saved: as it is written, There shall come out of Sion the Deliverer, and shall turn away ungodliness from Jacob: For this is my covenant unto them, when I shall take away their sins."*

What the Holy Spirit is telling us here is simply this: *"All Israel shall be saved"* as it is written, or prophesied, in God's holy Word. Everything Almighty God has promised must come to pass "as it is written." The Scriptures teach us clearly that a time is coming when Almighty God will save the *nation* of Israel—not just a remnant. This does not refer to the born again during the Dispensation of Grace, but the whole nation of Israel that will be alive when "that day" comes. It has nothing to do with the Israelites who died in unbelief during this Dispensation of Grace. The Jew is saved today just like the Gentile; and if the Jew refuses to receive the Lord Jesus, he will be lost just as will the Gentile who refuses to believe on the Lord Jesus Christ. But the nation will be saved.

"*. . . as it is written, There shall come out of Sion the Deliverer, and shall turn away ungodliness from Jacob.*" Here Paul quotes from Isaiah 59:20, where we read: "And the Redeemer shall come to Zion, and unto them that turn from transgression in Jacob, saith the Lord." Jesus came to the Jew, but the Jew rejected Him and had Him nailed to a cross. But "THE FOUNDATION OF GOD STANDETH SURE"—and since God's Word cannot be broken, since God's covenant cannot be broken, "ALL ISRAEL SHALL BE SAVED." David said, "Oh that the salvation of Israel were come out of Zion! when the Lord bringeth back the captivity of His people, Jacob shall rejoice, and Israel shall be glad" (Psalm 14:7). God has not forgotten His covenant with Abraham, He has not forgotten His promise; and in due time God will fulfill every jot and every tittle of His Word.

"*For this is my covenant unto them, when I shall take away their sins.*" In Jeremiah 31:31-35 we read the covenant, and the terms of the covenant, which God made with Israel:

"Behold, the days come, saith the Lord, that I will make a new covenant with the house of Israel, and with the house of Judah: not according to the covenant that I made with their fathers in the day that I took them by the hand to bring them out of the land of Egypt; which my covenant they brake, although I was an husband unto them, saith the Lord:

"But this shall be the covenant that I will make with the house of Israel; After those days, saith the Lord, I will put my law in their inward parts, and write it in their hearts; and will be their God, and they shall be my people. And they shall teach no more every man his neighbour, and every man his brother, saying, Know the Lord: for they shall all know me, from the least of them unto the greatest of them, saith the Lord: for I will forgive their iniquity, and I will remember their sin no more.

"Thus saith the Lord, which giveth the sun for a light by day, and the ordinances of the moon and of the stars for a light by night, which divideth the sea when the waves thereof roar; The Lord of hosts is His name." (Also read Isaiah 59:21.)

Hear this again: ". . . FOR THEY SHALL ALL KNOW ME, FROM THE LEAST OF THEM UNTO THE GREATEST OF THEM, SAITH THE LORD (JEHOVAH): FOR I WILL FORGIVE THEIR INIQUITY, AND I WILL REMEMBER THEIR SIN NO MORE"! (Jer. 31:34). Those words are the words of Jehovah God to *Israel*, and they cannot be broken, regardless of what some teachers and preachers say today . . . namely, those who teach and preach that we, the English speaking people, are Israel. Such a doctrine is being taught throughout the English speaking world. These teachers take the promises God made to Abraham and give them to the Church. Such a teaching is nothing short of spiritual robbery. One day God will fulfill every promise He made to Abraham.

Verses 28 and 29: *"As concerning the Gospel, they are enemies for your sakes: but as touching the election, they are beloved for the fathers' sakes. For the gifts and calling of God are without repentance."*

God's attitude to Israel in this Dispensation of Grace is determined by or with reference to *"the Gospel."* The nation of Israel rejected the Gospel, and in view of that rejection God counts Israel as *"enemies."* The attitude of God toward Israel with reference to *"the election"*—the elect remnant in that nation—is that those whom He counts enemies because of their rejection of the Gospel are still *"beloved"* ones, and this *for the sake of Abraham, Isaac, and Jacob,* with whom He made an everlasting covenant.

This is the age of the Gentiles, or the Gentile day—the day in which the Lord God is calling out a Gentile bride. (Read Acts 15:13-18.) But the Gentiles must take advantage of the opportunity afforded them through the blindness of Israel at this particular time. However, the Gentiles should not forget, lest they become proud, that Israel is still God's elect nation. The Gentiles should never forget that the promises God made to the fathers, God will keep:

"For the gifts and calling of God are without repentance." That is, the gifts and the calling God promised Israel will never be taken back. God does not make a promise and then take it back: "God is not a man, that He should lie; neither the son of man, that He should repent: *hath He said, and shall He not do it? or hath He spoken, and shall He not make it good?"* (Num. 23:19). God never changes . . . He is the same— yesterday, today, and forever. Therefore God will keep every promise and fulfill in full the covenant with faithful Abraham and the elect nation Israel.

Verses 30 and 31: *"For as ye in times past have not believed God, yet have now obtained mercy through their unbelief: Even so have these also now not believed, that through your mercy they also may obtain mercy."*

"For as ye in times past . . . ." The Gentiles once *disbelieved God* and were "dead in sins" (Eph. 2:1); but they *"have now obtained mercy"* by the unbelief of the Jews, as described in verses 11 and 12 of this chapter. And just so *"these"* (the Jews) *"have . . . not believed, that through your mercy* (the same mercy shown to you) *they also*

may obtain mercy." Through the inspiration of the Holy Spirit, Paul is assuring all that God in due time will fulfill every promise to Israel, and God will have mercy on His elect.

Verse 32: *"For God hath concluded them all in unbelief, that He might have mercy upon all."*

The thought here is that God has confined both Jew and Gentile within the scope of one kind of guilt—that of unbelief—that He might have mercy on all. *Wuest's* translation of verses 30 through 32 is very helpful: "For, even as you formerly disbelieved God, yet now have been made recipients of mercy through (the occasion of) their unbelief, thus also these now have disbelieved in order that through (the occasion of) the mercy which is yours, they themselves also might become the recipients of mercy, *for God has corralled all within (the state) of unbelief in order that He might have mercy upon all."*

In other words, both Jews and Gentiles are all in the state of unbelief, that God might have mercy upon ALL—not just upon one nation, Israel, or one people, the Gentiles; but upon Jews, Gentiles— or "whosoever." ALL are in the same boat spiritually, and until a person becomes a believer, whether he be Jew or Gentile, he is lost. The only way for anyone in this Dispensation of Grace to become a child of God is to believe on the Lord Jesus Christ, accept His finished work by faith.

In other words, if the Jews had fully obeyed God, they could have experienced no more than God's fidelity; grace and mercy wholly exclude privilege or merit.

To the Ephesians Paul declares: "But God, who is rich in mercy, for His great love wherewith He loved us, even when we were dead in sins, hath quickened us together with Christ, (by grace ye are saved)" (Eph. 2:4,5). In the first three verses of Ephesians chapter 2, Paul describes the Gentiles as walking "according to the course of this world," following the "prince of the power of the air," the devil; and as "the children of disobedience," following the lusts of the flesh, "the desires of the flesh and of the mind," who were "by nature the children of wrath"—or, the children of the devil. . . . "BUT GOD . . . ."

You see, *man*—whether Jew or Gentile—is totally and entirely depraved . . . hopeless, helpless, and hell-bound. *"But God"* . . . rich in mercy, extended His great love to us, even when we were dead in sins. Through the grace of the Lord Jesus Christ, God raised us to spiritual life. So we see that God included all within the state of unbelief, in order that He might have mercy upon all. I am so thankful salvation is offered to "whosoever" . . . ALL are included, none are excluded, regardless of race, color, or creed.

Certainly the "all" here in Romans 11:32 does not mean that all nations—Jews and Gentiles—

will be saved. It does not teach universal salvation. *"But the Scripture hath concluded all under sin, that the promise by faith of Jesus Christ might be given TO THEM THAT BELIEVE"* (Gal. 3:22). The Word of God is certainly clear that universal salvation is not a Bible doctrine, but a man-made dogma of religion. *God saves only those who believe on the Lord Jesus Christ.*

What the Apostle Paul realized and saw in his day is still a world-wide condition spiritually. The nations are still in sin and unbelief. Israel still refuses to believe on the Christ.

Praise to God

Verses 33-36: *"O the depth of the riches both of the wisdom and knowledge of God! How unsearchable are His judgments, and His ways past finding out! For who hath known the mind of the Lord? or who hath been His counsellor? Or who hath first given to Him, and it shall be recompensed unto him again? For of Him, and through Him, and to Him, are all things: to whom be glory for ever. Amen."*

This eleventh chapter of Romans closes with a song of praise to God. After considering the ways of God—in view of His mercies and His grace—Paul now bursts forth into praise: *"O the depth of the riches both of the wisdom and knowledge of God!"* The Apostle fully realizes his inability to sound the bottom of God's wisdom and knowledge with human reason and words. God is omnipotent, omniscient, omnipresent; *"His judgments"* are *"unsearchable," "His ways past finding out!"* "Past finding out" is literally "cannot be traced or found out." (Read Job 5:9 and 11:7.)

"For who hath known the mind of the Lord? . . ." Here Paul quotes again from the prophecy of Isaiah, where we find these words: "Who hath directed the Spirit of the Lord, or being His counsellor hath taught Him? With whom took He counsel, and who instructed Him, and taught Him in the path of judgment, and taught Him knowledge, and shewed to Him the way of understanding?" (Isaiah 40:13, 14).

"Or who hath first given to Him . . . ?" This verse is a quotation from Job 41:11, where God said to Job: "Who hath prevented me, that I should repay him? Whatsoever is under the whole heaven is mine."

I am so glad that in the very outset of this Epistle, Paul announced, "THE JUST SHALL LIVE BY FAITH" (1:17). *Faith accepts what God says BECAUSE GOD SAID IT.* Faith accepts what God promises, without feeling, without seeing, without tasting, without handling. Faith walks with God in the dark. Therefore faith never questions God. Like Abraham, men of faith *believe God.* And like *Paul,* believers "know whom they have believed."

408

God's grace is beyond man's understanding. Man could never understand how God could love wretched creatures such as we are, and permit His Son to die for us. God's grace is unsearchable. It is impossible for man to understand how Jesus Christ loved a whole world full of sinners, and laid His life down willingly, that we might be saved. God's ways are untrackable. Man tracks rockets through space, but man cannot track God; His ways are untrackable. God's judgments are unsearchable—and certainly God cannot be understood through man's wisdom and reason. God has been "from everlasting," and God will be "to everlasting" (Psalm 90:1, 2).

God's mercy has been extended to hell-deserving sinners through the sacrificial death of Jesus on the cross. The only way that you or I or any other person will ever stand before God and hear Him say, "Well done; enter into the joys of thy Lord," will be on the merit of Jesus' shed blood! In this day of liberalism and modernism, men scoff at the blood of Jesus. They declare that it is no longer necessary to believe in a "bloody Gospel." But I say in the words of Paul, "Without shedding of blood is no remission" (Heb. 9:22). And Peter says, ". . . ye were not redeemed with corruptible things, as silver and gold . . . *but with the precious blood of Christ, as of a lamb without blemish and without spot*" (I Pet. 1:18, 19).

"For of Him, and through Him, and to Him,

409

are all things: . . ." One commentary sums up
verse 36 in the following words:

"Thus worthily does the Apostle sum up this
whole matter. *'OF Him* are all things,' as their
eternal Source; *'THROUGH Him* are all things,'
inasmuch as He brings all to pass which in His
eternal counsels He purposed; *'TO Him* are all
things,' as being His own last End, the manifestation of the glory of His own perfections being
the ultimate, because the highest possible, design
of all His procedure from first to last."

*". . . TO WHOM (GOD) BE GLORY FOR EVER.
AMEN"!*

Chapter XII

1. I beseech you therefore, brethren, by the mercies of God, that ye present your bodies a living sacrifice, holy, acceptable unto God, which is your reasonable service.

2. And be not conformed to this world: but be ye transformed by the renewing of your mind, that ye may prove what is that good, and acceptable, and perfect, will of God.

3. For I say, through the grace given unto me, to every man that is among you, not to think of himself more highly than he ought to think; but to think soberly, according as God hath dealt to every man the measure of faith.

4. For as we have many members in one body, and all members have not the same office:

5. So we, being many, are one body in Christ, and every one members one of another.

6. Having then gifts differing according to the grace that is given to us, whether prophecy, let us prophesy according to the proportion of faith;

7. Or ministry, let us wait on our ministering: or he that teacheth, on teaching;

8. Or he that exhorteth, on exhortation: he that giveth, let him do it with simplicity; he that ruleth, with diligence; he that sheweth mercy, with cheerfulness.

9. Let love be without dissimulation. Abhor that which is evil; cleave to that which is good.

10. Be kindly affectioned one to another with brotherly love; in honour preferring one another;

11. Not slothful in business; fervent in spirit; serving the Lord;

12. Rejoicing in hope; patient in tribulation; continuing instant in prayer;

13. Distributing to the necessity of saints; given to hospitality.

14. Bless them which persecute you: bless, and curse not.

15. Rejoice with them that do rejoice, and weep with them that weep.

16. Be of the same mind one toward another. Mind not high things, but condescend to men of low estate. Be not wise in your own conceits.

17. Recompense to no man evil for evil. Provide things honest in the sight of all men.

18. If it be possible, as much as lieth in you, live peaceably with all men.

19. Dearly beloved, avenge not yourselves, but rather give place unto wrath: for it is written, Vengeance is mine; I will repay, saith the Lord.

20. Therefore if thine enemy hunger, feed him; if he thirst, give him drink: for in so doing thou shalt heap coals of fire on his head.

21. Be not overcome of evil, but overcome evil with good.

PART VI

THE CHRISTIAN LIFE AND TRUE SERVICE

Beginning with chapter 12, and through the greater part of the remaining chapters (through chapter 15), we are occupied chiefly with exhortations to the Christian—the walk and conduct of a

Christian—in accordance with what he has been taught. The strictly doctrinal chapters of this Epistle end with chapter 11. Doctrine determines Christian duty; what a man believes is revealed by what he does—"for as he thinketh in his heart, *so is he*" (Prov. 23:7).

The same thing is taught by Paul in Ephesians: "Ye were sometimes darkness, but now are ye light in the Lord: *walk as children of light*" (Eph. 5:8). Doctrine precedes the exhortations and furnishes the basis for a Christian walk. Before a person can live right, he must *think* right about God, Christ, the blood, and the Word; and if a person does not believe sound doctrine, he cannot produce sound Christian living. A real born-again experience, by grace through faith in the shed blood of Jesus, precedes a holy life; and apart from the new birth there is no such thing as holy living.

Verse 1: *"I beseech you therefore, brethren, by the mercies of God, that ye present your bodies a living sacrifice, holy, acceptable unto God, which is your reasonable service."*

"I beseech you . . . ." Greek authorities tell us that the verb used here is a strong word, and very hard to render into English. "I beseech you" could have been translated "I beg you earnestly," or "I entreat you," or "I exhort you." It has a deep meaning, as if God Himself were on His knees before His people, begging them to give

themselves over to Him and by so doing receive the fulness of the blessing of the Gospel of Christ. Jesus came that we might have *life,* and have it abundantly. But God cannot give us abundant life until we are fully yielded—soul, spirit, and body—to Him. So chapter 12 begins with God pleading, through the Holy Spirit, to the brethren.

The word *"therefore"* calls attention, or points back, to all that has preceded in the foregoing chapters of the Epistle . . . that is, because God has provided such a glorious salvation within reach of all, easily understood by all, received simply by faith in the finished work of Jesus, we should be willing to present our bodies as a living sacrifice.

We are saved by exercising faith in the finished work of the Lord Jesus Christ. We can give nothing in return for salvation. Salvation has been purchased and paid for by the precious blood of Jesus. Yet—as the eye needs the hands, the feet, and other members of the body physically speaking, so the spirit needs the members of our body, consecrated wholly and unreservedly unto God, if we would live the kind of life God would have His children live.

Please notice—the "begging" is directed to the *"brethren."* Only the born again can present their bodies to God. The unbeliever cannot give himself to God for service; and if he did, the offering would not be acceptable. The only thing for a lost man to do is to receive the Lord Jesus as his personal Saviour. After that is done, he may speak of making an offering.

Notice: It is *"by the mercies of God"* that we are asked to present our bodies. In other words, since God has been so merciful, the very facts presented in the previous chapters concerning God's mercy to hell-deserving sinners should cause us to want to present our bodies a living sacrifice, and we should desire to be holy brethren. We should desire to live, act, and conduct ourselves in such a way that our daily living in every minute detail would be acceptable unto God.

"Present" is a Temple term for the bringing of anything to God. So Jesus was *presented* (Luke 2:22), and so Paul would present each born again believer (Col. 1:28). Paul exhorts the Romans to make of themselves a sacrificial offering to God.

"Bodies" is the comprehensive term for the whole man—body, soul, and spirit. (Read I Thessalonians 5:23.) Every day men yield their bodies to physical service—but often with inner reluctance. This should not be so with a Christian's service to God. We are besought to present ourselves—that is, *willing* to do so—soul, spirit, and body.

People often say, "I am willing to die for Jesus." That is honorable—but let me say very humbly that God does not necessarily want you and me to die for Jesus in this Dispensation of Grace. He wants us to *live* for Jesus, He wants us to be *"a living sacrifice."* In our daily living

He wants us to be holy, and whatever we do—whether we eat, or drink, or *whatsoever* we do—God wants us to do it to His glory (I Cor. 10:31).

Under the old covenant, the sacrificial victims were slain. But since the one Sacrifice for sin, for all time, had been accomplished on Calvary, there is no further need for *dead* sacrifices. What God wants is that we present ourselves to Him a living sacrifice, putting ourselves into His hands for His pleasure. Therefore Paul is pleading for spiritual sacrifices in the name of Jesus. (Read I Peter 2:5.)

This "living sacrifice" is in glorious contrast to the legal sacrifices. The death of the one "Lamb of God, which taketh away the sin of the world" (John 1:29) has swept all dead sacrifices from off the altar of God, to make room for the redeemed themselves as "living sacrifices" to God, who "made Him (Christ) to be sin for us" (II Cor. 5:21). Every outgoing of a Christian's heart in grateful praise and every act prompted by the love of Christ, is itself a sacrifice to God of a sweet smelling savor (Heb. 13:15, 16).

"... *holy, acceptable unto God* ...." As the Levitical sacrifices when offered without blemish to God were regarded as holy, so believers, yielding themselves to God "as those that are alive from the dead, and (their) members as instruments of righteousness unto God" (Rom. 6:13) are, in God's eyes, not *ritually*, but REALLY, "holy" and "acceptable unto God." When we have done those things which are acceptable unto God, we should face the spiritual fact that what we have done is our *"reasonable service"!*

Verse 2: *"And be not conformed to this world: but be ye transformed by the renewing of your mind, that ye may prove what is that good, and acceptable, and perfect, will of God."*

This verse is more or less a command: *"Be NOT conformed . . . ."* "Conformed" refers to the act of an individual assuming an outward expression that does not come from within, nor is it representative of his inner life. The same Greek word for "conform" is translated "fashion" in I Peter 1:14: ". . . not *fashioning* yourselves according to . . . ." In other words, we are not to *fashion* our lives after this present evil age. "For all that is in the world—the lust of the flesh, and the lust of the eyes, and the pride of life—is not of the Father, but is of the world." And the world will surely pass away, "and the lust thereof: but he that doeth *the will of God* abideth for ever." (Read I John 2:15-17.) It is *God's will* that we present spirit, soul, and body unto Himself.

To be "conformed" to this age is to yield to the spirit of the age . . . that is, to follow the line of least resistance until we become like the age to which we conform; and when we do that, we give up "the good fight of faith." I did not say we give up our *faith;* I said we give up the *fight* of faith. You remember Paul's dying testimony contains the statement: "I have fought a good fight, I have finished my course, I have kept the faith" (II Tim. 4:7).

We are likened unto soldiers (II Tim. 2:3, 4); we are saved by grace through faith, and we are to "fight the good fight of faith" (I Tim. 6:12). *Demas* is an example of one who did not fight the good fight of faith. Paul said Demas forsook him, "having loved this present world (age)" (II Tim. 4:10). Demas forgot the One "who gave Himself for our sins, that He might *deliver* us from this present evil age, according to the will of God and our Father" (Gal. 1:4).

"... *but be ye transformed* ...." The word "transformed" is altogether a different word from "conformed." "Conformed" looks to the outward mold, "transformed"—or "transfigured"—to the inward man.

This spiritual miracle can happen only *"by the renewing of your mind."* The Greek word used here for "renewing" occurs but once more in the New Testament, and there in connection with regeneration. In Titus 3:5 we read: "Not by works of righteousness which we have done, but according to His mercy He saved us, by the washing of regeneration, *and renewing of the Holy Ghost."* This miracle of renewing is the work of the Holy Spirit. Man cannot renew himself in the spiritual sense. He can reform and try to make himself new, but the old nature will eventually take over again. The renewing of the mind comes about only when we surrender our body, soul, and spirit unto God.

". . . that ye may prove what is that good, and acceptable, and perfect, will of God." This means "that we may be able to discern, or to recognize, the perfect will of God for our life"; and until we do recognize the perfect will of God for our life, we can never enjoy our spiritual birthright, which is abundant life. If we hope to see the blessings of God, we must live daily, fully surrendered to God's will. We must allow Jesus to sit on the throne of our heart and control every minute detail of our life.

The Exercise of Spiritual Gifts
as Members of the Body of Christ

Verse 3: *"For I say, through the grace given unto me, to every man that is among you, not to think of himself more highly than he ought to think; but to think soberly, according as God hath dealt to every man the measure of faith."*

We can see very clearly that Paul is begging here for humility; he beseeches *"every man . . . not to think of himself more highly than he ought to think."* To himself, every man is the most important person in the world, and it always takes much grace to see what other people are, and to keep a sense of moral proportion. Whatever a person is, whatever he has accomplished, it is all due to the mercy of God. The more a person is dedicated to God, the more he will depend upon God, and the more he will lift up the Lord Jesus Christ. The more he is dedicated to God, the less he will magnify himself. God gives grace to the humble, but God "resisteth the proud" (James 4:6). There is no place for pride in the program of God. Paul declares that "no flesh should glory in His presence," and that *Christ* is our wisdom, righteousness, sanctification, and redemption (I Cor. 1:29, 30). Again Paul declares that we are complete in Jesus (Col. 2:10).

"*. . . God hath dealt to every man the measure of faith.*" We are to keep in mind that faith is here viewed as the inlet to all other graces. God has given to each his particular capacity to take in the gifts and graces which He designs for his general good. The idea seems to be that there are various degrees of self-estimation, for God gives one more and another less; but all should be fundamentally regulated by humility, for no one has anything he has not received (I Cor. 4:7; John 3:27).

Verses 4 and 5: "*For as we have many members in one body, and all members have not the same office: so we, being many, are one body in Christ, and every one members one of another.*"

All believers belong to one body—and that body is Christ. We are all "baptized into one body"

420

by the Holy Spirit of God (I Cor. 12:12, 13). Each of us belongs to the body of Christ. Jesus is the Head of that body, and we are "members of His body, of His flesh, and of His bones" (Eph. 5:26-30). However, even though we are all members of the same body, God does not give to each member *"the same office,"* the same gift, the same ministry.

In I Corinthians 12:18-20 Paul says to all believers: "But now hath God set the members every one of them in the body, *as it hath pleased Him.* And if they were all one member, where were the body? But now are they many members, yet but one body."

The most blessed day that will ever be in the lives of some Christians is the day they are willing to be what God wants them to be, and by so doing stop trying to be someone else. You remember, Peter said, "Lord, what about John?" And, in so many words, Jesus said to Peter, "That is none of your business. You let me take care of John, and you take care of your own ministry—and if you do that, Peter, you will have your hands full!" (Read John 21:20-25.)

In other words, if God calls you to be the janitor in your church, be the best janitor Jesus ever had, and do not covet the pastor's pulpit. By the same argument, if God has called you to direct the choir, *direct* the choir—and do not try to take the pastor's place. If God calls you to direct the music, *do that;* and let the pastor do the preaching.

421

There are a lot of believers who are willing to go to Africa or India, but they are not willing to win souls in their own back yard. There are a lot of believers who are willing to be Chairman of the Board—but they are not willing to serve only as a member of the Board. God help us to find the will of God for our lives, yield to God to direct our daily life and work—and when we find the place in life that God has for us, God help us to do what He calls us to do . . . in humility, simplicity, cheerfulness, and faithfulness. If we serve Him thus, when we get to the end of the way we will hear Jesus say to us, "Well done, thou good and faithful servant; enter thou into the joys of thy Lord!"

Verses 6-8: *"Having then gifts differing according to the grace that is given to us, whether prophecy, let us prophesy according to the proportion of faith; or ministry, let us wait on our ministering: or he that teacheth, on teaching; or he that exhorteth, on exhortation: he that giveth, let him do it with simplicity; he that ruleth, with diligence; he that sheweth mercy, with cheerfulness."*

We are given gifts *"according to the grace that is given to us."* Some have the gift of *prophecy*, some the gift of *ministry*, some the gift of *teaching*, some the gift of *exhortation*. Whatever gift God has given to us, we are commanded to do our best —with simplicity, cheerfulness, and humility.

". . . whether prophecy, let us prophesy . . . ."
The New Testament prophet is one who "speaketh unto men to edification, and exhortation, and comfort" (I Cor. 14:3). In I Corinthians 14:1, believers are exhorted to "follow after love (charity), and desire spiritual gifts, *but rather that ye may prophesy.*" It is a grand and glorious privilege to be a mouthpiece for the Spirit of God on earth, to tell men that Christ died to save sinners; but we are admonished to prophesy *"according to the proportion of faith."*

There is too much man-made "prophesying" today. Ministers make too many wild predictions in this age in which we live. We are to prophesy according to the proportion of faith God gives us as we study His Word, because faith comes by hearing and hearing by the Word. We are to rightly divide the Word, and it is a grave sin for God's teacher or God's preacher to *wrongly* divide the Word of truth.

Paul tells us that God "gave some, apostles; and some, prophets; and some, evangelists; and some, pastors and teachers." God gave these different ministries to the Church "for the perfecting of the saints, for the work of the ministry, for the edifying of the body of Christ" (Eph. 4:11, 12).

Any evangelist, prophet, pastor, or teacher who is not ministering the things of the Spirit to the edifying of the body of Christ and the building up of the faith of the saints, would be far better off out of the ministry. Every officer in the church should have a single eye, a single desire, a single motive—namely, to see what he or she can do to build up the body of Christ, to strengthen believers in the faith, and to advance the cause of Christ on earth. If that is not the motive that drives us on to do what we do in the church, then we would be better off to take a seat, fold our hands, and not attempt to do anything! There is entirely too much selfishness, too much self-righteousness, too much pride, too much vainglory, among church workers today. God help us, in all that we do, however humble the task may be or however outstanding it may be, to do what we do with simplicity and cheerfulness—and do it to the glory of God, not to the glory of man or to build up ourselves in the eyes of men!

"... *he that exhorteth, on exhortation* ...." This gift is sorely lacking today. The word means "to comfort fellow believers." *Vine's New Testament Dictionary* gives this explanation: "primarily a calling to one's side, and so to one's aid; hence denotes (a) an appeal, entreaty (II Cor. 8:4); (b) encouragement, exhortation (Rom. 12:8); (c) consolation and comfort." In other words, the exhorter is one who is able to comfort or encourage a fellow believer who is discouraged, or who is brokenhearted because of temptations or other reasons. Paul speaks of "the God of all comfort; who comforteth us in all our tribulation, *that we may be able to comfort them which are in any trouble, by the comfort wherewith we ourselves are comforted of God"* (II Cor. 1:3, 4).

Paul told Timothy, "Till I come, *give attendance* to reading, *to exhortation*, to doctrine" (I Tim. 4:13). Some who have been given the gift of exhortation have mistaken the calling God has bestowed upon them, and have desired to become pastors or evangelists instead of being God's exhorter in the church. Today we need men—ordinary men, laymen—who can exhort, and fill the place in the church that can be filled only by one capable of "exhortation."

". . . he that ruleth"—that is, "he who presides or superintends"—let him do it *"with diligence."* The person who is a leader (and there MUST be leaders in a church, in a home, in business) should be diligent. (Read I Thessalonians 5:12; I Timothy 3:4-12; 5:17.)

". . . he that sheweth mercy," let him do it *"with cheerfulness."* Here "mercy" has no reference to sins or the forgiveness of sins. It has reference to those in the church who have a special gift bestowed upon them by God . . . a gift to aid those who are in trouble. People who have the gift of helping those who are in trouble or overtaken with misfortune should do what they do with cheerfulness, with glad service. (Read I Corinthians 12:28.) This is a gift greatly needed in the church today.

Duties of Believers Toward Others

Verse 9: *"Let love be without dissimulation. Abhor that which is evil; cleave to that which is good."*

"Dissimulation" means to "play a part, to simulate, feign, pretend, play the hypocrite" *(Vine's New Testament Dictionary).* Therefore the Holy Spirit is here saying to believers, "Love without hypocrisy"—for the fruit of the Spirit, first of all, is *love* (Gal. 5:22). Feigned love is nothing but disguised hate. The command is to love sincerely in the Lord, from the heart. This caution about love is virtually the theme of the rest of the chapter.

We are further admonished to *"abhor (hate) that which is evil,"* but we are to *"cleave to that which is good."* In Psalm 97:10 the Psalmist says, "Ye that love the Lord, *hate evil* . . . ." Isaiah thunders out: *"Cease to do evil;* learn to do well . . ." (Isaiah 1:16, 17). Jesus said, "No man can serve two masters . . ." (Matt. 6:24). Believers are commanded to hate and despise (abhor) evil, and we are to express our hatred of evil by a withdrawal from it and loathing it.

The word *"cleave"* means "to join fast together, to glue, cement, or fasten firmly together." What a lofty tone of moral principle and feeling is here indicated. It is not *abstain* from one and do the other, or merely turn from one and be drawn to the other; but a much stronger meaning is implied: *abhor* the one, and *cling*—or be glued with deepest sympathy—to the other.

Verse 10:   *"Be kindly affectioned one to another with brotherly love; in honour preferring one another."*

It is not enough to SAY we love the brethren; we are to *demonstrate* brotherly love.   To feign affection with outward acts, when the heart does not possess love, is hypocrisy.   Of this kind of hypocrisy Paul has already warned the Christians (v. 9).   I believe the exhortation here is to love the brethren in the faith as though they were brethren of blood relation—*"with brotherly love."*

". . . in honour preferring one another"—that is, in respect shown another.   *Vine's New Testament Dictionary* states: "Primarily a valuing, hence objectively, a price paid or received.   The word here means 'as an advantage to be given to believers one to another instead of claiming it for self.'"

The word *"prefer"* means rather "to go before—take the lead; that is, show an example, in showing the honor that is due to the brethren of the church—showing honor to those whose gifts entitle them to respect in the church."   It is only those whom the love of Christ constrains to live not unto themselves (II Cor. 5:14, 15) who are capable of thoroughly acting in the spirit of this precept.

Verses 11 and 12: *"Not slothful in business; fervent in spirit; serving the Lord; rejoicing in hope; patient in tribulation; continuing instant in prayer."*

"Business" here does not mean secular business; the word means "zeal." I like the way the *Wuest* translation gives the meaning of these verses:

"With respect to zeal, not lazy; fervent in the sphere of the Spirit, serving the Lord; rejoicing in the sphere of hope; patient in tribulation; with respect to prayer, persevering in it continually."

The church life is to be characterized by energy and by warmth in serving the Lord. In other words, a person who is born again should be the most alert person in the community. If some people in secular work were no more zealous in their business transactions than they are in their spiritual life, they would be fired. It is disheartening to see the way some people carry on the work of the Lord! They drag along and act as if there is nothing to be excited about . . . "It makes no difference how we do it; if we must do it, let's get it done!" That is not the right attitude! Christians should be filled with zeal—zealous to do good works, *anxious* to do good works—and should do them cheerfully, praising God all the while, *"fervent in spirit"* (not lukewarm). (Read Revelation 3:16.) In our prayer life we should be fervent, for "the effectual fervent prayer of a righteous man availeth much" (James 5:16). In the Christian realm, in the business realm, in the realm of charity, or prayer, or whatever—we should always be *"serving the Lord"!* One great commentator states it like this: "Never let your zeal lag; maintain the spiritual glow; serve the Lord!"

". . . rejoicing in hope . . . ." We should always be rejoicing, because of the hope we have—"the hope of the Gospel" (Col. 1:23). We should rejoice because of the blessed hope of the soon coming of Jesus. Think of it! Today He may come! Today we may be caught up to meet Jesus in the air! What a hope . . . the happy hope . . . "the *blessed* hope"! (Read Titus 2:11-13.)

Then, we should always be *"patient in tribulation."* *Anyone* can be patient, happy, joyous, when everything goes well, when everyone speaks well of us, when everybody "pats us on the back" and tells us what a great fellow we are. But when people begin to curse us instead of blessing us, it takes grace, pure grace, GOD'S grace, to make us rejoice. But thank God, by grace it can be done! We should rejoice in hope, and we should be patient in tribulation. When we are tried, we should rejoice and be exceedingly glad (Matt. 5:12), because they persecuted the prophets, they persecuted Jesus, they persecuted the disciples—and Paul tells Timothy, "Yea, and all that will live godly in Christ Jesus shall suffer persecution" (II Tim. 3:12).

". . . continuing instant in prayer." Paul said

to the believers in Thessalonica, "Pray without ceasing" (I Thess. 5:17). Jesus taught "that men ought *always* to pray, and *not to faint*" (Luke 18:1). One translator gives it thus: "In your hope be joyful; in your sufferings be stedfast; *in your prayers be unwearied!*" It takes a real Christian to weep and laugh at the same time . . . to be sad, and filled with joy at the same time . . . to suffer severely, and yet be steadfast . . . to pray when seemingly no answer is even near, and yet be unwearied.

Jesus gives far above the ordinary. Everything Jesus does for us is extraordinary; therefore we should be far, far above average. The curse of the average church is too many "average" Christians, too many "ordinary" Christians. There is a great need for Christians who are zealous, alert, and anxious to be always serving God joyfully.

Verses 13-15: *"Distributing to the necessity of saints; given to hospitality. Bless them which persecute you: bless, and curse not. Rejoice with them that do rejoice, and weep with them that weep."*

"Distributing to the necessity of saints . . . ." "Saints" is the New Testament term for believers in Christ. Paul's injunction to the early Church was especially necessary when so many Christians were banished and persecuted.

A born again person should be an unselfish

person. Believers should be anxious to share with less fortunate believers. In the days of Paul this was much more needful than today—and yet, when we look outside the boundaries of our country, we can see much need among saints. As believers, we should be willing to share what we have with one another, that the needs of each may be met. (Read Hebrews 13:16 and I Timothy 6:17, 18.)

". . . *given to hospitality.*" Here we are admonished to be hospitable. We are to pursue hospitality; that is, we are to run after it, go out of our way to be hospitable. Greek authorities tell us that the word used here means that we are not only to furnish hospitality when sought, but we are to seek opportunities to exercise it. Hebrews 13:2 tells us, "Be not forgetful to entertain strangers: for thereby some have entertained angels unawares."

"*Bless them which persecute you: bless, and curse not.*" The best way in the world to win an enemy is to be good to him . . . be kind, and go out of your way to assist him. You will never win anyone by cursing him. Jesus taught this principle: "I say unto you, *Love your enemies, bless them that curse you, do good to them that hate you, and pray for them which despitefully use you, and persecute you*" (Matt. 5:44). (Also read Luke 6:27, 28 and I Corinthians 4:12). It is unnatural and humanly impossible to bless those who persecute you—but in the Holy Spirit it can be done. One

431

who possesses this grace is a happy and fruitful Christian.

"Rejoice with them that do rejoice, and weep with them that weep." Believers should rejoice with those who are happy, and weep with those fellow Christians who weep. The mother enters into the joys of her children and is sincerely grieved in their sorrows, for she is one with them and she loves them. Paul declares that the *Church* is one body—"and whether one member suffer, all the members suffer with it; or one member be honoured, all the members rejoice with it" (I Cor. 12:26).

It is to be noticed that Paul mentions rejoicing first. Perhaps it is because it is much easier to bewail another's sorrows, in that it does not excite envy and jealousy, than to congratulate him in his joy.

Verse 16: *"Be of the same mind one toward another. Mind not high things, but condescend to men of low estate. Be not wise in your own conceits."*

"Be of the same mind one toward another"—that is, believers are to have full sympathy with one another. They are to be so closely connected in love and fellowship that they sympathize with each other. They are to have the same respect one for another. They are to keep in harmony with one another, because Christians are one in

Christ and all belong to the same body. (Read Galatians 3:26-28.)

"Mind not high things . . . ." Believers are not to take hold of, or press forward to, high things; *"but condescend to men of low estate."* In other words, "Set not your mind on high things, but go along with the lowly; be guided by humility." The world neglects and usually despises men of "low estate"—but the Lord Jesus loved them and died for them. Many times there is more genuine worth, more genuine manhood, in the alleys and in the byways than on the boulevards and the avenues. Christian love should always go where love is most needed.

Jesus set the example. He was so interested in helping a fallen woman—a woman who had been married five times and who was at that time living with a man to whom she was not married—that He did not desire to eat. His appetite left Him. The disciples could not understand when they returned from the city where they had gone to buy bread; but Jesus said, "I have meat to eat that ye know not of" (John 4:1-32).

"Be not wise in your own conceits." This is the application of the command to "be of the same mind one toward another," to "mind not high things," and not to despise the lowly. In other words, "Think not too highly of yourself." Self-conceit, too high an estimate of oneself, is the chief hindrance to the three duties mentioned

433

in the first part of this verse. Solomon said: "Be not wise in thine own eyes: fear the Lord, and depart from evil" (Prov. 3:7). One outstanding commentator gives it thus: "Be not getting presumptuous in your own opinion." (Also read Jeremiah 9:23, 24.)

Verse 17: *"Recompense to no man evil for evil. Provide things honest in the sight of all men."*

Verse 14 forbade the *feeling*, and this verse forbids the *act*. In I Peter 3:9 we read: "Not rendering evil for evil, or railing for railing: but contrariwise blessing; knowing that ye are thereunto called, that ye should inherit a blessing." (Also read the words of Jesus in Matthew 5:38-48.) *Anyone* can do evil for evil—or, as the everyday expression puts it, "dirt for dirt." But it takes a real Christian—a real, humble, honest believer—to render good in return for evil. We are not to do to others as they do to us, but we are to do unto others as we would have them do unto us; and by so doing we will prove to them that in Christ we are much bigger than they are . . . and ONLY in Christ, because flesh recoils at doing good for evil.

"Provide things honest . . . ." We are to be honest in all of our dealings *"in the sight of all men."* We should be "of honest report" (Acts 6:3), of "good report" (I Tim. 3:7). (Read Proverbs 3:3, 4.)

Verses 18-21: *"If it be possible, as much as lieth in you, live peaceably with all men. Dearly beloved, avenge not yourselves, but rather give place unto wrath: for it is written, Vengeance is mine; I will repay, saith the Lord. Therefore if thine enemy hunger, feed him; if he thirst, give him drink: for in so doing thou shalt heap coals of fire on his head. Be not overcome of evil, but overcome evil with good."*

"If it be possible... live peaceably...." What Paul is saying here is simply this: If it is at all possible, be at peace *"with all men."* Seek peace. The other party may not yield, but let it be no fault of yours. The impossibility of this in some cases is hinted at to keep up the heart of those who, having done their best unsuccessfully to live in peace, might be disheartened by thinking the failure was owing to themselves.

"... avenge not yourselves"—but beloved, let the Lord God do the avenging. Be willing to *"give place unto wrath,"* because God has said, *"Vengeance is mine; I will repay"* (Deut. 32:35; Heb. 10:30). Since we have such a promise from Almighty God, *if our enemy is hungry,* we should *"feed him."* If our enemy is dying of thirst, we should *"give him drink."* When we feed our enemy and give him drink, through these kind acts of love we *"heap coals of fire on his head."* (Read Proverbs 25:21, 22.)

Believers are not to be *"overcome of evil,"* but believers are to *"overcome evil with good."* "Be not overcome with evil" as you would be if you cried for vengeance; you, yourself, would be conquered then. But if you "overcome evil with good," you have won a great victory in your own heart.

Before we leave chapter 12, just glance back through the verses. This chapter is full of human impossibilities. From the natural aspect, it is impossible to live chapter 12. Yet, in the Spirit, this chapter presents practical, normal Christian living. Spiritual victory comes to the believer through a definite yielding or surrendering of the body to God as a living sacrifice. God wants our body—all of it, every member of it; and when we have yielded our body to God in every minute detail, we have not done one thing to boast about. We have done that which is "OUR REASONABLE SERVICE."

When we yield ourselves unreservedly to God—spirit, soul, and body—then and only then can we overcome evil with good; and that is exactly what God wants us to do, as His believing children.

Chapter XIII

1. Let every soul be subject unto the higher powers. For there is no power but of God: the powers that be are ordained of God.

2. Whosoever therefore resisteth the power, resisteth the ordinance of God: and they that resist shall receive to themselves damnation.

3. For rulers are not a terror to good works, but to the evil. Wilt thou then not be afraid of the power? do that which is good, and thou shalt have praise of the same:

4. For he is the minister of God to thee for good. But if thou do that which is evil, be afraid; for he beareth not the sword in vain: for he is the minister of God, a revenger to execute wrath upon him that doeth evil.

5. Wherefore ye must needs be subject, not only for wrath, but also for conscience sake.

6. For for this cause pay ye tribute also: for they are God's ministers, attending continually upon this very thing.

7. Render therefore to all their dues: tribute to whom tribute is due; custom to whom custom; fear to whom fear; honour to whom honour.

8. Owe no man any thing, but to love one another: for he that loveth another hath fulfilled the law.

9. For this, Thou shalt not commit adultery, Thou shalt not kill, Thou shalt not steal, Thou shalt not bear false witness, Thou shalt not covet; and if there be any

other commandment, it is briefly comprehended in this saying, namely, Thou shalt love thy neighbour as thyself.

10. Love worketh no ill to his neighbour: therefore love is the fulfilling of the law.

11. And that, knowing the time, that now it is high time to awake out of sleep: for now is our salvation nearer than when we believed.

12. The night is far spent, the day is at hand: let us therefore cast off the works of darkness, and let us put on the armour of light.

13. Let us walk honestly, as in the day; not in rioting and drunkenness, not in chambering and wantonness, not in strife and envying.

14. But put ye on the Lord Jesus Christ, and make not provision for the flesh, to fulfil the lusts thereof.

Subjection to Human Government

Verse 1: *"Let every soul be subject unto the higher powers. For there is no power but of God: the powers that be are ordained of God."*

Some special reason must have given occasion to these exhortations in chapter 13. Undoubtedly there must have been an outbreak of disobedience to the civil authorities of that day. Paul had been dealing with Christians' responsibilities to the body of Christ. Now he abruptly begins a discussion of the Christian's duty to the local human government. There is nothing in the text to explain why Paul feels it necessary to give this exhortation, but many Bible scholars believe that although the Roman church was chiefly Gentiles, there were many Jewish members—and the Jews of the Roman Empire were bad citizens. They probably held, on the ground of Deuteronomy 17:15, that they were not to acknowledge a Gentile ruler. This was the spirit back of the question of the Pharisees who asked Jesus, "Is it lawful to give tribute unto Caesar, or not?" (Matt. 22:17).

In the days of Paul, the Jews had rebelled and had been expelled from the city of Rome, Aquila and Priscilla among them (Acts 18:2). Jews everywhere disputed the authority of the Roman government. Now Paul, knowing this, teaches that we are to be subject to civil government, for civil government has its origin in God.

A Christian is a citizen of the world as clearly as he is a member of the Church. Union with the body of Christ does not absolve him from a duty that belongs to men as men.

Notice, please, none are excluded from Paul's exhortation. He exhorts, *"Let every soul (every man) be subject"* to the rulers—and that takes in believers, preachers, evangelists, priests, and the pope.

Verse 2: *"Whosoever therefore resisteth the power, resisteth the ordinance of God: and they that resist shall receive to themselves damnation."*

Civil government has its source in Almighty God, and civil power and authority are appointed and ordained by Almighty God. That is, human

439

government is a permanent institution brought into being by God for the regulation of human affairs. The powers or authorities here are not seen as individual personalities, but as officers of the law, an institution ordained by God.

The structure of the government and the laws connected with it are appointed by God, but not all the officers of the government are always appointed by God. We know that there are ungodly, cruel officials energized by the devil, in places of authority. Yet the Christian is obligated to obey and honor the laws and officials under the jurisdiction in which he lives.

It is not intended to be taught here that the Christian is to do at the command of the government official that which is morally wrong. If civil power commands us to disobey the common laws of humanity or the sacred institutions of our country, or to violate the law of God, our obedience then is to a higher power—God. In Bible language, "We ought to obey God rather than men" (Acts 5:29).

"*. . . they that resist shall receive to themselves damnation (or judgment).*" That is, if we break the laws of the land we will be judged, we will be fined, and we will pay the penalty.

The same Greek word is used here that Paul uses in speaking to the Corinthians: "For he that eateth and drinketh unworthily, eateth and drink-eth *damnation* (or judgment) to himself, not discerning the Lord's body. For this cause many are weak and sickly among you, and many sleep. For if we would judge ourselves, we should not be judged. But when we are judged, we are chastened of the Lord, that we should not be condemned with the world" (I Cor. 11:29-32).

Therefore the teaching here is that God Himself will deal with believers who resist the civil authority of the land. If believers resist "the powers that be" they, in the true sense of the word, resist God, because He is the One who gives all power. They "shall receive to themselves judgment," and this judgment will come from God. True, the civil authorities would punish the violation of the law, but since their power is from God (and without God they would have no power), then the punishment is from God nevertheless.

You remember when Pilate said to Jesus, "Do you refuse to answer me? Do you not know who I am? I have the power to release you, and I have the power to crucify you!" Jesus answered Pilate, "You could have no power at all against me except it were given you by my Father." (Read John 19:10, 11.) ALL power is given by God, and He can take away kingdoms when He so desires; He can take away power (Dan. 2:21; 4:17, 34, 35).

When a nation has a leader who is ungodly, if believers would call on God in fervent prayer, without ceasing, God would remove that ruler; but as in the case of Pharaoh, God sometimes uses wicked rulers to chasten disobedient Christians.

Verse 3:   *"For rulers are not a terror to good works, but to the evil.   Wilt thou then not be afraid of the power? do that which is good, and thou shalt have praise of the same."*

As a rule (not always, though it should be always), *"rulers are not a terror to good works, but to the evil."*   In other words, the human government, instituted by God, is a means of regulating the affairs of the human race.   It is a protection to the innocent and a threat to evildoers, especially in the land in which we live. Policemen do not arrest men for being good—they arrest men for being evil. Civil authorities do not put us in the penitentiary for being honest and upright, but for being dishonest and sinful. So in the general sense, rulers are in accord with those who do good, and they are "a terror" to those who do evil.

". . . do that which is good, and thou shalt have praise of the same." It is implied here that those to whom he speaks will always be identified with good works, and so have the authorities on their side.   It is also taken for granted that the government will not violate its own idea, but will judge the evildoers and identify itself with those of good works.   (Read I Peter 2:13, 14, where we find a similar exhortation.)

Verse 4: *"For he is the minister of God to thee for good. But if thou do that which is evil, be afraid; for he beareth not the sword in vain: for he is the minister of God, a revenger to execute wrath upon him that doeth evil."*

This verse is a continuation of the last. There is no fear of the ruler when you do good, *"for he is the minister (or servant) of God to thee for good. But if thou do... evil,"* then *fear;* for God did not put *"the sword"* (a symbol of power to inflict punishment) in the ruler's hand *"in vain."*

Twice in this verse the ruler is given a very solemn title— *"minister* (or servant) *of God."* Every law-enforcing agency and every person who is a lawman should recognize that he is under the authority of Almighty God; and if a lawman misuses the power given him and abuses the position God has given him, his judgment will be greater— because "unto whomsoever much is given, of him shall be much required" (Luke 12:48). This is true in the spiritual realm, and also in the civil realm.

Verse 5: *"Wherefore ye must needs be subject, not only for wrath, but also for conscience sake."*

Believers should submit themselves to the civil authorities and obey the laws of the land, *"not only for wrath"*—because they fear the judgment that is sure to come if they break the laws, but they should be in obedience to civil authorities

443

"also for conscience sake"—for the sake of their own conscience.

We are children of light, and the Word of God teaches us that we are to walk in the light, not in darkness. Believers should obey the laws of the government "for the Lord's sake: whether it be to the king, as supreme; or unto governors, as unto them that are sent by Him for the punishment of evildoers, and for the praise of them that do well. For so is the will of God, that with well doing ye may put to silence the ignorance of foolish men: as free, and not using your liberty for a cloke of maliciousness, but as the servants of God. Honour all men. Love the brotherhood. Fear God. Honour the king" (I Pet. 2:13-17). Such Scripture needs no comment . . . it is clear.

Verse 6: *"For for this cause pay ye tribute also: for they are God's ministers, attending continually upon this very thing."*

"For for this cause," or "for on this account"—because civil government is God's appointment—there is a moral necessity for submission to authority, that is, to *"pay tribute."* ("'To pay' means 'to fulfil, complete,' carrying the sense of the fulfilment of an obligation."—*Wuest*)

The word *"ministers"* in this verse has a different meaning from "minister" in verse 4, where the word means "servant." Here it is a word used also of sacred religious services of the priest;

it is a word which means "of priestly character." As they are appointed by God, the tribute is to be paid for their support and the support of the government—as a matter of conscience. The act of paying tribute is ultimately an act performed in obedience to His will, and acceptable to Him.

I know there are some in office who are crooked and dishonest; but remember, our duty is to God. We must give an account to God for our stewardship—and they will give an account to God for theirs. And so if we do our duty toward God and toward the civil authorities of our country, we have a clear conscience toward God and we need not worry at the end of life's journey.

There could be much said here about present-day taxes; but I feel it would be time and energy wasted. Therefore, I simply say that we believers should pay our taxes. Personally, I thank God that I am an American, even though we do have taxes. I would not trade one square inch of America for a *square mile* of any other place I have ever been or heard of on this earth!

Verse 7:   *"Render therefore to all their dues: tribute to whom tribute is due; custom to whom custom; fear to whom fear; honour to whom honour."*

Whether it is *tribute, custom, fear,* or *honor* (respect)—as believers we are commanded not to fail in any respect toward those who are ministers

of God in civil affairs. By this statement I do not
mean that all civil authorities are Christians—but
the power they have, the office they hold, the
authority they have, is ordained of God, given to
them by God. As already pointed out, God sets up
whom He will and puts down whom He will. All
power and authority is given by God. That is a
Bible fact, and there is no need to deny it. Therefore, as a good Christian we are to *"render... to
all their dues."* We are to pay state taxes, county
taxes, customs on goods on which customs are due.
We are to fear men who are to be feared; we are to
honor men to whom honor is due. This is a Bible
fact, and we as believers should face it and not
try to dodge the issue.

I feel in my heart that there is a laxity among
believers today concerning civil affairs. Many
born again people refuse to vote. We may be
forced to vote for the lesser of two evils, but it is
our Christian duty to take our stand in civil affairs.
I believe with all of my heart that one reason the
government of our land is in the predicament it is
in today is that we born again people have not
prayed as we should for those who are in authority and have not gone to the polls and voted
as we should to put men whom God would have
in positions of authority. So let us not excuse
ourselves from civil affairs because we are Christians; for we are duty bound to render that which
is right to those who are in authority in the sec-

ondary matters of this life. (See Matthew 22:17-21.)

On the subject discussed in these seven verses the following principles seem to be settled by the authority of the Bible:

(1) Government is essential and its necessity recognized by God.

(2) God does not subordinate the church to the state. They are different in their character—the one natural, the other spiritual; and their aims are different—the state promotes moral living, the church spiritual living.

(3) Civil rulers are dependent on God. He has the entire control over them and can set them up or put them down as He pleases (as in Acts 12:23).

(4) The authority of God is superior to that of civil rulers. They have no right to make enactments which interfere with His authority.

Love—the Fulfillment of the Law

Verse 8: *"Owe no man any thing, but to love one another: for he that loveth another hath fulfilled the law."*

The Law given to Moses on Sinai provided against debt: "Thou shalt not defraud thy neighbour, neither rob him: the wages of him that is hired shall not abide with thee all night until the morning" (Lev. 19:13). Again we read, "The rich ruleth over the poor, and the borrower is servant to the lender" (Prov. 22:7).

Therefore Paul says: *"Owe no man any thing, but to love one another . . . ."* Love must still remain the root and spring of all your actions; no other law is needed. Pay all other debts; be indebted in the matter of love alone, for there is one debt that we can never fully pay or cause to be fully cancelled: that is the debt of love. We must go on loving continually— *"for he that loveth another hath fulfilled the law."*

Verses 9 and 10: *"For this, Thou shalt not commit adultery, Thou shalt not kill, Thou shalt not steal, Thou shalt not bear false witness, Thou shalt not covet; and if there be any other commandment, it is briefly comprehended in this saying, namely, Thou shalt love thy neighbour as thyself. Love worketh no ill to his neighbour: therefore love is the fulfilling of the law."*

When we love our fellow man as we ought to love him, we will treat him as we would want him to treat us. Love will restrain a man from making debts which he cannot pay. Love will restrain a man from adultery, murder, theft, bearing false witness, and covetousness. These are not all, but instances; for Paul adds the sweeping words, *"if there be any other commandment,"* love will fulfill it. It is all summed up in this: *"Thou shalt love thy neighbour as thyself."* Then Paul adds: *"Love worketh no ill to his neighbour: therefore love is the fulfilling of the law."*

You will recall that on one occasion a lawyer asked Jesus to name the greatest commandment, and Jesus declared that the greatest commandment is, *"Thou shalt love the Lord thy God* with all thy heart... soul... mind.... And the second is like unto it, *Thou shalt love thy neighbour as thyself."* Then Jesus said to the lawyer, "On these two commandments hang all the law and the prophets" (Matt. 22:35-40). Therefore, when we love God as we should, and when we love our neighbor as we should, we have fulfilled the law of God. (Also read Luke 10:25-37.)

The Walk of the Believer
in View of Christ's Soon Return

Verse 11: *"And that, knowing the time, that now it is high time to awake out of sleep: for now is our salvation nearer than when we believed."*

The truth Paul is pointing out is simply—"And let us do this: Live without debt except to love, *because now is our salvation nearer than when we (first) believed."* Peter speaks of a "salvation ready to be revealed in the last time" (I Pet. 1:5). The "salvation" here is not salvation from sin, but the *completion* of our salvation that began the moment we believed, and the glorification awaiting us at the coming of Christ, when we are "changed, in a moment, in the twinkling of an

eye, at the last trump" (I Cor. 15:51-53). At that
moment we will receive a glorified body just like
the Lord's glorious body. Paul is saying that *our
Lord's return* is nearer than the day we received
Him.

Salvation is in three tenses:

Past: Justification—the removal of the guilt and
penalty of sin from the believing sinner. The split
second we believed on Jesus and accepted Him by
faith, we were redeemed just as much as we will
ever be.

Present: Sanctification. We are saved daily
from the power of sin through the indwelling of
the Holy Spirit. We are delivered moment by
moment through the power of God.

Future: Glorification. We will be saved from
the presence of sin and from the corruption of the
body when Jesus comes in the Rapture. We will
see Him, and we will be like Him. (Read I Thessalonians 4:13-18 and I John 3:1-3.)

Verses 12-14: *"The night is far spent, the day
is at hand: let us therefore cast off the works of
darkness, and let us put on the armour of light.
Let us walk honestly, as in the day; not in rioting
and drunkenness, not in chambering and wantonness, not in strife and envying. But put ye on the
Lord Jesus Christ, and make not provision for the
flesh, to fulfil the lusts thereof."*

"The night is far spent . . . ." This is night,

insofar as the spiritual aspect of the day is concerned. The prince of darkness now reigns. We are the children of light, and we do not walk in darkness—but we are living in a dark world. But thank God this night is far spent and *"the day is at hand"*!

Since the night is far spent, and since our Lord's coming is imminent, believers therefore should *"cast off the works of darkness"* and *"put on the armour of light."* We should *"walk honestly"* every day—*"not in rioting and drunkenness, not in chambering and wantonness, not in strife and envying."* We are the temple of the Holy Spirit, who abides in our heart; and therefore we should *"make not provision for the flesh,"* to satisfy the lusts of the flesh. Whether we eat or drink, or whatever we do, we should do it all to the glory of God. We should never gratify the flesh by surrendering to the desires of the flesh.

There is no doctrine in the Word of God that will cause believers to live holy and spotless lives like the doctrine of the imminent return of Jesus Christ. John declares that "every man that hath this hope . . . *purifieth himself,* even as He is pure" (I John 3:3). If we are "looking for that blessed hope . . . the glorious appearing of the great God and our Saviour Jesus Christ" (Titus 2:13), we will abstain from the appearance of evil, and we will restrain the serving of the lusts of the flesh.

It is true that "of that day and hour knoweth

no man, no, not the angels which are in heaven, neither the Son, but the Father'' (Mark 13:32). We do not know the day. We do not know the hour. I have no respect for a date-setter—but we do know that according to the Scriptures *Jesus is coming*, and His coming (to the believer) is imminent. The certainty of the Lord's return is the Rock of Gibraltar on which our faith is grounded. The uncertainty of the *time* of His return stimulates our hope daily and causes our watchfulness to be aroused. Believers who are spiritually minded live in expectancy. We are not stargazers; we do not walk around looking up into the sky—but deep down in our heart we say, "Maybe this is the day that our blessed Lord will return in the air for His Church!" Spiritually-minded believers pray, "Even so, come, Lord Jesus!" (Rev. 22:20).

I would like to close this chapter by asking a question: "WHAT TIME IS IT BY GOD'S GREAT TIME CLOCK?" According to verses 11 and 12, "it is high time to awake out of sleep: for now is our salvation nearer than when we believed. The night is far spent, the day is at hand: ..." What time is it, insofar as you are individually concerned?

If you are a sinner, it is time for you to repent and be born again. *Today* is the day of salvation and *right now* is the accepted time. Five minutes from now may be eternally too late for you. Sinner, what time is it? It is time for you to repent and be born again! (Read John 3:3, 18, 36; James 4:14.)

Backslider, what time is it? For you, it is time to return unto the Lord, fall on your face before God and ask Him to forgive your backsliding. I warn you, Jesus may come today. John speaks of those who will be ashamed at His coming. Do you want to be one of those who will be ashamed? I am sure you do not. Then hear these words: "And now, little children, abide in Him; that, when He shall appear, we may have confidence, *and not be ashamed before Him at His coming*" (I John 2:28). Are you abiding in Jesus? If you are living in a backslidden condition, you certainly are not. It is time for you to return unto the Lord and renew your vows to Him. Do it, backslider, this moment. (Read I John 1:9; 2:1, 2.)

What time is it, believer, for you and for me, who profess to be faithful followers of the Lord Jesus? What time is it? It is time for us to be about our Father's business—to lift up our eyes and look on the fields that are white unto harvest, to see that the laborers are so few, and then to pray that the Lord of the harvest will send forth laborers! We need to be alert; we need to be "on our toes"; we need to be seeking the lost for Christ.

Christian, He may come today! Have you done your best to win your friends, your neighbors, and your own family to the Lord Jesus? If you have not, begin now. This is the time to become a soul winner. Get on your knees, present your body a living sacrifice, your members as instruments of righteousness unto God—and from this day forward go forth sowing seed that will bring forth a harvest of souls. God help us as believers to wake up and get on the job for Jesus. His coming is imminent!

Every minute detail of Scripture that needs to be fulfilled before the Rapture of the Church has been literally fulfilled. There is not one statement in the Bible that needs to be fulfilled before the Rapture of the Church. This may be the day that Jesus will descend from heaven with a shout, with the voice of the archangel and the trumpet of God. This may be the day we will be caught up to meet Him in the air!

Are you what you would like to be as a Christian if you knew you would meet Jesus today? Think it over! And if you are not, then do something about it!

Chapter XIV

1. Him that is weak in the faith receive ye, but not to doubtful disputations.

2. For one believeth that he may eat all things: another, who is weak, eateth herbs.

3. Let not him that eateth despise him that eateth not; and let not him which eateth not judge him that eateth: for God hath received him.

4. Who art thou that judgest another man's servant? to his own master he standeth or falleth. Yea, he shall be holden up: for God is able to make him stand.

5. One man esteemeth one day above another: another esteemeth every day alike. Let every man be fully persuaded in his own mind.

6. He that regardeth the day, regardeth it unto the Lord; and he that regardeth not the day, to the Lord he doth not regard it. He that eateth, eateth to the Lord, for he giveth God thanks; and he that eateth not, to the Lord he eateth not, and giveth God thanks.

7. For none of us liveth to himself, and no man dieth to himself.

8. For whether we live, we live unto the Lord; and whether we die, we die unto the Lord: whether we live therefore, or die, we are the Lord's.

9. For to this end Christ both died, and rose, and revived, that he might be Lord both of the dead and living.

10. But why dost thou judge thy brother? or why dost thou set at nought thy brother? for we shall all stand before the judgment seat of Christ.

11. For it is written, As I live, saith the Lord, every knee shall bow to me, and every tongue shall confess to God.

12. So then every one of us shall give account of himself to God.

13. Let us not therefore judge one another any more: but judge this rather, that no man put a stumblingblock or an occasion to fall in his brother's way.

14. I know, and am persuaded by the Lord Jesus, that there is nothing unclean of itself: but to him that esteemeth any thing to be unclean, to him it is unclean.

15. But if thy brother be grieved with thy meat, now walkest thou not charitably. Destroy not him with thy meat, for whom Christ died.

16. Let not then your good be evil spoken of:

17. For the kingdom of God is not meat and drink; but righteousness, and peace, and joy in the Holy Ghost.

18. For he that in these things serveth Christ is acceptable to God, and approved of men.

19. Let us therefore follow after the things which make for peace, and things wherewith one may edify another.

20. For meat destroy not the work of God. All things indeed are pure; but it is evil for that man who eateth with offence.

21. It is good neither to eat flesh, nor to drink wine, nor any thing whereby thy brother stumbleth, or is offended, or is made weak.

22. Hast thou faith? have it to thyself before God. Happy is he that condemneth not himself in that thing which he alloweth.

23. And he that doubteth is damned if he eat, because he eateth not of faith: for whatsoever is not of faith is sin.

Chapter 14:1

The Law of Love Concerning Doubtful Things

Verse 1: *"Him that is weak in the faith receive ye, but not to doubtful disputations."*

In this section Paul is dealing with the relations between the weak and the strong Christians. This weakness is in respect to faith: *"Him that is weak in the faith . . . ."* Faith is weak because of the lack of spiritual understanding. The weak Christian is one who does not fully appreciate what his Christianity means.

Paul is in no wise saying that Christians are at liberty to be too lax in their indulgence of natural appetites; but here Paul is speaking of the weak who have a tendency to be too scrupulous. The weak one here seems to be fettered by scruples in regard to customs dating to pre-Christian days. Such a weak one is blind to real love. He himself would not eat meat, and would condemn harshly the man who does, therefore exalting his own abstinence far above Christian love.

". . . receive ye . . . ." Paul directs this verse to the stronger brethren. In other words, recognize the weakness of a brother, but *receive* him because he *is* a brother. We who claim to be spiritually minded and strong in the Lord are not to demonstrate by our actions a "holier-than-thou" attitude, or a "more-spiritual-than-thou" attitude. If we are strong in the Lord, we are to receive the weak brother and encourage him. In Romans 15:7

we read, *"Wherefore receive ye one another, as Christ also received us to the glory of God."*

". . . but not to doubtful disputations." In the original Greek this reads, "not to judge his doubtful thoughts." This weak brother is to be received into fellowship—*but not to be disputed with* about his beliefs. This seems to be the meaning of "not to doubtful disputations." He cannot be argued out of his views; argument would only tend to make him more firm in his stand. He must *grow* out of them (by the Word of God), and in the meantime he is not to be criticized and judged, but loved.

Not all believers have the same knowledge, nor the same freedom from tradition, nor the same strength of appropriating faith. The weak brethren may be wrong, but we will never be able to help them by shunning them. We are to receive them as brethren. We are not to argue with them, but we are to receive them as Christ also received us, to the glory of God. We can agree to disagree if we are brethren, and still love each other and attempt to help each other in the Lord:

"Brethren, if a man be overtaken in a fault, *ye which are spiritual, restore such an one in the spirit of meekness; considering thyself, lest thou also be tempted.* Bear ye one another's burdens, and so fulfil the law of Christ" (Gal. 6:1, 2).

To the believers at Galatia, Paul admonished the brethren to restore those who fall by the wayside, or those who are "overtaken in a fault." We are to consider ourselves, realizing that the same temptation could come to us. Therefore weak brethren and brethren who do not live up to the standards we think they should, in the spiritual realm, are not to be shunned or ignored. They are to be received in the same spirit in which Jesus received us, while we were yet very unlovely; and through God's Word the weak in faith will be able to appreciate what his Christianity means: That he is saved by grace minus works, and that those who accept Christ are "free indeed" (Eph. 2:8, 9; Titus 3:5; John 8:32, 36).

Verse 2: *"For one believeth that he may eat all things: another, who is weak, eateth herbs."*

Here in this chapter, and also in I Corinthians chapter 8, the question is raised and discussed as to whether or not Christians should eat meat which had been offered to idols. In the early churches this was a big question—a burning question. Meat was brought in quantity to the heathen temples and presented in worship to the idols *in* the temples. Of course, the idols had no use for the meat; and even the priests were unable to consume all of the meat. Therefore it was sold to the public in the market places. This made it almost impossible for a believer to know every time he bought meat whether or not he was purchasing meat that had been offered to an idol in the temple of idol worship. The believers who were strong in the Lord paid no attention to this. They knew that in the Lord they were permitted to *"eat all things."* They knew that "an idol is nothing in the world, and that there is none other God but one" (I Cor. 8:4). "Howbeit, there is not in every man that knowledge . . ." (I Cor. 8:7). That is, not all believers had this knowledge of liberty, and these weak believers could not have a clear conscience and eat "a thing offered unto an idol." To go on eating these things was to defile their conscience, and in order to be on the perfectly safe side, they *ate "herbs";* that is, they confined their diet to vegetables.

Verse 3: *"Let not him that eateth despise him that eateth not; and let not him which eateth not judge him that eateth: for God hath received him."*

To me, this verse of Scripture is very clear. Those who are strong in the faith *("him that eateth")* have no right to set at nought a weaker brother *("him that eateth not").* The second part of this verse is directed to the weak brother: *"let not ⟮him which eateth not⟯ judge ⟮him that eateth."⟯* The weak brother has no right to criticize and condemn his stronger brother, who exercises his liberty in Christ. (This applies not to eating only, but to any other things people have scruples about.)

The sharpness of this rebuke shows that Paul, with all of his love and concern for the weak,

460

was aware of the trouble they could cause, and repressed it in its beginnings. *Wuest* says, "It is easy to lapse from scrupulousness about one's own conduct into Pharisaism about that of others." So the weaker brother is not to judge the stronger; and note, in the case of the stronger the Bible says, *"God hath received him."*

Verses 4 and 5: *"Who art thou that judgest another man's servant? to his own master he standeth or falleth. Yea, he shall be holden up: for God is able to make him stand. One man esteemeth one day above another: another esteemeth every day alike. Let every man be fully persuaded in his own mind."*

"Who art thou that judgest another man's servant?" Verse 4 utterly denies the right of the weaker brother to judge. The man who has confidence to eat meat is the *Lord's* servant, not the weak brother's. And *he stands or falls "to his own" Lord,* who is Christ. But he will not fall in the exercise of Christian liberty. *"Yea, he shall be holden up: for God is able to make him stand."*

Verse 5 presents another problem—one that may be a little more prominent in this day. Paul declares that *"one man esteemeth one day above another,"* and *"another esteemeth every day alike."* The strong believer regarded every day alike. Each day alike was an opportunity for him to be filled with the Spirit—in everything, by word or deed, giving thanks unto God the Father. Thus no day, in itself, was holy above another. Paul's instruction was: *"Let every man be fully persuaded in his own mind."*

Today there are those who worship on the Jewish Sabbath (Saturday) and those of us who believe that the Lord's day, the first day of the week, is the day to worship. But I believe in this Day of Grace that *every* day should be holy unto the Lord; and I believe the first day of the week should be a particular day in which we should rest and worship, attending the house of God.

In the true sense of the word and the strict spiritual aspect of the Gospel of the grace of God, no man has any right to judge another "in meat, or in drink, or in respect of an holyday, or of the new moon, or of the sabbath days: which are a shadow of things to come . . ." (Col. 2:16, 17). Believers are free from the Law. We enjoy liberty in Christ, and we are exhorted to *"stand fast therefore in the liberty wherewith Christ hath made us free,* and be not entangled again with the yoke of bondage"* (Gal. 5:1).

However, there are weaker brethren who cannot see this tremendous truth of liberty in Christ. These believers are fearful, and they are shocked at many things spiritually-minded believers say and do. These weak believers are very timid, and they have a spiritual inferiority complex; they never stand up and say, *"I know* whom I have

462

believed," and "We KNOW we have passed from death unto life." They say, instead, "I am living in hope, and I trust that all will be well at the end of the road." They pray, "Father, save us at last in heaven," and they insist that it is self-righteousness when one stands up and states that he knows he is saved.

Now, what are we supposed to do in such a case? Are we supposed to despise these weak believers? Are we supposed to continually dispute with them and argue and fuss? Definitely no! In Bible language, I say that since "God hath received them," let us also receive them in love. Let us pray for them and bear with them. Let us do all we can to strengthen these weak brethren. Paul teaches, "Let every man be fully persuaded in his own mind."

Thank God for the precious truth: "Brethren, *ye have been called unto liberty;* only use not liberty for an occasion to the flesh, but by love serve one another" (Gal. 5:13). Believer, "take heed lest by any means this liberty of your's become a stumblingblock to them that are weak" (I Cor. 8:9).

A spiritually-minded believer should be willing to refrain from anything that would cause a weak Christian to become weaker, or to become discouraged, or to stumble. Paul testifies: "In spite of how much I may like meat, in spite of how much I may crave meat, if eating meat will cause

463

one of my weak brothers to stumble, then I will not eat any meat." (Read I Corinthians 8:13.) That is the spirit Paul had—and if we would be what we ought to be for God, that is the spirit *we* will have. We should not eat or drink anything that would cause anyone to stumble. We should not go any place that would cause a weak brother to stumble. Whether we eat, or drink, or whatsoever we do, we should *"do all to the glory of God";* and if we do not, then we have sinned.

Verses 6-8: *"He that regardeth the day, regardeth it unto the Lord; and he that regardeth not the day, to the Lord he doth not regard it. He that eateth, eateth to the Lord, for he giveth God thanks; and he that eateth not, to the Lord he eateth not, and giveth God thanks. For none of us liveth to himself, and no man dieth to himself. For whether we live, we live unto the Lord; and whether we die, we die unto the Lord: whether we live therefore, or die, we are the Lord's."*

Paul is simply saying here that the man who keeps a certain day keeps it unto the Lord, and a man who eats certain things eats unto the Lord because he gives thanks unto God for the food. However, the same is true of the non-eater. The man who abstains from certain things gives thanks unto the Lord for the strength to abstain. The man who does not keep a certain day is convinced in his own conscience that the day he is keeping is the right day, and so he gives thanks to God for the day he *does* keep. Therefore it is not up to us to judge, for God knows the thoughts and the intents of the heart.

"For none of us liveth to himself, and no man dieth to himself." No man lives to himself, no man dies to himself; therefore, the things we do influence others. The things we eat, the places we go, have bearing on the lives of those with whom we mix and mingle. If we are a believer, *"we live unto the Lord"*; and if we are a believer, when we die *"we die unto the Lord."* Therefore, *"whether we live...or die, we are the Lord's."* The main thing is to know that the heart belongs to God. If you are born again, truly washed in the blood, whatever you eat (or do not eat) will not determine your eternal destiny. Our Lord Himself taught with clearness that "there is nothing from without a man, that entering into him can defile him..." (Mark 7:15). The thing that determines whether or not you belong to the Lord is personal faith in the shed blood of Jesus. If you have exercised faith in His shed blood, if you have accepted His finished work, you are the Lord's—and that is what counts!

Verse 9: *"For to this end Christ both died, and rose, and revived, that He might be Lord both of the dead and living."*

The meaning of this verse is simply that the Lord died and was raised from the dead, and therefore established His lordship over all, *"that He might be Lord both of the dead and living."*

Job asked, "If a man die, shall he live again?" (Job 14:14). In the New Testament we read, "Jesus said . . . *I am the resurrection, and the life: he that believeth in me, though he were dead, yet shall he live: and whosoever liveth and believeth in me shall never die"* (John 11:25, 26). Jesus also said, *"I am He that liveth, and was dead; and, behold, I am alive for evermore . . . and have the keys of hell and of death"* (Rev. 1:18). And Paul told the Corinthians: ". . . if One died for all, then were all dead: and . . . He died for all, *that they which live should not henceforth live unto themselves, but unto Him which died for them, and rose again"* (II Cor. 5:14, 15).

Jesus took a body, and in that body He fulfilled every jot and every tittle of the Law. He met every requirement of a holy God, and He conquered death, hell, and the grave. Today the Man Christ Jesus sits at the right hand of God the Father to make intercession for us (I Tim. 2:5).

Verses 10 and 11: *"But why dost thou judge thy brother? or why dost thou set at nought thy brother? for we shall all stand before the judgment seat of Christ. For it is written, As I live, saith the Lord, every knee shall bow to me, and every tongue shall confess to God."*

Paul asks the solemn, pertinent question: Why

will one believer judge another believer, or why will one believer *"set at nought"* a brother believer? According to the Word of God, we know that *all Christians will "stand before the judgment seat of Christ"* to receive their just reward. II Corinthians 5:10 plainly teaches that all will be judged for stewardship. The right and wrong in a brother's conduct are to be determined at the judgment seat, and not by individual opinion. In that solemn tribunal no man will judge his own case, much less that of his brother.

I Corinthians 3:11-15 clearly teaches that all believers will be judged and rewarded *according to their works. Redemption* is by *grace*—pure grace, *without* works; but *reward* is according to our *works.* We become sons of God by believing on the Lord Jesus Christ, but we will be *rewarded* for our *stewardship.*

"For it is written . . . ." Paul quotes here from Isaiah 45:23, and he points out the sure fact that *"every knee"* WILL *bow before God,* and *"every tongue"* WILL *"confess to God"* that Jesus is the Christ, to the glory of God. The statement *"As I live"* simply means "As surely as there is a God." And just so surely as He is eternal and will never die, just that surely will every individual appear before Almighty God.

In reading this verse we must distinguish between *the judgment seat of Christ* (Rom. 14:10; II Cor. 5:10) where saints will be judged, and the

Great White Throne judgment (Rev. 20:11-15) where *sinners* will be judged. Paul is speaking here primarily of the judgment of saints, but may I give to the sinner this solemn warning:

You may never bow your knee to God on earth. You may never humbly confess to Almighty God in this life. But I would like to warn you that if you never bow your knee to God here and accept His Christ as your Saviour, when you die God will bend your knee and He will COMPEL you to bow and to confess that Jesus is the Christ, the virgin-born Son of God. *Make up your mind:* If you confess Jesus *here,* He will save you and confess you before the heavenly Father. But if you deny Him here, He will deny you at the judgment (Matt. 10:32, 33)—but you will be compelled to bow your knee and confess that Jesus IS the Christ!

Verse 12: *"So then every one of us shall give account of himself to God."*

To me, there is much comfort in this verse. I am so happy that I will NOT give an account to God for the sins of another, for the conduct of another—but I will stand before God *for myself.* Children will not give an account to God for the conduct of their parents, nor will parents give an account to God for the conduct of their children. When I say this I am not minimizing the responsibility of the parents, for they are commanded to bring up their children "in the nurture and ad-

468

monition of the Lord" (Eph. 6:4) . . . to "train up a child in the way he should go" (Prov. 22:6). The fact I am pointing out here is simply this: Each individual will give an account to God for *himself* and for no one else.

Verse 13: *"Let us not therefore judge one another any more: but judge this rather, that no man put a stumblingblock or an occasion to fall in his brother's way."*

Since it is a Bible fact that every person will stand before Almighty God and will be judged for his own stewardship, then God forbid that we judge each other. There is a day coming when the Righteous Judge will judge righteously (Psalm 96:10). We poor, finite creatures could not judge right; so God forbid that we judge at all!

". . . but judge this rather, that no man put a stumblingblock or an occasion to fall in his brother's way." The judging that is needed is *self-*judgment rather than the judging of others.

Verse 14: *"I know, and am persuaded by the Lord Jesus, that there is nothing unclean of itself: but to him that esteemeth any thing to be unclean, to him it is unclean."*

This verse is self-explanatory. It simply states that Paul, insofar as he was concerned, did not feel that meat offered to idols in a heathen temple was unclean. He knew that those idols were dead;

he knew there was only one God (the true God), and he was *"persuaded by the Lord Jesus that there is nothing unclean of itself."* Therefore to him meat offered to idols was not unclean and he could eat it with a clear conscience.

However, the believer who was weak in faith and limited in knowledge, and who because of his weakness and limitation felt that the meat was unclean, should not eat the meat—for *"to him it is unclean."* In such a case it is better to abstain, because "he that doubteth is damned (condemned; that is, *self*-condemned) if he eat, because he eateth not of faith" (v. 23). If we are truly born again and have surrendered the inner man to God, we should follow the wooings of our conscience.

Verses 15 and 16: *"But if thy brother be grieved with thy meat, now walkest thou not charitably. Destroy not him with thy meat, for whom Christ died. Let not then your good be evil spoken of."*

Earlier in this series I suggested that we need more believers with the spirit and the practice of life that Paul demonstrated in his daily living. Here Paul teaches that if your brother is being injured because you eat certain food, then you are no longer living by the rule of love. Do not let that liberty of yours ruin a weaker Christian, *"for whom Christ died."* It is true that we cannot please everyone, and certainly not religious fanatics; but we certainly would not want to destroy the testimony of a weak believer just for the satisfaction of consuming food or for the satisfaction of wearing a garment that might offend a weak believer.

"Let not then your good be evil spoken of." This is good, sound Gospel admonition. The "good" here refers to Christian liberty, the freedom of conscience which has been won by Christ, but which will inevitably get a bad name if it is exercised in an inconsiderate, loveless fashion. That is, in doing good, be sure the things you do *are done* in such a manner that no man will be able to speak evil of your deeds.

The Wuest translation of the New Testament puts it this way: "Therefore, stop allowing your good to be spoken of in a reproachful and evil manner." Have you ever heard the old saying, "You certainly cannot put your finger on his (or her) life"? That is the way we should live—in such a manner that the world cannot criticize us or honestly speak evil of us; and we should live in such a way that weak believers have no cause to criticize us for the things we do and the places we go. Remember—"None of us liveth to himself, and no man dieth to himself." We influence others by the things we do, the places we go, the company we keep—and even by the things we eat and drink. Do not ever forget, however, that redemption is by *grace*, by the shed blood and finished work of Christ—not by our good works.

Verse 17: *"For the kingdom of God is not meat and drink; but righteousness, and peace, and joy in the Holy Ghost."*

The Bible is a wonderful Book. The Holy Spirit is the Author, and He is perfect in His dictation of God's Word to holy men. Notice how verse 17 is constructed: First of all, *"the kingdom of God is NOT meat and drink";* but the kingdom of God IS first, *"righteousness,"* then *"peace,"* and third, *"joy in the Holy Ghost."* There can be no peace apart from righteousness. There can be no joy apart from peace and righteousness. When we have been justified by faith we enter into peace with God, and this peace with God leads to joy *in* God: ". . . we have peace with God through our Lord Jesus Christ: . . . and rejoice in hope of the glory of God. . . . And not only so, but we JOY in God . . ." (Rom. 5:1, 2, 11).

One outstanding commentator says it this way: "You must not break down God's work for the mere sake of food! Everything may be clean, but it is wrong for a man to prove a stumblingblock by what he eats; the right course is to abstain from flesh—or indeed anything that your brother feels to be a stumblingblock. Certainly keep your own conviction on the matter, as between yourself and God. He is a fortunate man who has no misgivings about what he allows himself to eat; but if anyone has doubts about eating and then eats, that condemns him at once.

It was not faith that induced him to eat, and any action that is not based on faith is sin."

Verse 18: *"For he that in these things serveth Christ is acceptable to God, and approved of men."*

In verse 18 this truth is set forth: If we serve Christ in the matter of eating and in the things we wear, the places we go—in the habits of life—if we are conscientious in those things, we are *"acceptable to God" and Christ,* and we are *"approved of men."* I do not believe that any person can live a sinless, perfect life, as Jesus lived while here on earth. He did no sin. But I do believe we are duty bound as believers to live *blameless* lives. Paul admonished the believers at Philippi to "be blameless and harmless... without rebuke, in the midst of a crooked and perverse nation, among whom ye shine as lights in the world" (Phil. 2:15).

Verse 19: *"Let us therefore follow after the things which make for peace, and things wherewith one may edify another."*

Here Paul admonishes us to *"follow after the things which make for peace,"* the things which *"edify."* In other words, "Blessed is the peace-maker, and blessed is the man who edifies others by the practices of life—the things he does in his daily routine." On the job, believers can be a real source of edification to weaker brethren if they are happy and joyous, gentle and kind—and

473

if they serve the Lord fervently even on the job. We are to "follow after," we are to long for, the habits of life that will edify. We should never do anything to cause division and unrest.

Verses 20 and 21: *"For meat destroy not the work of God. All things indeed are pure; but it is evil for that man who eateth with offence. It is good neither to eat flesh, nor to drink wine, nor any thing whereby thy brother stumbleth, or is offended, or is made weak."*

"For meat destroy not the work of God." In other words, "Surely your God is bigger than your appetite. Surely your testimony is of more importance than satisfying the hunger of your stomach for meat. Surely your spiritual life is deeper than the hunger for physical food." And then again Paul reminds us that *"all things indeed are pure; but it is evil for that man who eateth with offence."* If we know we are offending others by the things we do, then we are definitely unchristian in our actions.

Paul clearly tells us in verse 21 that *we are not to do anything whereby a "brother stumbleth, or is offended, or is made weak."* His admonition is that we do not cause our brother, by the use of our liberty or any of our conduct, to stumble or fall. Do not obstruct or hinder his Christian growth by causing him to act contrary to his conscience. So, for the present, we are to accomodate our walk to his, lest he remain weak. (See I Corinthians 9:22.)

Let me say here what I have said many times in my meetings: There are a lot of things Christians can do that will not damn them; but there are a lot of things believers must *not* do because we are the representatives of the Lord Jesus on earth. We are saved by pure grace—but we do not live to ourselves; our lives influence others for good or bad.

Verses 22 and 23: *"Hast thou faith? have it to thyself before God. Happy is he that condemneth not himself in that thing which he alloweth. And he that doubteth is damned if he eat, because he eateth not of faith: for whatsoever is not of faith is sin."*

"Hast thou faith?" The faith here refers to the subject under discussion—the subject of meats, days, etc. The brother who is strong in faith has liberty in these matters because he knows he is saved by grace and grace alone. But there is a danger in this liberty, too. A man may not be as grounded as he supposed himself to be, and he may allow himself to do things which will cause his conscience to condemn him. The way to be happy is to have a clear conscience in what we do; or in other words, if we have doubts about a course of conduct, it is not safe to indulge in that course.

Paul is saying, "Are you saved by the grace of God through faith? Do you have faith? Then *have it before God,* and live a life before God so that when you lie down at night and close your eyes, your conscience will not condemn you for the things you have done during the day. *Happy is he that condemneth not himself in that thing which he alloweth."* Happy is the man who has a clear conscience toward God, because he has lived a separated, dedicated, Spirit-guided life.

"He that doubteth is damned if he eat...." This does not teach that if a believer eats meat, yet doubting whether it is right or wrong, he will be damned through the eating of that meat. Please do not accuse God of giving to us a salvation so weak and so cheap that a piece of meat could damn us. It simply means the man is *condemned by his own conscience "because he eateth not of faith"*—or "because it is not of faith." His act did not flow from his trust in Christ.

If you do things your conscience tells you NOT to do, and if you participate in things that are doubtful, then you will be judged, because the things you are doing are not in faith, but in doubt. God honors faith, and whatever we do that is *not* of faith is *sin.* Christ has certainly redeemed the believer from every ceremonial observance. But distrust of Christ in these matters equals to distrust of the perfect salvation Christ purchased with His blood. Therefore, *"whatsoever is not of faith is sin."*

Chapter XV

1. We then that are strong ought to bear the infirmities of the weak, and not to please ourselves.

2. Let every one of us please his neighbour for his good to edification.

3. For even Christ pleased not himself; but, as it is written, The reproaches of them that reproached thee fell on me.

4. For whatsoever things were written aforetime were written for our learning, that we through patience and comfort of the scriptures might have hope.

5. Now the God of patience and consolation grant you to be likeminded one toward another according to Christ Jesus:

6. That ye may with one mind and one mouth glorify God, even the Father of our Lord Jesus Christ.

7. Wherefore receive ye one another, as Christ also received us to the glory of God.

8. Now I say that Jesus Christ was a minister of the circumcision for the truth of God, to confirm the promises made unto the fathers:

9. And that the Gentiles might glorify God for his mercy; as it is written, For this cause I will confess to thee among the Gentiles, and sing unto thy name.

10. And again he saith, Rejoice, ye Gentiles, with his people.

11. And again, Praise the Lord, all ye Gentiles; and laud him, all ye people.

12. And again, Esaias saith, There shall be a root of Jesse, and he that shall rise to reign over the Gentiles; in him shall the Gentiles trust.

13. Now the God of hope fill you with all joy and peace in believing, that ye may abound in hope, through the power of the Holy Ghost.

14. And I myself also am persuaded of you, my brethren, that ye also are full of goodness, filled with all knowledge, able also to admonish one another.

15. Nevertheless, brethren, I have written the more boldly unto you in some sort, as putting you in mind, because of the grace that is given to me of God,

16. That I should be the minister of Jesus Christ to the Gentiles, ministering the gospel of God, that the offering up of the Gentiles might be acceptable, being sanctified by the Holy Ghost.

17. I have therefore whereof I may glory through Jesus Christ in those things which pertain to God.

18. For I will not dare to speak of any of those things which Christ hath not wrought by me, to make the Gentiles obedient, by word and deed,

19. Through mighty signs and wonders, by the power of the Spirit of God; so that from Jerusalem, and round about unto Illyricum, I have fully preached the gospel of Christ.

20. Yea, so have I strived to preach the gospel, not where Christ was named, lest I should build upon another man's foundation:

21. But as it is written, To whom he was not spoken of, they shall see: and they that have not heard shall understand.

22. For which cause also I have been much hindered from coming to you.

23. But now having no more place in these parts, and

having a great desire these many years to come unto you;

24. Whensoever I take my journey into Spain, I will come to you: for I trust to see you in my journey, and to be brought on my way thitherward by you, if first I be somewhat filled with your company.

25. But now I go unto Jerusalem to minister unto the saints.

26. For it hath pleased them of Macedonia and Achaia to make a certain contribution for the poor saints which are at Jerusalem.

27. It hath pleased them verily; and their debtors they are. For if the Gentiles have been made partakers of their spiritual things, their duty is also to minister unto them in carnal things.

28. When therefore I have performed this, and have sealed to them this fruit, I will come by you into Spain.

29. And I am sure that, when I come unto you, I shall come in the fulness of the blessing of the gospel of Christ.

30. Now I beseech you, brethren, for the Lord Jesus Christ's sake, and for the love of the Spirit, that ye strive together with me in your prayers to God for me;

31. That I may be delivered from them that do not believe in Judaea; and that my service which I have for Jerusalem may be accepted of the saints;

32. That I may come unto you with joy by the will of God, and may with you be refreshed.

33. Now the God of peace be with you all. Amen.

Believers to Receive One Another; Christ Our Example

Verses 1 and 2: *"We then that are strong ought to bear the infirmities of the weak, and not to please ourselves. Let every one of us please his neighbour for his good to edification."*

In chapter 15 we have a continuation of the law of love concerning a believer and doubtful things. Here, the rule of Christian love laid down in Romans 14:21 is amplified. To *"bear the infirmities of the weak"* is for a *"strong"* Christian to deny himself of meat—or of anything he knows is right—in order to help a weak brother who considers those things wrong. To deny oneself something that is legitimately his is a "burden" to be borne. It is a heavy weight, except where love gives the strength to carry it.

It is to be noted that Paul does not tell the weak Christian to reflect on the load and burden he is imposing on others; for if he had the power to reflect, he would not be weak.

Paul adds that the weak must be *pleased "for his good to edification."* To afford religious pleasure only to a fanatic (which does not build him up spiritually), is not for his good. To act so as to "please" a weak Christian "to edification," is for a strong Christian to forego something legitimate when it removes a source of temptation and helps the weak Christian to more easily live a life pleasing to God. This admonition in verse 2 has its reason in the next verse:

Verse 3: *"For even Christ pleased not Himself; but as it is written, The reproaches of them that reproached thee fell on me."*

Believers are not to be selfish, self-centered,

and always desiring the things that please themselves. Paul enforces his exhortation by referring to *the Lord Jesus Christ,* who *"pleased not Himself."* It should be a consolation to know that our Lord pleased not Himself, but bore the shame and agony of the cross that we might be saved. Since He did this for us, we should be willing to follow, as far as it is humanly possible, His example. Those who claim to be spiritually minded should be very patient with weak Christians and should bear with them, doing their best to help them become stronger Christians.

". . . as it is written, The reproaches of them that reproached thee fell on me." Paul quotes here from Psalm 69:9. Jesus took upon His own back the reproaches that were hurled at His followers. (Read also Acts 9:1, 4, 5 and I Peter 2:23, 24.)

Verse 4: *"For whatsoever things were written aforetime were written for our learning, that we through patience and comfort of the Scriptures might have hope."*

Paul told the young minister, Timothy: "All Scripture is given by inspiration of God, and is profitable for doctrine, for reproof, for correction, for instruction in righteousness: that the man of God may be perfect, throughly furnished unto all good works" (II Tim. 3:16, 17).

He says here in Romans, *"Whatsoever things were written aforetime"*—that is, all of the Old

Testament Scriptures (and the Gospels)—*"were written"* and given to us *"for our learning"* and instruction. The Old Testament abounds in instances of a self-denying life, redounding to the glory of God, and thus encourages the *"patience"* and gives the *"comfort"* which we need in this life. The record of these Bible instances Paul uses as authority to prove that as God dealt with His servants in the past, so He deals now. God does not change.

Verses 5 and 6: *"Now the God of patience and consolation grant you to be likeminded one toward another according to Christ Jesus: that ye may with one mind and one mouth glorify God, even the Father of our Lord Jesus Christ."*

"Now the God of patience and consolation grant you . . . ." Paul virtually prays that Christians in their use of the Scriptures may have granted to them by God their patience and comfort. These graces, after all, are gifts of God, but given by Him through His Word. It is by these two qualities, also, that God will make them *"likeminded one toward another,"* a mind according to Christ's.

". . . that ye may with one mind and one mouth glorify God . . . ." When the church glorifies God with one heart and one mouth, it will transcend all the troubles of chapter 14. This does not mean that all will come to a common view on meats—

or other doubtful things—but even though divided in dietary views, they must not be divided in their worship of God. This is true Christian union.

Verse 7: *"Wherefore receive ye one another, as Christ also received us to the glory of God."*

This is not now an exhortation to the strong to bear the weak, as in verse 1; but strong and weak alike are addressed. They are to *"receive...one another"* in fellowship and favor *"even as Christ also received"* *both* unto Him. If Christ accepts men with all their weaknesses and without any regard about their secondary matters, so should we.

If you profess to be a follower of the Lord Jesus, then practice in your daily living the humility, the unselfishness He practiced. Do all that you do *"to the glory of God"*—not to satisfy self, not for vainglory, but for God's glory. You are not your own, you are bought with a price. God wants your soul, your spirit, and your body...He wants *you!*

Verse 8: *"Now I say that Jesus Christ was a minister of the circumcision for the truth of God, to confirm the promises made unto the fathers."*

In this verse Paul is pointing out again *"that Jesus Christ was a minister to the circumcision...."* The Gospel was "to the Jew first," and then to the Gentile. Our Lord explains this Himself in His statement concerning the Syrophenician woman in Matthew 15:24, where He said, "I am not sent but unto the lost sheep of the house of Israel." This was in fulfillment of the Messianic promises to Israel—"*to confirm the promises made unto the fathers.*" But this was a means to an end, that the Gentiles might be reached through Israel and thus "glorify God for His mercy" (v. 9). The conclusion of the whole argument is based anew on the work of Christ in behalf of both parties. Christ broke down "the middle wall of partition" between Jew and Gentile (Eph. 2:14)—and He was the only One who *could* have broken down that wall between the two nations.

(It was primarily the Jew who refused to eat the meat referred to in chapter 14 of Romans; but now you will notice that the words "strong," "weak," and "meat" are not used again in this Epistle.)

Verses 9-12: "*And that the Gentiles might glorify God for His mercy; as it is written, For this cause I will confess to thee among the Gentiles, and sing unto thy name. And again He saith, Rejoice, ye Gentiles, with His people. And again, Praise the Lord, all ye Gentiles; and laud Him, all ye people. And again, Esaias saith, There shall be a root of Jesse, and He that shall rise to reign over the Gentiles; in Him shall the Gentiles trust.*"

Jesus came "a minister" first to the Jew, then to the Gentile—and He ministered to both, that through His shed blood Jews and Gentiles alike might be saved and *"glorify God for His mercy."*

". . . as it is written . . . ." Here Paul gives a number of quotations from the Old Testament. The references are as follows: *Psalm 18:49, Deuteronomy 32:43, Psalm 117:1,* and *Isaiah 11:1, 10.* These quotations have not the character of promises to Gentiles, but nevertheless they show that God's plan of mercy embraced, from the first, the Gentiles along with the Jews.

Verse 13: *"Now the God of hope fill you with all joy and peace in believing, that ye may abound in hope, through the power of the Holy Ghost."*

It is Paul's prayer that *"the God of hope fill"* the believers *"with all joy and peace"*—the opposite of the painful contention and disputing Paul has been discussing. In the discussion Paul has had much to say about bearing and forbearing, love and service. He now uses the word which gives the source of all these. All joy and peace come *"in believing."* And Paul longs for their joy and peace, *that they "may abound in hope, through the power of the Holy Ghost."*

Jesus came to bring joy. He said, "These things have I spoken unto you, *that my joy might remain in you, and that your joy might be full"* (John 15:11). Peter describes it as "joy unspeakable and full of glory" (I Pet. 1:8). This joy comes through the Holy Ghost, and until a person is saved—and knows beyond a shadow of doubt that he *is* saved

—he cannot joy in the blessings of the Holy Ghost.

Paul's Ministry and Coming Journey

Verses 14 and 15: *"And I myself also am persuaded of you, my brethren, that ye also are full of goodness, filled with all knowledge, able also to admonish one another. Nevertheless, brethren, I have written the more boldly unto you in some sort, as putting you in mind, because of the grace that is given to me of God."*

Here Paul has a good word for the believers at Rome; he commends them highly. He did not write this Epistle to condemn them or reprove them; he was *"persuaded"* that they, his *"brethren"* in the Lord, were *"full of goodness"* and *"filled with all knowledge."* In addition, they were spiritually minded enough *"to admonish one another."*

In verse 15 Paul says, *"Nevertheless . . . I have written . . . as putting you in mind . . . ."* He writes to the Roman believers not so much to instruct, as to "put them in mind" of what they already knew. In other words, "You believers at Rome are strong in the Lord. You are established in the Lord—that is, the greater part of you; but I must remind you that it is by grace we are saved, by grace we are overcomers, and we will be rewarded for faithful stewardship because of God's unmerited favor to us as hell-deserving sinners."

486

Verse 16: *"That I should be the minister of Jesus Christ to the Gentiles, ministering the Gospel of God, that the offering up of the Gentiles might be acceptable, being sanctified by the Holy Ghost."*

Remember, Paul was a freeborn Roman Jew; yet God called him to *"be the minister (the apostle) of Jesus Christ to the Gentiles."* As pointed out earlier in the study, Paul said, "I magnify mine office" (11:13). In chapter 9, verse 3, Paul cried out that he would be willing to be "accursed from Christ" if he could save *his own people.* In chapter 10, verses 1 and 2, he begged for their salvation; he said, "I bear them record that they have a zeal of God, but not according to knowledge." Yet he now praises God that He gave him grace (v. 15) to be the minister to the *Gentiles.* When the cry came, "Come over into Macedonia, and help us" (Acts 16:6-11), he was not disobedient to the heavenly vision. He obeyed, he went, and he ministered well to the Gentiles.

". . . that the offering up of the Gentiles might be acceptable . . . ." Wuest says: "The offering which Paul conceives himself as presenting to God is the Gentile church, and the priestly function in the exercise of which this offering was made is the preaching of the Gospel."

Verses 17-19: *"I have therefore whereof I may glory through Jesus Christ in those things which pertain to God. For I will not dare to speak of any of those things which Christ hath not wrought by me, to make the Gentiles obedient, by word and deed, through mighty signs and wonders, by the power of the Spirit of God; so that from Jerusalem, and round about unto Illyricum, I have fully preached the Gospel of Christ."*

In these verses, Paul is giving a personal testimony. He is not without confidence in writing to the Romans, for he says, *"I have . . . whereof I may glory."* But there is no personal assumption in this, for his confidence is only *"through Jesus Christ in those things which pertain to God."* He boasts only in Christ, in the grace of God, through the power of God and the Holy Spirit.

"For I will not dare to speak . . . ." Regarding the contents of verse 18, all other boasting Paul declines. In other words, Paul is saying, "I will not presume to speak of anything except *what Christ has wrought by me . . . ."* Wuest says: "The things which Christ did work through Paul He wrought with a view to obedience on the part of the Gentiles. This combination—Christ working in Paul, *'to make the Gentiles obedient'* to the Gospel—is the vindication of Paul's action in writing to Rome. It is not on his own impulse, but in Christ that he does it; and the Romans as Gentiles lie within the sphere in which Christ works through him."

". . . through mighty signs and wonders . . . ."

Paul was a worker of miracles—but only *"by the power of the Spirit of God."* He took no credit for anything he ever accomplished. On one occasion a young man fell out of a window at midnight "and was taken up dead" (Acts 20:9-12); Paul prayed for him and he was raised up. Paul himself was dragged outside a certain city for dead—but the very next day he continued on his journey (Acts 14:19, 20). To escape danger on another occasion, he was let down over a wall in a basket (Acts 9:23-25). On an island he was bitten by a very deadly serpent—but he did not die (Acts 28:1-6). God worked mighty miracles in his life—but he gave God all the glory.

In verse 19 Paul testifies that he *"fully preached the Gospel of Christ"*—not the Gospel he might have wanted to preach, but what Christ said preach. You will recall, Paul received instructions on the road to Damascus, to "go into the city, and it shall be told thee what thou must do" (Acts 9:6). He went . . . he was instructed . . . and immediately he began a series of revival services with a singular subject: *Jesus Christ the Son of God.*

Verses 20 and 21: *"Yea, so have I strived to preach the Gospel, not where Christ was named, lest I should build upon another man's foundation: but as it is written, To whom He was not spoken of, they shall see: and they that have not heard shall understand."*

Paul interpreted the commission to go into all the world and preach the Gospel (Mark 16:15) to mean, for him at least, not that he should follow someone who had already opened the way to the heathen, but that he should go *first*. It was his aim, his ambition, *"to preach the Gospel, not where Christ was named . . . ."* He searched for the place where the name of Jesus had never been mentioned, and to that place he went and preached Christ. We also need to search out those remote sections where the Gospel has not been preached, and we need to go there to lift up the blood-stained banner, to preach the pure Gospel as did the Apostle Paul.

". . . lest I should build upon another man's foundation." Paul considered it his work as an apostle to *lay* a foundation (I Cor. 3:10) and let others do the building. However he *did* preach a year to the church in Antioch after it had been established (Acts 11:19-26). Now he longs to visit the church at Rome—not with the view of staying among them long, but only on his way to Spain, as we shall see in verse 24.

"But as it is written . . . ." In verse 21 Paul refers to Isaiah 52:15, where we read: ". . . for that which had not been told them shall they see; and that which they had not heard shall they consider."

Verses 22-24: *"For which cause also I have been much hindered from coming to you. But now*

490

*having no more place in these parts, and having a
great desire these many years to come unto you;
whensoever I take my journey into Spain, I will
come to you: for I trust to see you in my journey,
and to be brought on my way thitherward by you,
if first I be somewhat filled with your company."*

Paul testifies here that he has had *"a great
desire these many years"* to visit the church at
Rome. (Read again chapter 1, verses 9-15.) But he
had been *"much hindered"* by abundance of work.
Now Paul had removed the obstacle by doing all
that was to be done *"in these parts."* He had
gone over "these parts" and established churches,
and now he was prepared to fulfill his desire of
many years to visit Rome. This he hoped to do
when he took his *"journey into Spain."* It is remarkable even here that Paul does not say his
principal object was to visit Rome, much as he
desired that, but to stop *in his journey*, on his way
to a higher fulfillment to preach the Gospel where
it had never been proclaimed.

Whether or not Paul ever reached Spain is not
certain; but we do know he finally reached Rome,
even though he arrived in chains, a prisoner. (Read
Acts 28:16-31.) He had the privilege of fellowshipping with at least some of the believers in Rome.

Verses 25-27: *"But now I go unto Jerusalem to
minister unto the saints. For it hath pleased
them of Macedonia and Achaia to make a certain*

contribution for the poor saints which are at Jerusalem. It hath pleased them verily; and their debtors they are. For if the Gentiles have been made partakers of their spiritual things, their duty is also to minister unto them in carnal things."

Paul could not go directly to the Roman brethren, for he had yet one duty to perform. He must *"go unto Jerusalem to minister unto the saints,"* to whom he was taking *"a certain contribution"* from *"them of Macedonia and Achaia."* Chapters 8 and 9 of II Corinthians show how Paul's heart was set on this contribution. This intended journey is also mentioned in Acts 19:21.

"It hath pleased them . . ."—that is, they had done it cheerfully and voluntarily. Paul points out that it pleased the believers in Macedonia to raise this money *"for the poor saints"* in Jerusalem, because *"the Gentiles have been made partakers of their spiritual things"*—the spiritual blessings of salvation—and they are *"debtors"* to the Jews for them, because our Lord said, *"Salvation is of the Jews"* (John 4:22). Since the Gentiles are partakers of the spiritual blessings because of the Jews, it is nothing but right that the Gentiles share their *"carnal things"*—that is, clothing, food, and necessities of life—with the needy Jews. Of course, Paul had great joy in being able to carry this offering to Jerusalem to present to the poor saints there.

Verse 28: *"When therefore I have performed this, and have sealed to them this fruit, I will come by you into Spain."*

The money contribution was the *"fruit"* of the Gospel among the Gentiles. *"To seal"* is to authenticate, to make one's own. "The point in the figure in the word 'sealed' cannot be said to be clear. It may possibly suggest that Paul, in handing over the money to the saints, authenticates it to them as the fruit of their 'spiritual gifts' which have been sown among the Gentiles; or it may mean only 'when I have secured this fruit to them as their property'" *(Wuest)*. At any rate, the simple fact here is that Paul states, "When I finish my ministry in Jerusalem, *I will come by you into Spain.*" As I have already said, it is not certain whether he ever reached Spain; but we do know he spent some time in Rome.

Verse 29: *"And I am sure that, when I come unto you, I shall come in the fulness of the blessing of the Gospel of Christ."*

Paul was a man full of faith, full of the Holy Ghost, completely yielded to God. He always preached the fulness of the Gospel—and the heart of the Gospel, to Paul, was the sufferings, the death, the burial, and the resurrection of the Lord Jesus Christ. He did not know when he would come to Rome, nor did he know the circumstances that would overtake him, but he was sure of the condition of his own heart and he had utmost confidence in Christ. Paul knew that when he arrived in Rome he would *"come in the fulness of the blessing of the Gospel of Christ."*

Verses 30-32: *"Now I beseech you, brethren, for the Lord Jesus Christ's sake, and for the love of the Spirit, that ye strive together with me in your prayers to God for me; that I may be delivered from them that do not believe in Judaea; and that my service which I have for Jerusalem may be accepted of the saints; that I may come unto you with joy by the will of God, and may with you be refreshed."*

Here Paul is pleading for prayer. He knew what prejudice against himself existed in Jerusalem, and he asks the Roman believers *"for the Lord Jesus Christ's sake"* and through the love the Spirit gives the saints one for another, that they *"strive together"* with him in their prayers for him. They were many miles apart, and they could not know any day just what his circumstances would be; but *God* knew, and their prayers would be effective. *Every* man of God needs and wants the prayers of God's people on his behalf.

Two things are to be prayed for concerning Paul's trip to Jerusalem: *"That I may be delivered from them that do not believe in Judaea; and that my service . . . may be accepted of the saints."*

494

Even though Paul was God's great apostle, he was not exempt from the hatred of men. His fear here is twofold: the unbelievers in Judaea may seek to destroy him, and the saints may refuse his gifts from the Gentile brethren.

To look at the history of Paul's visit to Jerusalem and his finally being sent to Rome in chains (Acts chapters 21-28), one might say his prayers were not answered. But the rough handling which Paul received shows most strikingly the way he was delivered and gives to us a useful lesson on the way God answers prayer. In answer to the prayers we know that God did not keep Paul *out* of the dangers, but He preserved him *in* them.

". . . that I may come unto you with joy . . . ." The chapter closes with Paul's desire to go to Rome. He looked forward to the time of joy and rest beyond the anxieties and dangers. He longed to visit the church at Rome, to share the joy and *"be refreshed"* in that wonderful assembly of believers. But after all of his desires and all of their prayers, it still depended upon *"the will of God."*

The closing verse of this chapter is the Apostle's prayer for God to be with the Roman believers:

Verse 33: *"Now the God of peace be with you all. Amen."*

Chapter XVI

1. I commend unto you Phebe our sister, which is a servant of the church which is at Cenchrea:

2. That ye receive her in the Lord, as becometh saints, and that ye assist her in whatsoever business she hath need of you: for she hath been a succourer of many, and of myself also.

3. Greet Priscilla and Aquila my helpers in Christ Jesus:

4. Who have for my life laid down their own necks: unto whom not only I give thanks, but also all the churches of the Gentiles.

5. Likewise greet the church that is in their house. Salute my wellbeloved Epaenetus, who is the firstfruits of Achaia unto Christ.

6. Greet Mary, who bestowed much labour on us.

7. Salute Andronicus and Junia, my kinsmen, and my fellowprisoners, who are of note among the apostles, who also were in Christ before me.

8. Greet Amplias my beloved in the Lord.

9. Salute Urbane, our helper in Christ, and Stachys my beloved.

10. Salute Apelles approved in Christ. Salute them which are of Aristobulus' household.

11. Salute Herodion my kinsman. Greet them that be of the household of Narcissus, which are in the Lord.

12. Salute Tryphena and Tryphosa, who labour in the

Lord. Salute the beloved Persis, which laboured much in the Lord.

13. Salute Rufus chosen in the Lord, and his mother and mine.

14. Salute Asyncritus, Phlegon, Hermas, Patrobas, Hermes, and the brethren which are with them.

15. Salute Philologus, and Julia, Nereus, and his sister, and Olympas, and all the saints which are with them.

16. Salute one another with an holy kiss. The churches of Christ salute you.

17. Now I beseech you, brethren, mark them which cause divisions and offences contrary to the doctrine which ye have learned; and avoid them.

18. For they that are such serve not our Lord Jesus Christ, but their own belly; and by good words and fair speeches deceive the hearts of the simple.

19. For your obedience is come abroad unto all men. I am glad therefore on your behalf: but yet I would have you wise unto that which is good, and simple concerning evil.

20. And the God of peace shall bruise Satan under your feet shortly. The grace of our Lord Jesus Christ be with you. Amen.

21. Timotheus my workfellow, and Lucius, and Jason, and Sosipater, my kinsmen, salute you.

22. I Tertius, who wrote this epistle, salute you in the Lord.

23. Gaius mine host, and of the whole church, saluteth you. Erastus the chamberlain of the city saluteth you, and Quartus a brother.

24. The grace of our Lord Jesus Christ be with you all. Amen.

25. Now to him that is of power to stablish you according to my gospel, and the preaching of Jesus Christ, according to the revelation of the mystery, which was kept secret since the world began,

26. But now is made manifest, and by the scriptures of the prophets, according to the commandment of the everlasting God, made known to all nations for the obedience of faith:

27. To God only wise, be glory through Jesus Christ for ever. Amen.

PART VII

THE OUTFLOW OF CHRISTIAN LOVE

Verses 1 and 2: *"I commend unto you Phebe our sister, which is a servant of the church which is at Cenchrea: that ye receive her in the Lord, as becometh saints, and that ye assist her in whatsoever business she hath need of you: for she hath been a succourer of many, and of myself also."*

"Phebe"—or *Phoebe*—is "described by Paul as *'our sister'* who is *'a servant of the church which is at Cenchrea,'* a helper of many, *'and of myself also.'* It is generally assumed that this letter (the Roman Epistle) was taken to Rome by Phoebe, these verses introducing her to the Christian community. In commending her, Paul asks that the Roman Christians *'receive her in the Lord,'* i. e., give her a Christian welcome, and that they *'assist her in whatsoever business'* (or matter) she may have need of them" (International Bible Ency.).

Greetings to Christians at Rome

As you read this chapter you will notice quite a

499

variety of greetings sent to those in Rome—saints with whom Paul was acquainted. Paul himself had never visited Rome (nor the church at Rome) until he was taken there as a prisoner; but you will remember the slogan of that day was "All roads lead to Rome." Without a doubt, many of the converts of Paul, possibly many of his personal friends, had gone to Rome for one reason or another and were fellowshipping with the believers in the church at Rome.

Verses 3 and 4: *"Greet Priscilla and Aquila my helpers in Christ Jesus: who have for my life laid down their own necks: unto whom not only I give thanks, but also all the churches of the Gentiles."*

Priscilla and her husband *Aquila* had toiled with Paul in Corinth, as we read in Acts 18:1-3: "After these things Paul departed from Athens, and came to Corinth; and found a certain Jew named Aquila, born in Pontus, lately come from Italy, with his wife Priscilla . . . and came unto them. And because he was of the same craft, he abode with them, and wrought: for by their occupation they were tentmakers." Here he calls them *"my helpers in Christ Jesus."* They had at some time *"laid down their own necks"* to save the life of Paul. On what occasion this was done is not known, but it was enough to call forth thanks not only from Paul, but also from *"all the churches of the Gentiles."*

500

Verse 5: *"Likewise greet the church that is in their house. Salute my wellbeloved Epaenetus, who is the firstfruits of Achaia unto Christ."*

In this verse Paul sends greetings to the church which Aquila and Priscilla had *"in their house."* (Notice also I Corinthians 16:19, where we read: ". . . Aquila and Priscilla salute you much in the Lord, with the church that is in their house.") Then he sends special greetings to his *"wellbeloved"* friend *"Epaenetus,"* one of the first converts of Asia.

Verses 6-15: *"Greet Mary, who bestowed much labour on us. Salute Andronicus and Junia, my kinsmen, and my fellowprisoners, who are of note among the apostles, who also were in Christ before me. Greet Amplias my beloved in the Lord. Salute Urbane, our helper in Christ, and Stachys my beloved. Salute Apelles approved in Christ. Salute them which are of Aristobulus' household. Salute Herodion my kinsman. Greet them that be of the household of Narcissus, which are in the Lord. Salute Tryphena and Tryphosa, who labour in the Lord. Salute the beloved Persis, which laboured much in the Lord. Salute Rufus chosen in the Lord, and his mother and mine. Salute Asyncritus, Phlegon, Hermas, Patrobas, Hermes, and the brethren which are with them. Salute Philologus, and Julia, Nereus, and his sister, and Olympas, and all the saints which are with them."*

None of the names mentioned in these verses are otherwise known than the record given here. It is quite a list of names to which Paul sends greetings, but there is no great difficulty in supposing that so active a traveling missionary as Paul would, in course of time, make the acquaintance of a considerable number of Christians then residing at Rome.

Verse 13 is very touching: *"Salute Rufus chosen in the Lord, and his mother and mine."* No doubt Rufus had been a very special friend to Paul, and because Rufus' mother had at some time ministered to Paul as a mother, he speaks of her as his own mother. This teaches us just how closely related believers are, one to another. After all, if we are saved we are members of the body of Christ, bone of His bone, flesh of His flesh. He is the Head of the Church into which all believers have been baptized, and we are very closely related one to another if we are born again. No wonder Jesus commands believers to love one another, even as He loved us . . . and then points out that "greater love hath no man than this, that a man lay down his life for his friends" (John 15:12, 13). We should love other believers, our brothers and sisters in Christ, just that deeply in the Lord.

Verse 16: *"Salute one another with an holy kiss. The churches of Christ salute you."*

Here Paul admonishes the believers to greet

one another in an affectionate manner—*"with an holy kiss"*; that is, treat each other with kindness and love. Wuest gives the following comment:

"Regarding the holy kiss, Denney says, 'The custom of combining greeting and kiss was oriental, and especially Jewish, and in this way became Christian. . . . By *"holy"* the kiss is distinguished from an ordinary greeting of natural affection or friendship. It belongs to God and the new society of His children. It is specifically *Christian.*' Robertson says, 'The near-east mode of salutation as hand-shaking in the western . . . Men kissed men and women kissed women.'"

A Warning and Exhortation

Verses 17 and 18:   *"Now I beseech you, brethren, mark them which cause divisions and offences contrary to the doctrine which ye have learned; and avoid them. For they that are such serve not our Lord Jesus Christ, but their own belly; and by good words and fair speeches deceive the hearts of the simple."*

Already at Rome there were men willing to bring about divisions among the saints; therefore in these verses Paul sounds out a solemn warning against *"them which cause divisions and offences"* and introduce schism in the church. He did not want the sweet spiritual unity demonstrated in the church at Rome to be disrupted. He warned the believers to beware of these people, to *"mark them."* And what was the remedy Paul subscribed? Was it torture? Imprisonment? No— simply *"avoid them,"* turn away from them, freeze them out by not listening to them. Christians today need this admonition as never before, for there are those who advocate that fundamental Christians and modernists should fellowship, rub shoulders, and walk together.

Paul warned that these ministers of Satan *"serve not our Lord Jesus Christ, but their own belly...."* (Compare here the words of Paul in Philippians 3:18, 19.) *"... and by good words and fair speeches deceive the hearts of the simple."*

The church at Rome was extraordinary, and Paul wanted it to stay that way. So he solemnly warned, in this last chapter: "Avoid false teachers, false prophets... those who would cause divisions and stir up trouble, bring about offences and teach false doctrine. Practice what you have learned from the teachers of the pure Gospel; avoid anyone who teaches anything you have not heard from the Holy Scriptures."

Verse 19: *"For your obedience is come abroad unto all men. I am glad therefore on your behalf: but yet I would have you wise unto that which is good, and simple concerning evil."*

In this verse, Paul states that the obedience of the believers in the church at Rome was known to all men. Paul rejoiced in that, but he sounded out a solemn warning. He said, "I want you believers to be *wise unto that which is good, and simple concerning evil.* Be alert." Peter puts it this way: "Be sober, be vigilant; because your adversary the devil, as a roaring lion, walketh about, seeking whom he may devour: whom resist stedfast in the faith . . ." (I Pet. 5:8, 9). If the devil cannot devour our soul and damn us in hell, he then sets about to devour our testimony, our influence, and our usefulness as a servant of God.

Verse 20: *"And the God of peace shall bruise Satan under your feet shortly. The grace of our Lord Jesus Christ be with you. Amen."*

With these words Paul encourages the believers in patient waiting: *"God . . . shall bruise Satan . . . shortly."* Note that it is *"the God of peace"* that "shall bruise Satan." How contrary to Him are those who cause divisions and deceive the hearts of the simple. "Shall bruise Satan" refers to the promise in Genesis 3:15. God told the serpent in the Garden of Eden: "I will put enmity between thee and the woman, and between thy seed and her seed; *it shall bruise thy head,* and thou shalt bruise his heel."

Friendly Greetings;
Benediction and Praise to God

Verses 21-23: *"Timotheus my workfellow, and*

505

Lucius, and Jason, and Sosipater, my kinsmen, salute you. I Tertius, who wrote this epistle, salute you in the Lord. Gaius mine host, and of the whole church, saluteth you. Erastus the chamberlain of the city saluteth you, and Quartus a brother."

In the first part of chapter 16, Paul himself is sending salutations to the Christians in the church at Rome. In verses 21 through 23 he sends salutations from his fellow workers who are with him as he writes this Epistle to the believers in Rome.

"Timotheus" is *Timothy,* Paul's young understudy. It has been suggested that *"Lucius"* is the same as Saint Luke, but this is merely conjecture. These two and *"Jason"* and *"Sosipater"* send greetings. Of *"Tertius"* nothing more is known than is mentioned here. It is evident that he *"wrote this epistle"* as Paul dictated it and added his own greeting.

"Gaius," in whose home Paul was staying, sends greetings. Apparently the church in that city met in the house of Gaius, because we read that he was *"host...of the whole church."* Also *"Erastus the chamberlain of the city"*—a very high official in the city of Corinth—and *"Quartus a brother"* send Christian greetings.

Verse 24: *"The grace of our Lord Jesus Christ be with you all. Amen."*

Here we have a repetition of the benediction

506

found in verse 20, except that in this verse it is invoked on all.

Verses 25-27: *"Now to Him that is of power to stablish you according to my Gospel, and the preaching of Jesus Christ, according to the revelation of the mystery, which was kept secret since the world began, but now is made manifest, and by the Scriptures of the prophets, according to the commandment of the everlasting God, made known to all nations for the obedience of faith: To God only wise, be glory through Jesus Christ for ever. Amen."*

In this closing paragraph, we have a great doctrinal declaration: God, the only *true* God, is *"of power to stablish"* those who believe in Him and receive Him as their God. Paul says that God establishes them *"according to my Gospel and the preaching of Jesus Christ . . . ."* Paul, like all other God-ordained, God-sent ministers, preached the Gospel of Jesus Christ—and the Gospel is the death, burial, and resurrection of Jesus "according to the Scriptures." Writing to the Corinthian believers, Paul said:

"Moreover, brethren, I declare unto you *the Gospel which I preached unto you,* which also ye have received, and wherein ye stand; BY WHICH ALSO YE ARE SAVED, if ye keep in memory what I preached unto you, unless ye have believed in vain. *For I delivered unto you first of all that which I also received, how that CHRIST DIED FOR OUR SINS according to the Scriptures; and that HE WAS BURIED, and that HE ROSE AGAIN THE THIRD DAY according to the Scriptures"* (I Cor. 15:1-4).

Paul had a singular subject: *The death, the burial, the resurrection of Jesus according to the Scriptures.* When Paul preached, words like these fell from his lips: "God forbid that I should glory save in the cross. I am determined not to know anything among you save Jesus Christ and Him crucified. I am crucified with Christ; nevertheless I live . . . yet not I, but Christ liveth in me."

No wonder when Paul came to the end of his earthly life, he could look death squarely in the face and testify: "I am now ready to be offered, and the time of my departure is at hand. *I have fought a good fight, I have finished my course, I have kept the faith:* Henceforth there is laid up for me a crown of righteousness..." (II Tim. 4:6-8).

The preaching of Jesus Christ, by which and through which God establishes His people, must be *"according to the revelation of the mystery...."* In this day of liberalism and modernism there is much preaching which does not establish God's people nor build them up in the faith. This modern, liberal preaching is not according to Paul's Gospel, nor is it "according to the revelation of the mystery" which was hidden, or *"kept secret since the world began, but now is made manifest"* by

508

revelation to the Apostle Paul. Paul tells us of the revelation dictated to him by the Holy Spirit:

"For this cause I Paul, the prisoner of Jesus Christ for you Gentiles, if ye have heard of the dispensation of the grace of God which is given me to you-ward: How that *by revelation He made known unto me the mystery;* (as I wrote afore in few words, whereby, when ye read, ye may understand my knowledge in the mystery of Christ) *which in other ages was not made known unto the sons of men, as it is now revealed unto His holy apostles and prophets by the Spirit; that the Gentiles should be fellowheirs, and of the same body, and partakers of His promise in Christ by the Gospel:* Whereof I was made a minister, according to the gift of the grace of God given unto me by the effectual working of His power.

"Unto me, who am less than the least of all saints, is this grace given, that I should preach among the Gentiles the unsearchable riches of Christ; and to make all men see what is the fellowship of the mystery, which from the beginning of the world hath been hid in God, who created all things by Jesus Christ: to the intent that now unto the principalities and powers in heavenly places might be known by the Church the manifold wisdom of God, according to the eternal purpose which He purposed in Christ Jesus our Lord: in whom we have boldness and access with confidence by the faith of Him" (Eph. 3:1-12).

In Colossians 1:26, 27 Paul speaks of *"the mystery which hath been hid from ages and from generations, but now is made manifest to His saints:* to whom God would make known what is the riches of the glory of this mystery among the Gentiles; *which is Christ in you, the hope of glory."* Every believer is a possessor of Christ, a possessor of divine nature, a possessor of the Holy Spirit. (In the Old Testament era, the Holy Spirit came upon men and departed. He came for a special ministry, a special service, and then He departed; but in this dispensation He abides in the bosom of every born again child of God.)

"... and by the Scriptures of the prophets...." By these "Scriptures of the prophets" is *"made known"* that the Lord Jesus Christ, He who was born of a virgin, is "Immanuel, God with us"— that is, God in flesh (Isaiah 7:14; Matt. 1:21-23). He is "The mighty God" from eternity (Isaiah 9:6; Psalm 90:1, 2). And this Christ—very God in flesh— became "our Passover... sacrificed for us" (I Cor. 5:7). Jesus was "the Lamb slain from the foundation of the world" (Rev. 13:8), whose suffering was imperative, that we might escape the sufferings of hell. (Read Exodus 12:1-28.) The Old Testament prophet prophesied concerning the sufferings and the glory that should follow (I Pet. 1:10-12). The Old Testament prophet did not understand what he prophesied, but to Paul it was revealed in full.

Jesus is "that great Shepherd" in His resurrection (Heb. 13:20, 21). He is the "High Priest over the house of God" (Heb. 10:21). Jesus once for all forever offered His own blood. He entered into the holy of holies with His own blood; therefore we who believe in Him now enter boldly by a new and living way. The Old Testament prophet could not understand this mystery, but God revealed it clearly to the minister to the Gentiles, the Apostle Paul.

The prophecy of the coming King who will reign over the whole earth (Jer. 23:5, 6; Zech. 14:9) was not understood by the prophets who prophesied in the Old Testament; and when Jesus came, humble and lowly, a "root out of dry ground" with no form or comeliness, *the Jews* would not accept Him as their king. They shouted, "We will not have this Man to reign over us!" They were looking for a gigantic superman to deliver them from the power of Rome; and when the Lamb came, they refused to receive Him . . . they crucified Him instead. But they did it in ignorance, not understanding the prophecies concerning the coming of their Messiah. They did not see that the cross preceded the crown. They did not understand that the sufferings of Jesus preceded the glory, and that He must die for the sins of the world before He sat on the throne of David to reign over the entire earth. The mystery was hidden from the beginning, until Paul received from Almighty God the revelation, the unveiling of the mystery.

In closing this Epistle, Paul speaks of "Him that is of power to *stablish* you...." I trust that these studies have helped you as a believer to a clear understanding of the wonderful truths set forth in Romans, and that the things you have learned may establish you. If the lessons given in this book have failed to build you up in the faith and strengthen you in the inner man, then my time in preparing them and your time in studying them has been wasted. My purpose in preparing this study is that believers might be blessed and made better Christians, and that the unsaved might be brought to repentance and faith in the Lord Jesus Christ. It has taken many long hours, and the hours have run into days and weeks; but if one Christian is strengthened or one sinner is born again, then the hours, the days, the weeks have been well spent.

You can rest assured that the Epistle to the Romans, which we have been studying, speaks to us with authority. The words in this Epistle are *God's* words, written by God's appointed man as he was moved by the Holy Spirit. *All* Scripture is God-breathed (II Tim. 3:16).

I would like to close our study with the last words of Paul in this Epistle:

"To God only wise, be glory through Jesus Christ for ever. Amen."